Two for Boarding

A WORKPLACE COLLEGE HOCKEY ROMANCE

LASAIRIONA MCMASTER

DRAMA LLAMA PUBLISHING

Copyright © 2022 by Lasairiona McMaster

The moral right of Lasairiona McMaster to be identified as the author of this work has been asserted in accordance with the copyright, designs, and patents act of 1988.

All rights reserved.

No part of this book may be reproduced in any form or by any electronic or mechanical means, including information storage and retrieval systems, without written permission from the author, except for the use of brief quotations in a book review. Your support for the Author's rights is appreciated.

All the characters in this book are fictitious and any resemblance to actual persons living or dead, are purely coincidental.

Dedication

For Amber, my lighthouse in a raging storm: for not leaving me when things got hard and for turning up on my doorstep during a pandemic with matching Golden Girl's pj bottoms because I was having a mental health crisis and needed my best friend.

CHAPTER 1
Mackenzie

"Heavens to Betsy, y'all, are we in a... a... sex club?" As it turned out, Mackenzie's whisper, hadn't been much of a whisper at all. Her blurted-out question drew narrow-eyed, suspicious looks from the two women leaning on the bar to her right. The taller, skinnier one with a striking inverted bob dressed in a skin-tight, PVC French maid's outfit, smirked at her corset-and-collar-wearing friend who rolled her eyes.

Kenzie's traitorous bestie, Addison, shook with laughter and grabbed Paige's arm as though she might collapse from the hilarity of it all. "Uh... Surprise? Welcome to Protocol." Addison reminded her of her sister Bea; she was the light to Kenzie's dark, headstrong, beautiful, and lived for the smug satisfaction of being right.

"So this is why I'm dressed like I'm performing at a burlesque show." Kenzie tugged at the hem of her studded leather skirt. It barely covered her ass cheeks. And while she wasn't a prude, she also didn't think the whole world needed to see her booty. "This is the last time I follow y'all blindly into the unknown. No more ride-or-die. I'm done with you bitches." She waved her hand at them. "When I get home I'm finding new best friends on Craigslist."

Her friends' giggles continued as she made her way to the bar. Her heart pounded in her ears and pulsed in her temples as she attempted to take in the bustling crowd clad from head to toe in leather and PVC, trying desperately not to stare too hard, or seem too out of place. "Bitches."

The French Maid raised her eyebrows as a wave of heat flashed across Kenzie's cheeks. "Not y'all. Y'all aren't bitches. They..." She pointed over her shoulder. "They are the bitches."

French Maid and Corset-and-Collar picked up their drinks and fled out of sight before Kenzie could suck in another breath to explain any further. She didn't blame them, she was acting a little odd and needed to calm the fuck down. While she wasn't generally someone to yuck someone's yum, as a former Sunday school attending, pageant girl from Pearland, Texas, she was most certainly in over her head.

Her body-hugging purple corset with black lace trim grew tighter as three men in dress pants and pressed shirts walked by her. "How come they didn't have to wear pleather skirts that barely cover their butt crack?"

The giant, bartender with a blond man-bun to her right, laughed. "You didn't either. Can I get you anything?" He placed a black, square drink napkin with an emblem printed in silver and the word 'Protocol' above it, on the shiny black bar top in front of her. It looked like a yin yang symbol with three of the darker, yin shapes. She traced her fingers over the three "arms" curving out from the center and merging with an encompassing circle.

"Yes sir. New best friends?" She groaned, dropping her forehead to the back of her hands on the cool surface.

"We don't serve those here. At least not behind the bar. But I could provide you with a delicious beverage that might take the edge off. Who knows, maybe your new best friend is out there waiting." He jerked his stubble-encased chin at the space behind her. "Give it a chance. I get that it can be intimidating, but you passed the first hurdle of getting in the door and not peeing yourself or running away screaming."

She pointed her index finger at him as someone bumped her from behind with a muttered apology. "You don't know that I haven't peed myself. And maybe I haven't yet bolted because my legs don't work anymore 'cause I'm frozen in place. Have you considered that... Thor?"

His broad shoulders shook as he laughed. "I get that a lot."

"Must be because you look like a Viking."

He winced and covered his heart. "I always thought it was because I look like a god."

She rolled her eyes. Another bartender, seemingly half the size of the blond giant and in every way his polar opposite appeared and patted Thor's expansive chest. "He likes to think that. Thor, Melissa called in sick. It's just you and me tonight, your god-ship." The second bartender's lip rings glinted in the light as he grinned and the much narrower man, with wild short red hair bowed at Thor and smiled at Kenzie.

He made his way past Thor to the far end of the bar where he took orders from the three men in dress pants without a notepad. She envied people who could keep everything in their head. There wasn't a day that went by when her to-do lists didn't sprout to-do lists just to keep her on the path to successful adulting.

She narrowed her eyes. "Is your nickname really Thor?"

The blond giant with almost inhuman blue eyes shrugged his shoulders. "Maybe I'm the real Thor of Asgard and I'm here to protect you from all the PVC and kinky fuckery that's afoot behind you with my massive hammer. Maybe I really am the God of Thunder." He waggled his eyebrows and pointed behind her. "Ask anyone, they'll corroborate my identity."

In her haste to get to the bar, and cover her behind with a high-backed barstool, she hadn't truly stopped to take in her surroundings. She'd glanced around and panicked at her instant overwhelm. She wasn't sure she was ready to look at what was behind her, no matter how curious she might have felt. She groaned and her head thudded against the bar. "Ugh."

"I'd ask if it was your first time, but you have this blinding neon sign right above your head. It's kinda distracting."

She sat up as he leaned on his forearms in front of her. "What can I get you, sugar?"

"Three margaritas. Espolon if you have it. Salt rims."

"She likes her rims good and salty." Paige snorted as she and Addison joined Kenzie at the bar.

The corner of his lips twitched.

"What?"

"Most clubs with play are dry spaces." He grabbed a glass from the rack overhead. "Sometimes they are BYOB. We have timekeepers and dungeon monitors to ensure that anyone in the play spaces is not under the influence. It becomes risky for consent as well as activities that require coordination. As a general rule, most believe that there is no space for alcohol or drugs in the kink community during play, or introductions, for safety reasons. A common mantra at the places that do have a serving option is 'kink then drink'. We are not one of those places."

"No tequila?"

He shook his head. "'fraid not."

"I hate you both." She flipped her friends the bird.

"If that were true, you'd have ordered only one margarita, not three." Adi slipped her arm across Kenzie's shoulders. "Admit it, you love us."

"Maybe I planned on drinking all three. Fine. Virgin margaritas then. I'll imagine the tequila."

"So... you want lime juice and sugar syrup?" Thor was

doing a terrible job at hiding his amusement at the situation unfolding in front of him.

"Do you have a better suggestion?" She shivered as someone opened the door behind her, sending a blast of frigid November air through the bar area. She was already regretting her outfit choice even despite her heavy coat, which she was clinging to like a life raft.

"Pfft. Don't insult me." Thor flashed a grin. "I make the best virgin cocktails in the city."

"It's true." Paige nodded. "We'll take three citrus sippers please, Thor."

"What the fuck is a citrus sipper?" Kenzie folded her arms. The night was going downhill fast.

"Lime, cranberry juice, ginger ale, and white grapefruit juice." Thor answered, as he assembled the ingredients on the bar in front of them.

"Sounds distinctly lacking in tequila."

He was already making their drinks and shook his head. "Give it a chance, lady. If you hate it, you can always leave, no one's tying you up unless you want them to." He winked at Addison whose eyes bugged out of her head. "Plus, you can always grab a 'don't fucking talk to me' wristband if you want to."

"A wristband?"

Both Paige and Addison waved their arms in front of Kenzie's face. She grabbed Adi's arm. "What does orange mean?"

Addison squared her shoulders, casting a furtive glance at the tall, blond, and totally-her-type bartender. "It means taken but exploring submissive. It means I'm not all the way in the 'don't fucking talk to me' camp. I mean, I'm single…" She batted her eyes at Thor who did little to hide his approving gaze as it traveled down Addison's face, landing on her ample cleavage. "But I want to play it safe for the night. If that means pretending I'm in a relationship to ward off the throngs of potential suitors..." She shrugged.

She also wore a corset, but hers was brown, steampunk in style, and had leather straps crisscrossing under her bust. Her cheeks pinked. "This way I have an out for not hurting anyone's feelings. I can just flash my band and say I'm taken. Just cause I'm single doesn't mean I'm open to just anyone. A girl's gotta have standards."

Thor handed her a tumbler of pinky orange liquid. "She does indeed, my lady. And if anyone gives you any hassle here tonight, you come find me. Thor of Asgard will take care of you."

"With his massive hammer." Kenzie tugged at the top of her corset and turned her head to avoid the come-fuck-me eyes her friend was giving the giant bartender they'd just met. One of the three dress-pant-clad guys at the end of the bar looked vaguely familiar from his profile, but she couldn't place him, and he and the two men he was with were gone before she had a chance to confirm.

"See?" Paige elbowed Kenzie in the ribs. "Thor here says it's all good. If you wanna play you can play, if you wanna watch you can watch, if you want to leave... we'll be very sad about it, won't we, Adi?"

Addison still made gooey heart eyes at Thor, but she nodded.

"Y'all made me dress up like this when I didn't have to. If I wasn't so dang self-conscious about what I'm wearing, it wouldn't be so bad."

Paige snorted. "Lies. If you were wearing jeans and a Brett Young tour T-shirt from five years ago you'd still feel out of place and even more self-conscious. This is better." She clutched her glass and gestured it up and down in front of Kenzie's corset. "This is hot as fuck. And you do have to. There's a dress code."

"She's not wrong." Thor handed Kenzie her glass and she ignored the straw in favor of chugging half of the cold, bittersweet mixture in one go. "Dress codes keep people from showing up who are not part of the community."

"What is the dress code?" The more he talked, the more her curiosity grew.

"A good rule of thumb is "no pink" should be visible on men or women. For men, a well-tailored suit is often all that is required. Black and red are often easier to pass. That is the easy entry. I have also worn chest harnesses with jeans and button down shirts, carried a rope, or worn other leather gear on the outside of my clothing. The biggest piece of importance is that the clothing fits. If it looks like you borrowed someone else's suit, you will likely not get in."

Kenzie tugged on her corset, thankful it was hers from the previous year's Halloween costume and that she hadn't gotten turned away at the door for her overwhelming ignorance at what she was about to walk into.

Thor mixed more of their mocktail and refilled their glasses. "Men and women have to meet the dress code alike. Even still there are often boys who enter the club with a thought process of getting the opportunity to beat on a woman and a guaranteed line up of vaginas in front of them."

Kenzie gasped, but Thor continued. "Often the DM's will spot and remove these individuals quickly, but there are cases where people have been seriously injured."

"Dungeon masters." Paige correctly guessed that the abbreviation was lost on her.

"Are all clubs the same? Do they all have dress codes?"

He shook his head. "Entry to dungeon spaces typically requires a strict dress code. The more the location focuses on targeting swingers vs general kinksters, the more likely it will have a vanilla vs strict dress code. If you have stocks and gags, it is likely a dungeon and there is also likely a dress code in place." He sighed and threw his cloth onto the bar. "I feel like I need to adequately prepare you since your friends were idiots and didn't."

"Hey." Addison's protests were drowned out by Thor not pausing for breath.

"There's a staircase that takes you to the basement." He pointed over her left shoulder. "Most of the time play happens in private and there are a lot of rules around more public play and what is allowed. A good rule is also to ensure you ask prior to using any equipment."

Two men called out their drinks order, and Thor grabbed their alcohol-free beer without missing a beat. "There are a lot of signs around the club to remind you of the rules. Even sober, people have a tendency to forget it's generally not a free-for-all play space where you can let loose anywhere. Penetrative activities and those that would result in body fluid etc. are in more enclosed areas. For safety reasons. But you're still going to see things."

Her heart quickened. Watching people do... things... was one thing, but all out intercourse? Or rather all-in-tercourse? Shit. Her face burned. If her mama could see her now she'd have her hauled down to Pastor Mullholland's church for a conscience cleanse.

"A sex dungeon." Addison clapped her hands, her eyes wide and sparkling and a grin that could light up the Houston power grid spread across her face.

He nodded, returning her grin. "We have 'house doms' resident in the club. They will be more front and center in a shared space to perform some acts for those interested. It's a way to introduce spanking, flogging, whipping, shibari, wax play..." His approving gaze swept over Addison, making Kenzie blush.

"Shibari is rope play," supplied Paige, sipping on her second drink.

"Consent, as always, remains important, even with our house doms who have a release you sign prior to engaging. When you leave the dungeon, you enter a lounge with traditional drinks. The lounge also has a separate entrance where you can choose to only attend there for drinks without passing the dungeon. No play is allowed in that space. I'd suggest you get a wristband like your friends – unless you're into being dominant rather than submissive, in which case you'll need a different color to both of them."

She sipped her drink in silence as her friends both turned to stare at her with round, hopeful eyes. Addison kicked the heel of Kenzie's over-the-knee black leather boots. "Come on K-K. Pleeeeease? You've been so busy since you started working with those fucking Snow Pirates that we hardly get to hang out anymore." She threw a pointed glare at Paige as if to encourage her to join in.

Thor quirked his brow. "You a student at the U?"

Kenzie snorted and rolled her eyes. "My college days are far behind me."

"She's right, Kenz." Paige slurped at the remaining liquid in the bottom of her glass. "I've wanted to check this place out for ages. If we'd waited for you to get on board, we'd have grown old and died."

They weren't wrong. As it turned out, working as a physiotherapist for the local college hockey team was sucking her of all her energy.

"All work and no play makes Mackenzie a dull girl. And by extension, her friends." Addison sipped her drink. "If you really wanna leave, we can. But Paige and I will go take a quick look around first."

Kenzie stared at the slow melting ice cubes in the bottom of her glass. She'd played by everyone else's rules for so long when she lived back in Texas – her estranged husband, her family, society – everyone and their grandma had their own opinions of how she should look, talk, act. But in Minnesota she could be anyone she wanted to be. She'd left that old life behind.

She'd changed her name, her hair, and her attitude. In Minnesota she could be the fun-loving Mackenzie Abbottt who went to the local sex club with her friends and wasn't embarrassed to admit to herself she was all-the-way curious, and more turned on than she expected to be.

"Fuck it." She drained the last of her drink. "I'm in."

Paige bounced on the balls of her feet and clapped her hands. "Whoop! If you get uncomfortable and want to leave, just holler. We should give her a safe word." She rolled her lips between her teeth. "If you need to escape the kinky sex dungeon just say... uh... starfish."

"Starfish?" Kenzie tipped her head.

Paige shrugged. "It's mine."

Thor wiped the bar with a washcloth. "And if you end up comfortable and want to have sex with a stranger, the dungeon has cleaning stations with safe sex supplies, spray, towels, wipes, etc. You are expected to clean a space before you leave so the next person can enjoy it safely. The monitor or timekeeper quality checks before allowing the next person in the space."

A shiver rattled through her from head to toe. Clean up team. Condoms. Kink. If the entire room wouldn't see them every time she moved in such a short skirt, she'd have hurried home to put on her Big Girl Panties. But for the moment, she, and the only black thong she owned, had to pray everyone else had better things to look at than her big butt.

Paige looked like all her Christmases had come at once. She slipped her red velvet jacket off her shoulders to reveal a black dress. A tulle panel across her chest exposed her breasts, and she had diamanté crystals covering her nipples under the sheer fabric.

Under her bust, a leather insert pulled her waist in with

what looked to be a corset – held together with braided leather and golden hoops. There was more tulle at the bottom to create a pleated skirt.

Coupled with her boob-length, jet-black wavy hair and blood red lips the look had even Kenzie questioning her sexuality for a moment. "Wow. You came prepared. Wait. You're not wearing an orange band." She grabbed her friend's arm. "What does green mean?"

"Available switch." Paige's grin was hungry and wicked.

Addison's arched eyebrow suggested she was every bit as lost as Kenzie was. "What the fuck is a switch?" She handed her empty glass to Thor.

"A switch is someone who goes back and forth between dominating and being submissive depending on their mood, circumstances, and the vibe between partners." Thor smirked. "This isn't your friend's first rodeo."

Paige shrugged. "It was time for you guys to see my dark and twisty side." She jabbed a finger at Addison and Kenzie. "No judgment from you bitches, or I will cut you."

Addison held her palms up to Paige. "Girl, you didn't judge me for that abomination of a dye job I got last year. Or that guy who brought his mom to our first date. Let that freak flag fly. Maybe I'll find my kink tonight."

A jolt of excitement rippled through her. Maybe Kenzie would, too.

CHAPTER 2
Mackenzie

Armed with an orange armband, and on shaky legs, Kenzie followed her friends through the double doors leading to the staircase, clutching the banister like it was her lifeline. What lay at the bottom of the stairs was anyone's guess and she couldn't quite discern whether she was more excited or nervous to peek behind the kink-curtain.

Three steps from the bottom, her foot missed the edge. Her stomach tightened as her lungs forced a squeak to bubble up into her throat and break free.

Was this how she died? Falling down three stairs in a sex dungeon? If nothing else it sounded like a pretty cool death, right? Shrouded in mystery. It was what everyone could only dream about, an honorable demise – wasn't it?

A firm hand clasped the right side of her ribs from behind, supporting her until she found level ground again. "Easy." The low male voice close to her ear spread goosebumps across her skin.

Her heart stuttered. Could you climax from a man's voice? Easy. He'd only said one word but the gruffness that laced his tone, the confident, firm grip he had on her body despite being a stranger, and the intoxicating smell of sandalwood and citrus sent her body into overdrive.

She resisted the urge to turn over her shoulder to see who had saved her from the embarrassing fate of landing on her ass in front of a roomful of people. "Th-thank you, sir." Whose voice was that? She sounded like a breathless, prissy princess from a cartoon who'd just been saved by some gallant white knight on a noble steed. Other than her southern-bred manners, there was no sign of her strong, Texas badass self.

She cleared her throat to speak again, but the hand around her waist tightened and pulled her to a stop. Did he just growl at her? An honest-to-goodness growl. Feral. Animalistic. Raw. And against her skin. Her brain stopped working, though her body somehow fought the urge to lean into whoever the intoxicating man was at her back. The goosebumps that still pebbled her body were joined by a wave of heat like someone had dipped her into a vat of hot oil like a turkey on Thanksgiving.

"Be careful who you say that to this evening. It does things to a certain type of person."

Thank you? People had a kink hearing other people say thank you? Was gratitude really such a rarity? Something tugged at the back of her brain. The voice was almost familiar somehow but stayed just out of her grasp.

Paige snapped her fingers in front of Kenzie's face. "You good?"

Swallowing down the lump in her throat, Kenzie forced herself to nod.

Addison stood next to her, glanced over Kenzie's shoulder, and did a double take. So her white knight was attractive after all. With a voice like melting honey, and a grip that would probably make her daddy wince, how could he not be?

She smoothed out her skirt with clammy palms. "I slipped, but I'm good."

The girls linked arms with her once she stepped off the bottom step. "Falling to your death won't get you out of this experience Mackenzie Abbott, nice try." Paige planted a kiss on her cheek and led her away from her mystery Good Samaritan and into the kinky unknown.

The first room they got to was a wide open space, like a hotel ballroom. Large wooden frames littered the room, with a few feet between each. "They're individual play spaces." Paige stage-whispered.

Addison nodded, but Kenzie couldn't take her eyes off the woman who was gagged and bound to the frame in front of her. Trails of mascara lined her cheeks, and red welts covered her almost-nude butt as the shirtless man behind her smacked her with a riding crop.

Kenzie clenched her thighs together. She'd learned horse riding as a child. She'd used a crop in one of her most favorite hobbies and here it was being used to mark a person's skin for fun... for *pleasure*. What did it feel like?

The thwap of leather meeting skin made her jump, but the woman's eyes rolled back in her head as though consumed by a wave of bliss. Kenzie's clit throbbed. She'd been sexually curious in the early days with her husband, Garrett. She'd asked him to spank her once, but he'd declined saying he didn't want to hurt her, and when she'd asked him to slip her tiny vibrating bullet into her butthole he'd called her a deviant. She'd never asked him for anything else in the bedroom after that. Or for anything at all for that matter.

"I wonder if I can find someone to do that to me tonight." Paige's voice had a wistful quality to it, like it would be a dream come true to find a man to smack her butt with a crop. "I'd rather a paddle tonight though."

A... paddle? "Doesn't it hurt?" Didn't it all hurt?

Paige's smile turned sympathetic as she nodded. "First lesson: pain can be pleasurable. Very pleasurable." She moved to step away but stopped. "Look, it's hard enough to find someone who likes the same music, or living room furniture as you do. It's harder still to find someone who shares your particular flavor of kink. This is a safe space to find out what those kinks are and maybe even find someone who likes the same kinks *and* music as you without judgment."

Kenzie nodded. She knew what it was like to have to force herself into a box, to make herself small, to do things people said she should do, rather than what she wanted to.

Having the opportunity to express yourself so freely, to be supported and not judged... while foreign to her, was equal parts enticing and overwhelming. She'd love to be as confident, as sexually aware and engaged as the woman still shuddering and mewling with every smack of the crop against her angry red skin.

But years of never being good enough for her family, her husband... years of being told to diet, to conform, to sit pretty and stay quiet had left her unsure of who she even was anymore.

The flutter in her chest, her hard nipples brushing against the soft fabric of the corset with every breath, and the heat blooming in her cheeks and low in her belly suggested she should perhaps find her lady balls and investigate further.

"If you see something you don't understand, ask, or make a mental note to ask me later, okay? There are no stupid questions and I'm only too happy to help explain something to you." Paige's sincerity was heartwarming. "You'll find that pretty much everyone is friendly and approachable if you can't find me and have a question. And if you're traumatized and want to leave, that's okay too."

Kenzie shook her head as a man in little more than a loincloth was placed in stocks to her left. A tall, curvaceous woman with blood red lipstick to match her impossibly high heels and a high ponytail the 90's would have been proud of, stood next to him with a long, leather whip.

While she had no desire at all to dominate a woman, her curiosity about being dominated by one surprised her. "I'm not traumatized. Sexually confused. But not traumatized."

Paige nodded. "It might take a while to figure out what you like, and that's cool. You might not like any of it. Maybe you simply like watching – that's okay too." Paige winked as Addison walked toward another play space where a couple were having sex.

"This is... a lot."

Paige rubbed Kenzie's bicep. "If you need a time out, you can always go back upstairs for another drink, or over there." She pointed over Kenzie's shoulder. "To the social room. You can take a lap around the smaller rooms back there, too. They're often quieter."

"Thanks, P Diddy." Kenzie bumped her hip against Paige's. "I wouldn't have picked this activity for girls' night, but I can't deny I'm curious."

Paige bumped her back. "And turned on, right?"

She was most definitely turned on. It had been an age since she'd slept with anyone, and she'd already replaced two of her well-used and cherished vibrator collection in the last few months. Self-service was expensive. "More than I'm willing to admit in polite company."

"I don't see any polite company around here." Paige elbowed her. "That's my girl."

For the first forty minutes, Kenzie stayed close to Addison's side. Paige quickly found someone to play with, but there was only so much Kenzie could watch one of her besties getting it on before it got awkward on the ride home.

She made her way to the almost empty social area to take a breather. Her cheeks were still every bit as ablaze as her panties, and no amount of deep breathing could slow her racing heart.

Plush leather couches and recliners with small coffee tables next to each filled the first part of the room.

A slim man wearing wire-rimmed glasses sipped a beer as he stroked the hair of a curvy, red-headed woman whose head was on his lap. Her chest rose and fell with even breaths and her eyes were closed. Kenzie envied the woman's chill when all she wanted to do was dry hump one of the benches in the common space to find some relief from her aching clit.

She offered a small smile to the man, who tipped his beer at her as she made her way through the couch area and toward the tall tables dotted around the snack bar. The lights had been dimmed up front, but a neon sign lit up the snack bar in back. A perfectly chilled, delightfully sweet Dr. Pepper would take the edge off her anxiety.

A small metal object on top of one of the tables caught the light, glinting under the warm glow. Was it a wine bottle stopper? She took a step toward it, pursing her lips and frowning. It didn't look like any stopper she'd ever seen before.

Just as she started to move her arm to reach for it, warmth met her back. "That's a butt plug."

Despite the familiar orange-lemon scent mixed with something woodsy, something masculine, and the honey-voice of her white knight being so close to her ear she could almost feel his lips, her insides withered. A butt plug? That huge chunk of metal was something people shoved in their... Jesus, Mary, and Joseph. What in the world? Ouch.

She folded her arms, heat snaking up her spine. "I knew that."

His low chuckle vibrated through her corset, peaking her nipples. She hadn't even seen his face but his scent and voice alone was sending emergency signals to her most important body parts. "Of course you did. That's why you were going to touch it."

"For all you know it's my butt plug." It certainly wasn't,

and her butthole puckered at the very thought of sticking something quite so large up there, but the swell of indignation in the pit of her stomach wouldn't let her back down. She would be damned if she let her inexperience show. Even if he already knew she was as vanilla as Madagascan vanilla bean paste.

Though he remained silent, his warmth still radiated through her clothes, making her clench her thighs. She turned to face him, her stomach looping in knots and her mouth running dry.

The guy at the bar that nagged at the edges of her recognition stood in front of her. Austin Morgan. #69 on the Snow Pirates roster. Defenseman. Enforcer. Tall dark and handsome drink of perfectly chilled water stood in front of her.

She hadn't spoken to him directly since the first time they'd met at the rink when she'd flipped him off for offering her the little kid's skating apparatus to get her back on the ice. Obnoxious asshole. But what a delicious asshole he was. And a 'no' for every professional reason under the sun. She worked with him. She couldn't compromise her integrity at work for dropping her panties for a player she worked with. No matter how delicious he was.

A cold drip trickled down her spine. His dark hair had been freshly clipped close to his head, and she noted a drop in her stomach at the idea he'd left nothing to be pulled on.

Her pulse sped up. The space around her was getting to her. While she'd been attracted to him at the rink, her body was reacting to his presence in a much more aggressive manner. It had to be because of the environment, right? The club was charged with pheromones, desire, and sex.

When they'd first met, she'd mistaken his eyes for blue. But it must have been a trick of the light because his eyes were the most exquisite shade of brown. She could get lost in those mocha eyes that sat above a perfectly sloped nose, and a jaw so chiseled you could cut glass. The top two buttons on his crisp, black dress shirt that stretched across his deliciously broad shoulders were open. The shirt pulled in a bit as his waist narrowed, tucked into pressed dress pants, and was fastened in place by a black leather belt with a polished buckle.

What was it about a man in a dress shirt that turned her into a puddle?

She blinked. Was he talking to her?

His brows tugged into a frown over those warm eyes swirling with unreadable emotion. "Mackenzie? Are you okay?"

Was she okay? She'd almost picked up a stranger's butt plug in front of the hottest guy she worked with, while half naked, and in a sex dungeon. Sure. She was absolutely fucking peachy. "Peachy keen."

His expression didn't change. "Do you need to sit down?"

"I'm good." She wrapped her arms around her middle, and sent up a prayer to ask God to strike her down with a lightning bolt.

He brushed a wisp of hair from her face, leaving a blur of energy dancing across her cheekbone from the contact. "You're panicking. If it's because you think I'm going to out you at work..."

Sweet baby Jesus, all the angels and saints she was going to vomit on the man's shiny dress shoes if he didn't stop talking.

"You have nothing to worry about. Discretion is an important part of the kink community."

Her tight chest twitched. She held his gaze, searching for any trace of insincerity, but she found none, looking away before his eyes set her soul on fire. What was it about him that made her want to tell him her life history after only a moment of interaction?

"Can I get you a drink? Mackenzie?" The knuckles of his

finger and thumb sandwiched her chin and turned her head back to him. "Are you sure you're okay?"

"I'm fine, Austin. I just..." She glanced over his shoulder. "I guess I'm just processing everything, that's all." Realization dawned and she smacked a hand over her mouth as she gasped. "I almost fell on you on the stairs earlier. I'm sorry. Thanks for saving me from the mortification of landing on my ass."

The lazy smile that tugged on his lips almost undid her. But it was controlled, practiced, every bit as poised and stoic as the rest of him. Did he ever let go and just laugh or do something silly and fun? Did he ever find something so funny he threw his head back and guffawed out loud?

"Don't mention it."

She'd watched him play on the ice. Despite being the team's enforcer, their 'heavy', their fighter, he was the most composed man she'd ever met. And yet his jersey number suggested a humorous side to him that she found hard to imagine. Her core twitched as she imagined sixty-nining with him. She swallowed hard. She needed to get outside, to stand in the cold winter air and let it blast her dirty thoughts right out of her mind.

When she dared meet his eyes again they were still on her. "Can I get you a drink, Mackenzie?"

No one called her Mackenzie. It was always Kenzie, or Kenz, Mickey, Mac and Cheese, Big Mac, Mac Machine... Paige and Addison took great pleasure in coming up with nicknames for her. He'd said her name a few times already and each time, he'd said the whole thing. While no one knew it wasn't her real name, the way it fell from Austin's lips like that... *Mackenzie*... made her glad she'd picked it.

"I'll have a soda, please. Dr. Pepper."

He screwed up his face. "You should have some water."

"Sure. And I should eat more vegetables and do more exercise than amble to the freezer for a pint of Bluebell, but that ain't happenin'." Her eyes flinched wide as he pursed his lips, but he didn't say anything. He simply nodded and went to the bar.

She stared at the tall bar stool next to her. Should she attempt to mount it? Hoping that her ass – and dignity – remained covered as she did? Or did she stay standing next to the table and avoid any additional possibility of falling at Austin's feet for the second time that evening?

A hand clutching a bottle of Dr. Pepper brushed against her arm sending tingles through her extremities and she fought a shudder. "Thank you."

He nodded and uncapped his bottle of water, taking a long drink. Water had never been so sexy. He mounted the stool with ease and leaned his forearms on the table. "I'm glad to see you took precautions for your first time."

"E-excuse me?" She paused, twisting the cap off the bottle, a rash of heat prickled across her chest, climbing up her throat. "Precautions?"

A smirk danced on his lips, and when the light caught his dark brown eyes, all she saw was amusement. He enjoyed the fact she was on edge. He gestured to her armband with his bottle.

Squaring her shoulders, she nodded. "Thor said it would be smart until we figured out what we were doing."

He arched an eyebrow. "Already on first name terms with Thor."

"I do that."

"So it would seem."

Behind him, the guy and girl who had been sitting on the couch, left the room, passing two women and a man on their way out. The small group made their way past her and Austin and stood at the bar.

The heavy air sizzled and her chest rose and fell far harder than she'd like while in the presence of someone she saw regularly in her day job. She was panting like a dog in the Texas sun. He was affecting her, and he probably knew it, too. With luck, he'd think she was simply affected by the club in general and not his deliciously kissable lips she couldn't peel her eyes away from.

What was he doing there? He was obviously into kink but he seemed to be alone. Wasn't he with the two other guys dressed like he was? Did he have a girlfriend? Wasn't it creepy for a guy to go to a sex club alone?

"Ask your question, Mackenzie." He took another drink.

"How do you know I have a question?" Her fingertip caught a bead of perspiration on the cold bottle and she dragged it back up the side of the label.

"The cogs turning in your brain are quite loud."

She smiled. "You speak weird."

He nodded. "I get that a lot. English isn't my first language."

She tilted her head and searched for humor in his intense gaze. "It's not? Then what is?"

"French. My mom is French. We lived there for a number of years when I was young."

There was no trace of anything other than American in his tone. "You don't sound in any way French." She folded her arms. Was he mocking her? She hated being the butt of people's jokes.

He shrugged. "It often only comes to the fore when I am speaking with my mother."

The amount of time her stare lingered on the man's mouth was probably considered a crime in some places, but she couldn't help it. She squeezed her thighs together at the idea of French spilling from his lips. Such a romantic language from such a delectable mouth.

"Do you visit often?"

His lazy smile was back, accompanied by an arched

eyebrow. "Nice try, Mackenzie. But I have not forgotten you have a different question to ask."

She swore internally, and stared at the metal plug still lying discarded on the table between them and braced her foot on the rung of the stool next to her.

"Do you need assistance getting onto the stool?"

She crinkled her nose. This guy. Who even spoke like that? "I don't need help, thanks." Her cheeks heated. She absolutely needed help, but she wouldn't let him know that. She'd stand until her legs went numb and gave out from under her before she'd ever voice the words 'I need help.'

He stood, the feet of his seat scraping across the floor with a loud screech as he did. "Stop being stubborn, Mackenzie and accept *help*."

Before she could blink, he gripped her by her waist, picked her up, and plopped her onto the stool. Who did he think he was? And who did that? Who just picked up a near stranger and dropped her onto a chair like she weighed less than a bag of Lays?

She wasn't skinny, not by a long stretch since her injury and the stress and depression surrounding running away from home. Her body had drastically changed over the past few years. She was 200lbs of curves for days, and he had lifted her like she weighed nothing. She couldn't deny it: it was hot as fuck. She opened her mouth to scold him for having touched her.

She'd already said she didn't need his help and he'd done it anyway, but something about the way he narrowed his eyes, and the warmth that scorched her skin as he stared at her gave her pause. She snapped her mouth shut. The corner of his twitched and his nostrils flared.

Asshole.

"Is this...?" She swept a hand around the room. "Your guilty pleasure?"

"I take pleasure in many things. I choose not to feel guilty about it."

A rumble vibrated in the back of her throat. What the hell was his deal? Was he always so cagey and aloof?

She pulled her arms tighter across her chest. "Do you have a girlfriend?"

He tilted his head, smirking, and her eyes widened. "I just mean it's a little creepy for a single guy to be in a BDSM club by himself, isn't it?"

"It is no creepier than a single woman being in a BDSM club by herself." He leaned forward on his forearms, clasping his hands together as he did.

Intense dude sort of had a point. She was making assumptions based on his gender, which wasn't very kind of her to do.

"I know those men you saw me with, yes. But I did not come here with them. People come to places like this alone for a number of reasons, if they are not well integrated, for example."

The people standing at the snack bar behind them carried drinks to two couches facing each other and took a seat. Their easy smiles and flowing conversation suggested they were friends. Something pinched in her chest at how unapologetically themselves everyone surrounding her was. The realization jerked her corset tighter, making it harder to breathe.

She swallowed down the bitterness in the back of her throat and sipped on her soda. Austin seemed way too self-assured to not be well integrated.

"They go solo if they are meeting someone."

Her eyebrows rose. Was he there to meet someone? If so, why would he be talking to her? Saving her from the mortification of falling on her tuchus, and from picking up a stranger's – probably used – butt plug was one thing, but they were beyond that. They were having a conversation as though they were friends, or even on a date. Her heart spluttered at the thought, but a guy like Austin didn't date girls like her.

He didn't answer her silent question, instead, he kept talking as though she wasn't doing a whole thing in her head by herself.

"They go with a friend... if they are looking for new partners... often there are themed events or classes..." He paused as though waiting for her to ask what classes there might be at a sex club, which only served to make her even more determined to stay silent.

"If you have questions you should ask them, Mackenzie." He paused again, and when she pursed her lips he continued. "Sometimes people come here alone if they simply want to be in a place where they do not feel judged by their thoughts."

Her eyes met his, the sincerity with which he spoke made something stir in her chest. "Do you think people would judge you for your thoughts?"

He made zero effort in hiding the fact he was taking her in as his eyes swept from her head, to her toes, and all the way back up, landing on her hot face. His confidence was intoxicating.

Was she sweating? If he could make her feel this undone with only an appraising look, just how undone could he make her feel if—

"Perhaps." He sipped his almost empty bottle of water.

Perhaps.

Perhaps what? She'd asked him something, hadn't she? Yes. She tried to blink through the lust-filled haze which had settled over her, but it was slow to clear.

She had asked if he felt as though people would judge his thoughts. She wasn't judging. She was curious. So curious, in fact, she wanted to shrink like Alice in Wonderland, climb into his brain, and find just what he was thinking about her as the intensity of his stare somehow grew stronger.

She reached to pull her shirt from her neck, only to be met with bare skin. There was nothing there constricting her neck, but it was as though he controlled the very oxygen in the room. Her blood raced to the surface of her skin, spreading a ripple of heat across her chest.

His eyebrow twitched. Was he evaluating her? Watching to see how she'd react to the fact he was overtly eye-fucking her in a place where she could fuck-fuck him while everyone watched? She coughed to hide the fact she'd choked on her own spit at the thought.

He wasn't at all flummoxed by her presence like she was his. And while mortification squeezed her ribs like a vise, she couldn't help the heat pooling at the apex of her thighs. She needed air. She needed space. She needed to not sit staring at the enforcer for the team she worked with as though she could take a bite out of him and it wouldn't get weird at work.

Beyond that, there were probably rules. It would be unprofessional for a team physio to lick a player's jaw simply because it appeared to have been carved by a greater being, especially considering she was still relatively new to the team. But damn did she ever want to drag her tongue along the smooth line of his jaw and nibble on his ear lobe.

He even had perfect ears. Who had perfect ears? Who *noticed* someone's perfect ears? She tried to tear her eyes away from his perfect ears but found she couldn't. Maybe he was some kind of mind-controlling freak. That would explain the fact she couldn't stop staring at him. It was almost as though Disney had drawn this guy, and the kink community had claimed him for their own.

Her feet met the floor and she stood. "I should go." Standing gave little relief from the heat radiating from him. Her fingers twitched. She needed to stroke his cheek to see if his skin was anywhere near as hot as hers felt.

"There you are." Addison burst into the snack bar with a

wicked grin and smudged lipstick. "I thought you might have left."

"I was just leaving."

"Paige is staying, but I'm ready to leave if you are." Addison glanced at Austin, back to Kenzie, then back to Austin, before offering him her hand. "Addison. Kenzie's best friend."

"Austin." While he shook Addison's hand, he didn't take his eyes off Kenzie.

She needed to get home, take the damn corset off, suck in a few dozen full and cleansing breaths, and things would be better. She wouldn't feel so compelled to get naked and dry-hump Austin Morgan's leg in a sex club once she'd taken off her corset. There had to be some kind of kinky fuckery laced into its stitching.

Austin rose to his feet, his chair didn't scrape the floor as loudly. "I will walk you out."

She covered her chest with a splayed palm, and held another up like a stop sign. "You don't have to do that, Austin. We'll be okay."

He didn't answer her right away, but his brows knotted into a frown, and his eyes narrowed. "I said I will walk you out."

Addison waggled her eyebrows at Kenzie. "Don't be rude, Kenz. Let the man be chivalrous."

She bit her lip so as not to smack her best friend and took a step toward the door. Warmth radiated through the small in her back as Austin's hand met the soft fabric of her corset and her feet stuttered. He was so close his breath tickled the bare skin of her neck and shoulders. Despite herself, she pressed into his hand, aching to close her eyes and tip her head back.

He was confident, well-mannered, and his eyes set her on fire with even the most cursory of glances. She was sure if he ever smiled he'd have one of those panty-dropping, Colgate smiles from romance novels – which would be an issue because she already wanted to drop her panties for him.

She fanned herself with her hand as she walked, but it did little to quell the burning ache building in her body. Oh what she would give to have a fan for her vagina.

He walked them to the coat check to collect their things, helped slip her coat over her shoulders, then escorted them outside and waited until their Lyft arrived to take them home. He opened the door for her, too. A perfect gentleman.

A perfect gentleman with a dark and twisty side. A shiver rolled through her muscles making her twitch against his palm as he guided her into the car.

"Get home safely, Mackenzie. This evening has been a pleasure." He brushed his lips against her cheek, then he was gone.

She plopped onto the leather backseat with a huff of air. Addison shoved her bicep. "Spill. What the fuck was that?"

Heaving out a relieved sigh, she shrugged. "I have no idea." But she wanted to find out.

CHAPTER 3
Austin

"The fuck is your deal tonight, Tin Man?" Johnny White, fellow Snow Pirate and resident asshole, shoved Austin's shoulder as he stepped off the ice and onto the bench. "Where the fuck is your head at? I got creamed against the boards and you let that fucker get away with it."

Finn O'Brien sniggered and raised an eyebrow that said 'he deserved it,' but he kept his mouth shut.

"I told you not to call me that." Austin dropped onto the bench and squirted cold water into his mouth from his water bottle.

"I'm not the only one." He shrugged. "And the shoe fits." Johnny had been calling him Tin Man for as long as they'd known each other. It was a nickname for a mean, cold-hearted Austin.

"We use it affectionately." Russell Stewart growled out every word as his intense stare held Austin's.

"Yup." Finn popped his P and reached over Austin's head to rub his glove on his chest. "We know he's warm and squishy under all those fuck-off vibes he puts out."

"You're just a dick."

He smirked as Lincoln Scott joined the discussion. Austin didn't need his teammates to have his back, but it felt good that they did all the same. He could handle himself. A black belt in Krav Maga who regularly fought at the cages in the warehouse district downtown, he was more than capable. And there wasn't a single player in the league who didn't know as much.

On the ice, he reined it in. On the ice, he played good cop – have the skills but never need to use them. It was how he liked it and it worked. He couldn't afford to let his anger lead to injury – either his or someone else's – or to muddy the precious Morgan name. The cages were his pressure valve. In the cages, he released the stress and tension that coiled in his stomach like a serpent and wound its way around his muscles.

"Change it up." Coach Swift smacked his clipboard off the edge of the bench and bodies launched themselves onto the ice as the previous shift made their way back to base.

"You doing okay, Auzzy?" Finn's low voice was close to Austin's ear.

He grunted in reply. He'd been off balance since he'd seen the firecracker trainer at the club the night before, and no amount of meditating or breathing exercises seemed to be able to ground him. His lack of inner peace only grew when daddy dearest had woken him up at 4.30am to talk about the family business.

Austin almost choked on the snicker that escaped his mouth. His father was more concerned with public perceptions of his family than he was with the family itself. He forced a cleansing breath through his body to center himself. He couldn't afford to let dear old dad upend him any more than he already had.

"Here if you need to talk, man." Finn patted his shoulder as Coach called another change. Austin took pride in not needing anyone. He was there for people if they needed someone, but he handled his business himself. He certainly wouldn't be talking to Finn I'm-in-love-with-my-best-friends-sister-and-think-no-one-has-noticed O'Brien about a woman who captivated him with her sass and curves.

Austin threw his leg over the boards and hit the ice. He shook his head, but it didn't clear the striking, wide, olive-green eyes from his mind.

#71, the player who'd thrown a dirty check at JW skated past with a smirk twisting his lips around his mouth guard. Austin glanced at the ref and linesmen, and shouldered him into the boards with a snarl. Shots fired.

His opponent groused, but didn't retaliate, instead opting to skate across the ice and back to his bench. A twinge of pain in Austin's shoulder gave him pause. He was in peak condition. His body was a temple. He ate well, slept well, and exercised – often multiple times – daily to maintain a clean and healthy lifestyle. He had no time for injuries, no matter how inconsequential.

Rolling his shoulder he shoved down the irksome flash of pain and intercepted the puck at his defensive line, playing it forward to Johnny who gave a sharp nod. It was as close to an acknowledgement or a thank you as Austin would get from the asshole, but he'd take it.

Finn skated up the left wing, he'd been having trouble with his knee on and off and had gone to see Mackenzie about it at least once. Mackenzie. Why couldn't he get the woman out of his head?

Obi passed to Linc who lit up the lamp with a slapshot no one saw coming and the crowd went wild.

Austin stepped into Pucks and cringed. It was country night. They'd cleared a dance floor and placed a few hay bales around the edge and pop-country blasted from the speakers. He couldn't do it. He hated country music, and despite the fact the team had won their game, he still felt like he'd somehow let them down by having an off night.

A hand clasped over his shoulder with a firm grip. "Let's get a drink." Russ tugged him forward, but Austin held his ground.

"I think I'm heading out."

Russ raised an eyebrow. "You good?"

Austin started nodding, his eyes scanning the bar. He'd just opened his mouth to answer his friend when a familiar nose ring caught the lights overhead and glinted like a beacon. Mackenzie and one of her friends from the club the night before sat at a table on the edge of the dancefloor. Okay, so maybe he could tolerate a little country.

Russ raised questioning brows over his still expectant stare. "Austin? You good?"

"I hate country."

"Same. But we like beer, so let's drink."

He couldn't really argue when Russ was right, so instead, he followed him to the bar and accepted the cold bottle of Sam Adams that was handed to him when he got there. Mackenzie and her friend sat a few feet away side-on to him, sipping on margaritas. She had one leg slung over the other and her boot-clad toes tapped in time with the music.

Linc and his girl, Cleo, stood off to the side, heads close together in a bid to hear each other over the loud music.

He couldn't believe the change in Linc since he'd met Cleo. She was good for him. Encouraged him to just be who he was instead of who his father tried to craft him to be.

A sour taste coated his mouth. For all his strength on the ice, and in the ring, even after years of trying, Austin still couldn't find the most important strength of all: the strength he needed to stand up to his own father.

Taking over the family business might not be so bad, it just wasn't what he wanted to do. While his father lived and breathed corporate America – a qualified lawyer who'd gotten rich off his father's coattails and wise investments in the stock market and who owned a major aviation company – Austin was cut from a different cloth entirely.

Movement in his periphery dragged his attention back to the trainer. Her blonde hair was braided in neat pigtails that hung over her shoulders. If her reaction to the plug on the table in the club was anything to go by, she was vanilla, and not at all into the kink lifestyle. But that didn't stop his dick from twitching at the 'safety first' hairstyle that made his fingers itch to reach out and tug on them.

She wore a green and blue plaid checkered shirt tied under her cleavage, layered over a blue tank top and jeans that hugged her in all the right places. She watched the line dancing that had begun on the floor in front of her, a wistful smile on her face like her surroundings transported her somewhere other than a cold November night in Minnesota.

Her mouth moved in time with the lyrics being sung by some heartbroken cowboy as she placed both feet flat on the ground and moved them in time with the people dancing.

The movement which had caught his attention was a man approaching her. He'd tucked his cowboy hat under his arm and reached a hand out to her. As Austin sipped on his drink in the hockey honkytonk from hell, Mackenzie simply flitted her eyes between the man's outstretched hand and his face as though trying to figure out his intentions.

The dance on the floor ended, the band fell quiet for a blissful moment, and Mackenzie's polite 'no thank you' met his ears.

"Don't those boots know how to two-step?" The stranger tilted his head and studied her feet with a wry smile.

With a spark of indignation in her eyes, she folded her arms. "Yes, sir. Every self-respecting Texan woman worth their salt knows how to fucking two-step."

The man pursed his lips, clearly fighting a grin. "Prove it."

A muscle in her cheek twitched as the band started the next song. She placed her drink onto the table and stood, brushing her palms along the denim on her thighs before taking the man's still outstretched hand and following him to the dancefloor.

"What do you think, Auzzy?" Finn waved his beer in his direction.

While the luscious blonde being spun around the room had captivated Austin's attention, he'd still half-listened to the conversation happening next to him between his teammates Finn, Russ, and Cory.

"I think it was rightly disallowed. No goal."

Finn whooped and Russ shook his head. "You don't know what you're talking about."

Turning back to the dancefloor, Mackenzie's head was tossed back as she laughed, a wide and beautiful smile lighting up her face. He'd thought the tug to her at the ice rink when they met was fleeting, that he'd been drawn to her because she was everything that his ex, Brittney, was not. But everything from her quirky clothes and oversized glasses to her perfect curves called to him.

He needed to put himself in her path, to get to know her better. The man holding her as they danced leaned closer to her neck. Did she still smell like lemons? He'd had to lean back from her when he'd caught her on the stairs, assaulted by nostalgia from his childhood when the scent of lemons invaded his nose.

It reminded him of happiness and sunshine. His mom in the kitchen baking his favorite dessert, teaching him her secrets. Almost every good memory he had was laced with lemon. He'd fought every urge in the club to bury his nose deep into Mackenzie's golden waves and inhale.

Was it a one off? Or did she still smell like lemons? It bothered him that he didn't know the answer, but the stranger spinning her around the dancefloor probably did. His phone vibrated in his pocket. His father, Malcolm Edward Morgan was calling again, probably to berate him for the game, or his hair being too short, or his grades not being high enough for a Morgan. He jammed the phone back into his pocket and gripped the cool glass in his palm.

"What'd the bottle ever do to you, man?" Lincoln's concerned eyes made Austin's stomach churn. He hated pity, sympathy, anything that suggested weakness. Hated. He didn't need his friend's pity, he needed his father to get off his case and let him live his life the way he wanted.

Except it wasn't quite that simple. If he chose to distance himself from the family it meant being cut off financially, and although that would have stung, it wouldn't have been the worst thing to happen. The worst that could happen would be that his father would likely insist that his mother cut him off completely as well. His gut twisted. Not an option.

"You okay? You seem... off." Lincoln held up two fingers to the bartender to request another round.

"Wishing I'd stayed in Europe." Austin drained the dregs of his beer. He'd taken a year out to play hockey and travel Europe before starting at the University of Minnesota, so he was one of the oldest in his year and on the team. He raked a hand over his face, stopping short when he remembered he'd cut his hair and there wasn't much to drag his fingers through.

Linc whistled. "That bad, huh? If you hadn't come back from Europe you'd never have met us. And not to toot my own flute or anything, but we're pretty rad."

Austin shook his head and put his empty bottle down on the bar. "Flutes do not toot, Linc."

"Yeah but horn doesn't rhyme." He accepted the two beers from the bartender with a 'thank you.' "Wanna talk about it?"

Austin took the second beer from Linc and took a sip. It

was no secret that he had daddy issues, too. Living in the shadow of a great NHL superstar came with its own baggage.

"Dad stuff."

Linc took a long pull from his bottle and nodded. "Must be tough."

Austin made a non-committal noise in the back of his throat.

"As the son of a successful man, I know what the pressure can be like, Austin."

At the use of his name, his head snapped up. Linc's face was pulled into a frown, his lips pursed into a grim line.

"I can only imagine the level of pressure involved when you're the son of a billionaire."

Austin snorted. His family fortune was no secret. Nor was his father's disdain for Austin's decision to travel abroad, play hockey, and study psychology at the U. Morgans went to Brown, or Yale, Dartmouth, Harvard, Cornell, Princeton... they were all acceptable options. Stanford at a push. Hell, even MIT or enlisting in the military would have gone down better than psychology at the U.

He had almost buckled under his father's pressure to attend an Ivy League school. Father had said if he didn't attend a school of his choosing, he wouldn't pay for tuition. Mercifully, Maman had intervened on his behalf and talked Father down, but Father wouldn't let it happen a second time.

"He's... something. I'll give you that."

Linc nodded, his face still serious like he knew only too well what Austin was talking about. "Not gonna push you to talk. We all know you're a man of few words. But if you need to take a load off..." He patted his chest. "I'm here and a good listener."

"Thanks."

Linc hesitated, like he wanted to say more, but left with another nod. When Austin turned back around, Mackenzie was gone. She wasn't on the dancefloor, she wasn't in her seat, and her empty glass taunted him from the table. He'd missed his chance to talk to her again. It probably wasn't the worst thing since he was surrounded by his teammates. Perhaps she was afraid he was going to out her as some dirty little kinkster. The thought made him chuckle as he remembered the look on her face when she'd seen the plug at the club.

"You know, they say talking to yourself is a sign of madness, but I think laughing to yourself is even worse." Her southern drawl poured over him like top shelf liquor over perfectly formed ice cubes. He closed his eyes and sucked in a breath. Lemons.

"Good evening, Mackenzie. How are you?"

"So formal, *Monsieur*." Her pronunciation of the word surprised him. Perfect. Those who didn't speak French often butchered the language. But this southern surprise nailed it. "Don't you think we're a little past 'good evening' considering you saw me half naked last night while almost caressing a stranger's ass-plug?"

He couldn't help but smile. She had a point.

"Ah ha!" She pointed at him. "So you do smile. Good to know." She picked up her fresh margarita and took a sip as he turned to face her. His eyes drifted over her plump lips, her rosy cheeks, and the tiny diamanté stud glittering in her nose.

"I'm out." Will, the team captain, smacked Austin's bicep. "Don't stay out too late, okay? And make sure these degenerates don't get themselves in trouble." With an easy smile at Mackenzie, Will left.

When he turned his attention back to Mackenzie, her entire demeanor had shifted. Her eyes turned downward, she fidgeted with the straw in her drink, and her shoulders rolled forward.

"I haven't told anyone about last night, Mackenzie. Nor do I plan to. You can breathe easy. I would never betray anyone's trust like that." He meant it, too. Even beyond the rules of the kink community, he was a trustworthy man.

She nodded and stirred her drink. "Have you ever used one?"

His desire to reach out and pull her to him inched him closer to insanity. What was it about the woman that was so alluring?

She arched an eyebrow when he didn't reply. "Well? Have you?"

"Used what?"

She cast a wary glance over both shoulders before putting her hand next to her mouth and stage whispering. "A butt plug. Have you ever used one?"

A wisp of hair loosened itself from her braid and fell across her face. Her innocent, green eyes with flecks of gray around the edges held his. He nodded. "Yes ma'am, I have."

She held up an open hand. "Did you just... ma'am me?"

He shrugged. While she'd called him 'sir' the previous night, she'd also called Mr. Cowboy sir when he'd asked her to dance. "It would seem that your southern manners bring out my honorifics. My father would be pleased."

She pursed her lips and squinted. "You can take the girl out of Texas..."

"But good manners always shine through."

"Yes, sir."

He covered his unintentional groan at her words by taking a drink of beer as she watched him quietly.

"What?"

He quirked a brow.

"That look. What was it?"

He leaned toward her. "Sir is a term many submissives bestow on their dominants."

She held his gaze, her fingers still idly stirring the straw around her glass. "I'm not your submissive." She picked up the glass and tilted it toward him. "And you are not my dominant." The flush in her cheeks darkened. The more the pink blossomed across her skin, the more he desired to see that flush spread across her entire body.

He nodded and drank again. "This is true, you aren't. And I am not. That doesn't mean the words don't affect me when spoken from the mouth of a beautiful woman, though." He reached out and swept her stray hair behind her ear, gliding his fingers over the apple of her cheek, not missing the flutter of her pulse at the base of her neck. Warmth spread up his arm and into his chest.

She was fire, he was the moth. No one else existed in the bar, not his teammates, not the bartender, not the other patrons in the bustling, busy space around him. There was only Mackenzie.

He wanted to lean into her magnetism, to learn everything there was to know about her. He couldn't seem to fight the urge to plant himself in her orbit.

He swallowed. It wasn't like him, and he needed to find the emergency exit before things got complicated with the woman who didn't belong in his world, and who didn't date guys like him. His curiosity burned. Was she truly vanilla? Or had she simply never had the chance to explore her every desire?

"Why?"

"Why do they affect me? Or why do submissives call their dominants 'sir'?"

Sipping her drink with a slurp, she nodded. "Yes."

"It used to be that almost every dominant was called 'sir' right off the bat as a mark of respect."

"But it changed?"

He nodded. Somewhere in the bar, someone broke a glass, or two. Mackenzie started beside him, covering her chest and laughing it off, but there had been a moment of sheer panic in her features that sent shards of ice into his soul.

"Yes ma'am."

She stiffened, and her chest rose faster.

"It changed. Pretenders who were not really dominant at all demanded the title be used. When it's used so frequently, it loses its meaning, its importance. And it wasn't fair to submissives." He brushed her braid over her shoulder, exposing the column of her neck. "It isn't right to assume that just because someone is submissive, that they are submissive to all. Some demanded the title even when showing a complete lack of respect for their submissive."

"And you?" Her eyes sparkled under the bar lighting, the gray specks seeming almost blue when she moved, turning her head to stare back at her half-empty glass.

He dragged his thumb along her jaw, enjoying the almost imperceptible hitch in her breath and shudder through her body that followed. "When my submissive calls me 'Sir' it is because I have earned the title, earned her trust, and earned her respect. When she calls me 'Sir,' it means she trusts me and what I have to say. But I don't demand it. And I don't expect it bestowed on me if I do not deserve it. It is something I endeavor to earn every single day."

When she finally let out her breath it was ragged and shaky. He enjoyed knowing that his proximity to her affected her in some way, as hers did him. She remained quiet for a moment, as though churning things over in her mind. Silence didn't bother him, though he'd give almost anything to shut the persistent twanging country music up. She enjoyed it though, tapping her finger against the side of her glass, or her foot on the floor, and she'd sang along with every word of every song that had played since he'd arrived at the bar.

"Wait." Her head snapped to him on a gasp, her eyes wide, and eyebrows high. "You've used a butt plug?"

There was no judgment in her eyes, only surprise and maybe a hint of inquisitiveness. She hadn't recoiled in horror at the idea that he'd had a chunk of cold, hard metal in his butthole, nor had she run away screaming. He'd misjudged her. Perhaps he'd even buy her a plug of her own to see what she thought of it.

CHAPTER 4
Mackenzie

Kenzie clutched her Starbucks hot chocolate in one hand, and her phone in the other as she entered the elevator at the arena.

Monday mornings were a special kind of hell. A gallon container of milk had fallen on her counter and sprayed her kitchen, she'd left the house without her keys and had to get the spare from her neighbor, and she'd gotten a ticket on her way to the office.

> Kenzie: There are not enough middle fingers for this Monday morning.

> Paige: Uh oh. It's barely 9AM and you're already out of fucks? What the hell happened?

> Addison: When life gives you Monday, dip it in glitter and sparkle all day.

> Kenzie: I'mma dip my foot in glitter and stick it up your ass so your shit sparkles for days.

> Paige: Period?
>
> Addison: Lucky for you, I don't mind stuff being stuck up my ass.
>
> Paige: Same, girl. Same.

Kenzie winced as the doors to the elevator slid closed.

> Kenzie: TMI, y'all. T-M-fucking-I! And no, I don't have my period.

The door stopped at the last second and rebounded open. Austin stepped inside, wearing sweats and a faded Snow Pirates t-shirt. "I love you."

Kenzie's heart stopped beating. He loved her? How could he love her? She glanced over her shoulder at the wall behind her to make sure he was talking to her. There was no one else in the elevator. She cleared her throat. "I... uh, love you too?" She frowned. Something weird was happening and once again she was convinced he was playing some kind of trick on her.

His brow crinkled and he rolled his lips. Slowly turning the right side of his head toward her, he pointed at the Airpod lodged in his ear.

Fuck. She buried her head in her phone while a swarm of bumble bees took flight in her chest.

> Kenzie: Fucking fuckety fuck.
>
> Kenzie: DIDN'T YOU HEAR ME? I SAID FUCK, GOSH DARNIT.
>
> Kenzie: I'm fixin' to set off the fire alarm in the building as a distraction.
>
> Paige: I love when your Texan shows.

> Kenzie: Anyone know how to summon a demon? Or a portal? If the ground could swallow me whole right now that'd be peachy.

Addison: What the hell is going on over there? Do you need adult supervision?

> Kenzie: Only every damn day. One of the players got in the elevator and said 'I love you.'

Paige: You didn't.

Addison: She totally did.

> Kenzie: I didn't want to be rude.

Paige: Can you hear that noise from across town? That's me laughing like a hysterical hyena on laughing gas.

Addison: I think I peed myself a little.

A throat cleared. His throat to be precise. But she refused to take her eyes from her screen.

"Mackenzie?"

Maybe she could pretend she was someone else. Or that she didn't speak English. Or that she was on the phone talking to someone, too.

Shit.

Her entire body was hot. Her face was probably so red they could see it from satellites in orbit.

Fingers hooked under her chin and tilted her head. "Are you going to stay in the elevator all day, Mackenzie?"

"No, sir." She sucked in a sharp breath, then coughed. "I mean, Austin. I have things, work, stuff to do. Groins and stuff."

If the fact she wasn't at all kinky wasn't enough to turn the stunning man in front of her away, the bumbling idiot pouring from her lips like molasses would do it.

"Groins?" His lips twitched, but she couldn't bring herself to look any higher to see what his eyes held.

"Shoulders, too." She shrugged like it was totally normal for her to be frozen in place in the elevator, talking about doing groins to a near stranger she'd said 'I love you,' to.

He slipped his hand into hers and tugged, pulling her away from the wall of the elevator and out into the corridor. She retracted her hand, but followed him a few steps before realizing she was going the wrong direction. She stopped dead, hooked a thumb over her shoulder. "I'm uh... I'm going to... my office is..."

She spun on her toes, wincing as her foot squeaked against the floor.

"Mackenzie?"

She stopped, but didn't turn to him.

"Have a good day."

She waved a hand back at him over her head and forced the hysteria bubbling in her chest out of her voice. "You, too."

Her temples throbbed as she pushed through the double doors and kept walking, dumping her half-full paper cup of hot chocolate in the trash. Her stomach churned. The door to the restrooms smacked off the wall as she shoved her way into the bathroom. She checked the stalls were all unoccupied before she splashed water on her face, gripped the cool edges of the sink, and let out a loud groan.

He had to think she was a few sandwiches short of a picnic. How could she ever look him in the eye again? He was hotter than a honeymoon hotel, his mere presence tied her in knots. Woah. Did he like bondage? He probably liked bondage. Rope probably saw him coming and tied itself in knots.

Heat lapped low in her belly as she splashed her face a second time. Her phone chimed, and again. Three more chimes made her swipe the phone from the counter and open the group chat.

> Paige: So, are you married now?
>
> Addison: Do we need to buy hats?
>
> Paige: Dibs on maid of honor.
>
> Addison: No argument from me there. Too much responsibility.
>
> Paige: I wonder who our new brother in law is. Is he hot?
>
> Addison: Maybe she died of embarrassment.
>
> Addison: Kenz… replacing our best friend will be grossly inconvenient, so we'd prefer if you weren't dead. Reply please.
>
> Kenzie: Dangnabbit it I'm not dead. No thanks to you bitches. But I need to move away and change my name.

She dropped her phone. That was exactly what she'd done when she left Texas. Studying herself in the mirror, she steadied her breathing. Embarrassing herself in front of Austin Morgan was nothing compared to the shit-show ex and family drama she'd left behind. Maybe running away and changing her name for a second time was overkill.

> Addison: Twenty bucks says it was the hottie from the bar.

Kenzie groaned. How did they always just know?

Addison: OMG it WAS Mr. Hottie McDom wasn't it?

Kenzie: I plead the fifth.

Addison: Called it.

Kenzie: It's too early to drink, right?

Paige: I try to wait till noon.

Kenzie: I have never been so embarrassed in all my life.

Addison: Twenty bucks says this is the beginning of a beautiful love story.

Paige: I can see it now… gather round grandkiddies, it's time for meemaw to tell all y'all about when she met y'all's granddaddy, Austin.

Addison: Where would you even start? The almost falling on your ass part?

Paige: The plug, obvs.

Kenzie: I hate you both.

Addison: Austin offering her the kiddie assist at the rink.

Paige: I forgot all about that. It was a while ago, right?

Addison: Right.

Paige: Saying 'I love you' in the elevator…

Kenzie: I swear, I'm opening Craigslist. I composed the ad after our trip to kink-town.

> Paige: Wanted: two badass bitch best friends.

> Addison: Must be able to make you laugh, so you temporarily forget the crushing embarrassment of telling a man you wanna get nasty with, that you love him, in an elevator.

> Paige: That's a bit wordy.

> Addison: True, no one will read all that.

> Kenzie: How can I go back out there?

A toilet flushed behind her and she shrieked. The stall door creaked as it opened.

"Sorry. I didn't see you come in." Kenzie cupped her hot cheek with her cool palm as the woman washed her hands and left.

> Addison: Did you bring snacks into the bathroom?

> Kenzie: Who does that?

> Paige: Then you're going to have to leave the bathroom to eat at some point.

> Addison: Poor planning, K-K.

> Paige: Sucks to be you.

She shook her head and tucked her phone away. Her cheeks were still flushed but she'd faced worse. What was a little workplace embarrassment? They were both professionals, right? Maybe she could just avoid him. His file said he was fit and healthy, he didn't need her for her professional services, she was too plain Jane, girl-next-door for him in bed, and the arena was big enough that they could co-exist without her having to face her mortification every day.

She nodded to herself in the mirror, twisted her nose stud twice, and picked up her bag. That was all she had to do: avoid Austin Morgan forever and things would be fine. Bye, bye embarrassment. Hello avoidance. Simple.

She charged through the halls, not stopping until she reached her office, dropping her bag on the floor next to her desk and her butt in her office chair. She spun around to face her desk and squeaked.

A pink, glass butt plug with a decorative flared end lay on her desk with a bow stuck to it and a dangling ribbon attached to a gift card.

The card simply had a cell phone number printed in neat lettering with the initial A written beneath it.

That arrogant son of a bitch had left a butt plug on her desk.

She picked up a pen and used the end to roll over the pretty pink glass object. Her heart thrashed. Did he expect her to use it? Her hand fluttered to her mouth smothering a gasp. Who the hell did he think he was?

Who in their right mind just sent someone a fucking butt plug? He hadn't even sent it, he'd walked into her space and dropped it on the desk like he was dropping off a glass of ice tea. She yanked the top drawer of her desk open and picked the plug up by the gift tag, dangling it over the open drawer.

"Kenzie?"

She squealed, dropping the plug with a soft clunk, and spun to face Coach Swift.

"You okay?"

She rolled her lips, nodding, and willed her heart to stop thundering. "Yes sir, you just gave me a fright that's all. I was in a world of my own." She waved a hand as though he didn't almost catch her with a sex toy in her office. The skin on her cheeks prickled with heat and she was sure a bead of sweat was weaving a path down her lower back and into her butt crack.

"What can I do for you, sir?"

"Just checking that everything's going okay? We haven't really seen much of each other, but I wanted to make sure you're settling in and the guys are treating you right."

Sure they were treating her right. Absolutely. Yes sir. If treating her right meant one of his biteable players leaving inappropriate gifts in her workspace, then sure thing. Everything was absolutely fine.

"Mmhmm. S'all good, Coach. Everything's going great. I really am grateful for the opportunity to work with the Snow Pirates."

"And we're glad to have you. You got Finn this morning?"

"Yes sir, I do."

"Hmmm." His phone rang out from his polo shirt pocket. "I gotta take this."

"No problem." She turned her attention to the offensive item still laying on top of a stack of multicolored Post It pads in her drawer. Asshole. What was she supposed to do with it? She could hardly throw it in the trash, the cleaning crew might see it. She'd have to take it home and dispose of it there.

She picked it up by the tag again and stared into the pink glass as it spun. It wasn't all that big. In fact it looked delicate and feminine. It was actually quite beautiful. She dropped it onto her open palm and closed her hand around it. Cold and hard. A shiver rattled through her.

People wouldn't put them in their butts if they didn't enjoy it, right? She clenched her ass cheeks.

She rolled the pretty object around in her hand. Her phone rang, probably Paige or Addison checking she hadn't run around the arena with her underwear showing or something else grossly embarrassing.

A number she didn't recognize appeared on the screen,

perhaps Paige was calling from someone else's line at work – as she often did. "Yes, I have all my clothes on, no I haven't done anything embarrassing in the past four minutes."

"Mackenzie." One word chilled her entire body to the bone. She turned over the gift card, read the digits printed in perfect black ink, and pulled the phone from her ear.

Fuck. "Austin." She breathed out his name hoping the fire flickering in her veins would escape with her exhale.

"Yes ma'am." His voice was laced with amusement.

"What can I do for you?" Her words sounded like they were rolling around with a mouthful of marbles.

"I'm not sure if I'm relieved or disappointed to learn that you have all your clothes on."

She groaned, a wave of heat licking at her skin. Fuck. His confidence and self-assuredness was enthralling and way more of a turn on than she wanted to admit.

"I see you got my gift."

She turned to find her door still open and Austin standing about twenty feet away, his hand tucked into his sweatpants pocket.

"Shit." She dropped the plug back into her drawer and slammed it shut. His chuckle reverberated through the line, making her clit tingle. "You know that's inappropriate workplace behavior, don't you, Austin?"

"No ma'am. Inappropriate workplace behavior would be if I bent you over your desk and inserted it myself."

Her jaw hung open. She should have been affronted at his forwardness. She should have been disgusted at his implication, but it only served to fuel the fire in her underwear.

Her brain no longer functioned. She couldn't remember how to form coherent thoughts and she was pretty sure she was suffocating as she forgot how to take oxygen into her body.

The half-smile that both drove her crazy, and warmed her

insides appeared on his face. He jerked his chin. "Use lubricant for the plug, Mackenzie. It'll make it easier." And with that he hung up, turned to his left, and walked away.

She hated him just a little. Because they both knew she was going to try the damn thing as soon as she got a chance.

CHAPTER 5
Mackenzie

Austin: Have you tried it yet, Mackenzie?

Kenzie coughed as she swallowed a mouthful of her margarita, sending tequila into places tequila had no right being. Her throat burned, her nose burned, and her eyes watered. She had saved Austin's number in her phone, but she hadn't yet used it, or the plug still burning a hole in her purse.

"Who is it?" Paige snatched her cell from her hand and ran the few feet across Kenzie's living room to Addison. "Austin. Ooh!"

"I told you. The start of a beautiful romance."

Kenzie snorted and tossed a throw pillow at them as they huddled together on the love seat.

Paige pointed the phone at Kenzie. "What? What is...?" She waved her hand in the direction of Kenzie's face. "What is that look? And tried what? What is he talking about?"

"I am not nearly drunk enough for this discussion, y'all."

"Spill." Addison leaned forward in her chair.

"No ma'am." Kenzie gulped down her drink. "Glasses are

almost empty, I gotta make more 'ritas." She bounced up from the couch and darted into the kitchen, swiping her phone back as she passed her friends.

Her electric juicer was the greatest gift she'd ever given to herself, not because she was some juicing heath fanatic, but because the best margaritas were made with freshly squeezed limes and she refused to do it by hand.

Ain't nobody got time for that shit.

She pulled the sharp knife through the flesh of a lime and placed the two halves into the juicer, pressing the button as her friends entered the room speaking to her. Pointing her fingers at her ears, she mouthed 'I can't hear you' to them, ignoring their scowls.

Her two friends pulled stools out from her breakfast bar. She loved her kitchen. Sure, she was an average cook at best and didn't use it anywhere near its potential, but it was her happy place.

Paige and Addison shared a look she couldn't decipher before Addison nodded. Pointing a knife back and forth between them she tilted her head. "What was *that* look?"

Paige nodded to Addison, who swallowed hard and placed two empty glasses on the counter between them. "It's time, Kenz. We want you to tell us what happened."

She'd met them in a bar on her first night in the city two years ago. Adrenaline pumped through her veins at finally having the strength to leave her abusive husband, her family, her entire life and everything she ever held dear in Texas. She had found herself propping up the bar with the worst margarita she'd ever tasted and on a trip to the bathroom she walked in on Paige and Addison reapplying makeup in front of the sinks.

Adi had complimented her boots, and for the first time in a long time it had felt like a genuine compliment. Not a back handed, sarcastic, "bless your heart," kind of compliment, but something real. They'd started talking, became fast friends, and by the time she'd peed and washed her hands, the dynamic duo had adopted Kenzie-the-newcomer into their circle.

They'd never pried too hard or too deep about her past. They'd accepted there were things she didn't want to talk about and had given her the space to exist the way she needed to. She'd tell them when she was more comfortable. But weeks turned to months and the unanswered questions still hung between them, a weight pressing down on her shoulders. They'd never brought it up, and she was content to live under its shadow, keeping that piece of her life to herself.

"Can't we go back to the awkward Austin questions?" She gave a nervous laugh as she free-poured tequila and Cointreau into a drinks dispenser.

"Two years, K-K." Paige put her glass down next to the other two. "You've been here for two years. It's time to share. We're your friends and we love you. We aren't going to leave you, no matter what."

"Translation: you waited for me to be merry on margaritas before staging an interrogation?" She added sugar syrup to the concoction in the dispenser.

"It's not like that, girl. You know we're your ride or die."

She sighed and sliced two more limes. "Why now?" She'd known it would happen at some point. And in fairness they'd given her two years, but why out of the blue and all of a sudden?

"Austin." Paige trailed her finger along the small, square tiles on the breakfast bar.

Austin? What did he have to do with anything? "What about him?"

"Like I said, the beginning of something special. I feel it." Adi reached across the counter to a bowl of salted peanuts and scooped up a handful, popping one into her mouth. "Your dating history is grim, Kenz. When you're not celibate, you meet a nice guy, go out on a few dates, keep them at arm's length, and never let them get too close. You either ghost them or they get tired of waiting for you to take the next step and leave."

Paige snagged a couple of pretzels from another bowl, pointing one at Kenzie. "The boyfriend step."

"We don't want you to make the same mistake with Austin."

Paige crunched on a pretzel. "We like him for you."

"Y'all don't even know him."

"We know how he makes your cheeks go pink. And that smile..." She pointed at Kenzie's face.

"And he's hotter than Hades." Addison dusted her palms together after finishing her peanuts.

"And all this means I need an intervention?"

Both her friends arched a single brow, Paige folded her arms. "We can't help you if we don't know what you're running from."

Kenzie folded her arms, maybe it would protect her from the shards of agony floating through her heart. "How...?" She cleared her throat. "How do you know I'm running from something?"

Addison rolled her eyes. "So we're doing this? You're gonna make us lay it out for you?"

"We're not stupid, Kenzie. You left Texas, and came to Minnesota. I don't know a single Texan who loves the cold and snow and who would volunteer to live there permanently unless something "big bad" was down south." Paige counted on her index finger.

She smirked. "How many Texans do you actually know, Paige?"

"Never talk about your family." Addison held up two fingers.

"Never talk about your life in Texas. Period." Paige tapped

on her third finger.

"Never visit Texas." Adi counted four.

"No one from Texas ever visits Minn-e-so-ta." Paige dragged out the word, making Kenzie giggle.

"Have you ever heard her talking about calling someone in Texas?"

"Nope. As far as I know, they don't call her either."

She'd kind of hoped they hadn't noticed her distinct lack of engagement with her prior life, but she couldn't fault them for being either observant, or concerned. She tipped the lime juice into the dispenser and mixed it with a wooden spoon before adding ice to two of the empty glasses and half-filling them with the delicious cocktail.

She gave herself a full glass, no ice, and chugged it down. If they were going to do this, she needed to grease the wheels just a little more. She needed the Dutch courage to tell her friends about her past.

When she'd finished, she dropped ice into her empty glass and filled it to the same level as her friends. Meeting their concerned eyes, she nodded. "Okay." After a stretched pause she nodded. "I can't get involved with anyone. Not seriously. Because I'm married."

She waited for the gasps and 'what the fuck's to erupt from her friends, but to their credit they remained silent.

"His name is Garrett. His daddy and my daddy..." Daddy. Her chest constricted. She missed him more than anything. She swallowed down the bubbling at the back of her throat. "They work together, in oil and gas. It was always just kind of understood we'd be together. Since high school. It was a good move for the families. His daddy owned a small oil company, and so did mine. Uniting the companies was good for business. Uniting the families was good for the company's future. The next generation when retirement came 'round."

Addison sipped her drink, clutching the glass with white

knuckles. Her friends had to know that nothing good would come from the story she was telling, and the anger was already spilling from their pores as she told her truth.

"I tried to tell mamma. Y'know? Garrett and I never worked. He was a stoic, silent type. And me..." She gestured to her favorite, bright yellow sweater. "I don't do silent. I guess they hoped he'd rub off on me and I'd settle down." She sipped from her glass.

"Like his daddy, Garrett was fond of bourbon. He and JD were besties, and he was a mean drunk."

Paige slammed her glass onto the counter. "Did he hit you, Kenzie? So help me God, I'll—"

"He hit me once. It was the night I left and came here." She couldn't meet their eyes. Her hands trembled and tears welled. "I told mamma. I told her he was a nasty drunk. The things he said, about my clothes, my appearance, my... everything. Constantly henpecking. Never enough and yet too much. I was just never enough for him."

She shrugged. "I guess he found 'enough' elsewhere. In Miss Sugar Land's pants."

"That sleazy son of a bitch."

"Mamma downplayed it. Looking back knowing what I know now, she gaslit me. She said it wasn't all that bad, so many people had it worse. It was what it was and I just had to take it. And I'd never dream of doing anything to hurt daddy and the business, you know? Be a good girl. Never speak out of turn. Always leave the house in nice clothes, make up done, and every hair in its place." Her Texan accent grew thicker as she spoke.

She swirled the drink around in her glass. "I drew the line at physical violence, though. I called him on his bullshit, accused him of cheating, told him I wasn't okay with it and he backhanded me like it was nothing. Got in the car, drove to that hussy's house, and by the time he got back I was gone."

"And your family?"

Kenzie shrugged. The misery of leaving in the night without so much as a trace lived in her daily. "They wouldn't have understood. They'd have convinced me to do the right thing for the family, for the business. They'd have made excuses. Apologized for him. But I was trapped. The only way out was either death or fleeing."

"Oh K-K." Addison was on her feet and rounding the table, arms wide open. "I wish you'd told us sooner. Not that we could change anything. But so we could just sit with you, and so you could have felt like you didn't need to hide a piece of yourself from us."

She accepted her friend's warm hug, allowing herself to sink into the sentiments swirling in her tight chest, her face warm from the emotion as much as from the tequila. "I was scared, I guess. And I didn't want y'all to look at me with pity."

Paige reached across the table and grabbed her hand from Addison's side. "Girl, we don't pity you at all. In fact, I think you're a freakin' badass. Finding the strength to leave a situation like that? That requires a vibranium vagina."

"Wakanda forever." Addison mumbled against Kenzie's shoulder making her laugh. She straightened up. "So you can't date a guy in case you fall in love, because you can't divorce Garrett without him finding out where you are, and what you're doing?"

"And you're afraid your parents will try to convince you to go back to him? Even after all this time?"

Kenzie bit her lip and shook her head. "They probably won't even talk to me now that I've disgraced the family by leaving. Mamma would have been madder'n a wet hen, y'all."

"I'm sure they'll have calmed down by now, Kenz. Two years is a long time to worry about your missing child." Paige still held Kenzie's hand and gave it a squeeze. "I wouldn't write them off completely."

Kenzie stiffened.

"Hey, I don't mean you need to run back and play happy families. I just mean they might surprise you. If my kid ran away and was who knows where for two years, I wouldn't give a shit what happened, I'd just be glad to have them back."

Kenzie shook her head. "You don't know my folks. Daddy… maybe. But mamma would dig her heels in. I brought shame on the family by being a quitter and running when things got hard – that's what she'd say."

Addison tightened her grip around Kenzie's chest. "You are not a quitter, Mackenzie Abbott. And things didn't *get hard*. They got abusive. You feared for your safety. And I'm even more proud of you now. It takes real stones to recognize when you're in a toxic relationship."

Something tightened inside her and she shook her head. "I'm going to have to disagree with you. It takes… luck sometimes. I was lucky. It took me months *after* I left to recognize it. It did take balls to step away from the relationship everyone thought was perfect. But by saying it takes stones… that makes it sound like those who stay are cowards. And they're not."

Addison squeezed her even harder. "That's not what I meant, I'm sorry. I just meant that it takes a lot to step away from that, even if it means leaving everything you're familiar with. All that and only twenty eight years old? Fuck. That's huge."

"Y'all gon' make me cry." Tears burned behind Kenzie's scrunched shut eyelids. "But I'm twenty seven. I'm not owning that extra year until I have to in a few months."

Paige wrapped her arms around Kenzie from behind. "Maybe you need to cry. God knows you've kept it all inside you for so long. We've got you."

She believed them. For the first time ever, she'd spoken her truth out loud to people who loved her. Her chosen family. And it loosened the knots in her chest, just enough to feel like she could breathe a little easier.

She still wasn't inclined to call Daddy by any means, but knowing that her friends knew her, the *real* her, shifted something into place inside her.

After a long, squishy hug, the girls separated and went back to their seats.

"So." Adi picked up her glass and took a sip. "What are we going to do about Austin? I mean, you guys are totally going to be end-game, I feel it in my bones. I've already picked out my dress for the wedding."

Kenzie opened her mouth to protest, but Addison held up a hand to stop her, and continued. "It's not something you need to deal with right now. Right now, we just gotta get you two together. We'll deal with the future stuff in the future."

Kenzie reached under the breakfast bar and pulled out her purse. The plug landed on the breakfast bar with a shrill 'ding.' "He left a butt plug on my desk at work."

Both her friends cracked up laughing. "You're kidding?" Paige picked it up and examined it. "This is nice. Not too big, not too small, just right for our Goldilocks."

Addison snorted. "And they say romance is dead." She wiggled her eyebrows. "So he clearly wants in your pants. I think you should totally let him."

Kenzie downed the rest of her drink and refilled her glass. She wasn't nearly drunk enough for the conversation. Talking about her abusive ex and her family? Sure. She could handle that. Talking about the fact the tall drink of water from work wanted to bend her over her desk and put a plug in her ass? Not so much. "I can't."

"Can't and won't aren't the same thing."

Addison lifted her glass to clink it against Paige's at her announcement. "She's right, K."

"No. I mean, I can't."

"State your reasons." Paige took a drink.

"And make them good please." Adi folded her arms.

"He was in that club. He's a Dom. He clearly wants a submissive."

Paige extended her hand as if to say 'go on...'

"Y'all, I am the least submissive person we all know. I'm stubborn, sassy, and southern. It's the trifecta of hell-to-the-no when it comes to the type of women Austin Morgan wants in his bed. And speaking of his bed, we *all* know I'm too boring for him, too."

"Wow." Paige's eyes were wide.

"You see? I told you." Kenzie shrugged. "I can't."

"Oh. No. I don't agree with you. I think you're an idiot." Paige threw a peanut from the bowl at Kenzie's forehead.

"Ow!" She rubbed her head with the heel of her hand. "What the hell?"

"First." She ticked off a finger. "Don't you think he should get to have a say in who is and isn't right for him?"

Before Kenzie could answer, she continued. "Not having experience, and not being kinky are two totally different things. You've never been exposed to kinks to know if you have any."

She raised her third finger. "Three, just because you're a badass boss bitch in your day to day life doesn't mean you won't love getting on your knees for him. Giving yourself over to someone entirely is hugely freeing. Saying 'yes Sir' when he tells you all the nasty things he wants to do to you? So fucking hot. Don't rule it out until you've tried it."

"Seconded." Addison raised her glass to 'cheers' with Paige again.

"Four. BDSM isn't always all about the pain. Don't get me wrong, there are definitely people out there who dig the pain. There are definitely pain Doms. And pain plays a factor – but that's not all it's about. Kink is about trust, finding that which brings you the most pleasure, pushing your limits, and trying new things." She threw the plug into the air and caught it. "Seems to me that your boy knows you're vanilla, and is keen to see if you have any kinks. The plug is in your court."

Addison coughed, choking on her mouthful of margarita.

Paige waved the plug at Kenzie. "But don't make assumptions. There's no such thing as 'all doms' or 'all submissives.' Each submissive and every dom is different. There are no rules. The real beauty is finding someone whose kinks match, and you can't stand there and tell me you don't match him. Because you're letting fear of the unknown color your judgment. And fear itself isn't a good enough reason not to do something."

Addison's jaw dropped open. "Damn. I love when you get all prophetic and shit. Prophetic? Is that the word I'm searching for? Philosophical? I'm pretty sure it begins with P." She sipped her drink. "Penis. You're getting Kenzie some peen. And I'm here. For. It."

Kenzie pursed her lips, letting her friend's words roll over her. "I dunno y'all..." No matter what her friends said, it was their job to see the very best in her. But she'd been too much for her husband, too loud, too brash, too individual. She'd been too much for her family. She was wild and free. If both were cut in half, she'd still have too much.

"Well. You won't know until you try." Paige rolled the glass plug across the counter to Kenzie and raised her eyebrow. "Will you?"

CHAPTER 6
Austin

Mackenzie: Yes Sir, I did.

He stared at the screen for what must have been a solid minute before he sucked in a breath or blinked. It had taken her almost a full day to respond. She was mocking him with her 'Sir,' he knew that much, but was she pulling his leg about the plug? Or had she really tried it?

Austin: Your sass is not lost on me, Mackenzie. But I hope you really did try the plug and more so that you enjoyed it.

Mackenzie: It was… cold.

He smiled as the 'she's typing' dots continued to flicker on his screen.

Mackenzie: I expected it to hurt. Or be uncomfortable when it was in.

> Mackenzie: OMG I can't believe I shared that.

> Austin: How long did you wear it for?

> Mackenzie: I feel the need to remind you that this is a grossly inappropriate workplace discussion, Austin.

> Mackenzie: And before you say it's not a workplace discussion, I know we're both in the same building right now. It's game night.

> Mackenzie: Inappropriate.

> Austin: Noted. Now tell me how long you kept the plug in for.

> Mackenzie: Ask me nicely.

He growled at his phone, a familiar tingle working its way across his palm.

> Austin: If you were here you'd pay for your sass.

> Mackenzie: Pay for it, how?

> Austin: I'd put you over my knee and spank that perfect ass.

The little dots moved on the screen. They stopped, started, stopped, started, and stopped again. She didn't reply. Dragging his thumb across his bottom lip he scowled. Perhaps he'd misjudged her. He'd been drawn to her fire, and while he had no desire to tame it, he wanted to push her out of her comfort zone. Perhaps he'd pushed too fast.

He tossed his phone into his kit bag and continued pulling on his hockey gear. She was right, it was game night, and he needed to stay in the right frame of mind to guarantee the win. Centered. Calm. Focused. Not distracted by idle thoughts of spanking one Miss Mackenzie Abbott's perfect ass.

The door to the locker room opened, and Austin had to blink to make sure he wasn't seeing things. Mackenzie stood clutching a clipboard to her chest.

"Cover your goodies, gents. There's a lady in the room." Finn cupped his bare cock with his hands as he waddled toward Mackenzie.

Over his dead body. "Finnegan. Back up."

Finn froze and reversed course. "I was only trying to see what Kenzie needed."

Her gaze raked over the locker room like she was searching for something before she shrugged. "Just wanted to make sure your knee felt good before the game, Finn." While she spoke to Finn, her twinkling eyes never left Austin's face. She shook her phone in her hand by her side as if to call attention to the fact it was there.

"I'm all good. No issues."

She nodded like that was really the reason she was standing in the doorway taunting Austin. He reached into his bag, a text from her lit up his screen.

> Mackenzie: Who said I took it out?

Another growl rumbled in his chest. She was playing with fire. She threw him a wink over her shoulder and sashayed out of the room. Sashayed. Swaying her ass from side to side like she had no idea what it was doing to him.

Oh. She fucking knew. He was on his feet and out the door, shirtless and barefoot, in a heartbeat. "Mackenzie."

She froze in her tracks, but took her sweet time turning to face him. Rolling her lips between her teeth did little to hide the smile on her face. She looked up at him with wide, fake-innocent eyes. "Yes, Austin? What can I do for you?"

He stepped toward her until her back met the concrete wall of the corridor and she huffed out a surprised puff of air.

"It would seem you've forgotten your shirt." She pointed at his bare chest as he boxed her in, palms on either side of her shoulders.

"It would seem you've forgotten your manners."

"No, *Sir*. I remember my manners just fine." She blinked, slowly. Once. Twice. Her nostrils flared as she clearly fought the smirk tugging on her mouth.

He lowered his head so his mouth was close to her ear. "You're playing with fire, Mackenzie."

A shudder rippled through her as his breath kissed her neck and she inhaled deeply, bringing her chest flush with his. "Actually, I'm playing with glass, Austin." She wiggled her goddamn hips against his. "And I kinda like it." Her sweet southern voice had a gravelly quality that scraped over his skin like sharp fingernails.

If she read the phone book out loud to him he'd probably find a way to get off without effort. His hand twitched again. She lifted her head in defiance. Intensity flaring in her eyes.

He couldn't figure the woman in front of him out. One minute she was turning down a man on the dance floor and abhorred by a glass butt plug on her desk, and the next she was being a brat. He liked it. He more than liked it.

"Mackenzie Abbottt. It is taking every ounce of self-restraint right now not to slide my palm over your neck. I want to drag my thumb along your jaw, slip my thumb into your mouth, and squeeze your throat ever so slightly."

She gasped.

"Morgan! Get your naked ass out of the corridor and ready for the game."

"Yes, Coach."

Mackenzie's hand had flown to her face to cover her mouth and her eyes were wide. "Did he see me?"

"I don't think so. I'm pretty big. He might have seen feet, but I doubt he'd know whose they were."

She placed an open palm on his chest and pushed. "This... this can't happen. They'd fire me. I need this job, Austin. I can't..." Her hands shook and her lip trembled.

"Hey. Hey?" He wrapped his arms around her and held her for a moment until her breathing evened out. "You good?"

She nodded against his chest.

He whooshed out a deep breath. "Steady breathing, okay?"

Another nod, but he didn't let her go.

"Everything is okay."

She hesitated, but nodded for a third time.

"I'll agree to nothing else happening at the arena. But what happens outside of the arena is our own business."

She shook her head. "It's too risky." She stared up at him. He could get lost in those impassioned green eyes.

"Persévérance arrive à récompense." He resisted the urge to reach out and touch her. He was a man of his word and no matter how difficult it was, he'd respect the workplace boundaries. But as he backed away from her toward the locker room, he regretted having ever said it in the first place.

Two periods and two goals down. The more the Snow Pirates dug deep, the more they seemed to bury themselves. Alabama dominated the game, both on the scoreboard and on the ice, and that fly lil fucker Jeremy Lewis seemed to be everywhere all the motherfuckin' time.

Wiping sweat out of his stinging eyes, Austin landed on the bench with a grunt. Fucking 'Bama.

On the ice, AJ Williams – Alabama's boy-next-door enforcer – slammed Russ into the boards. Russ lost his footing and ended up on his ass.

Austin couldn't hold it against Russ, AJ was a broad-assed dude who hit like a freight train and landed his hits with precision more often than not. The home crowd booed and AJ smirked around his mouth guard. He was a nice guy, the very definition of a lover not a fighter, yet as team enforcer the role often required an element of badass and DGAF.

The lines changed. Coach Swift mixed them up during the period break in a bid to turn the shit show on the ice into something... less shitty. It wasn't working. They stunk pretty bad. His head wasn't in the game, which was part of the problem, but he couldn't focus.

Austin slugged some water and tossed his bottle down with an unnecessary amount of force. With a growl, he hit the boards and jerked his head at Clement, calling for a change.

He darted off the bench and skated to his defensive zone with a renewed vigor. 'Bama might be winning the game, but he wasn't going to make it easy for them. Maybe a change of attitude would be enough to change the tide of the game. A win would be pretty sweet. Jeremy Lewis dug the puck out of the corner, jabbing his stick at the ice as the rubber disc refused to budge.

Austin cruised toward him. Throwing a shoulder at Lewis wouldn't do much to keep him from scoring – dude could score with a hand tied behind his back and a blindfold covering his eyes, but it would at least make Austin feel better. At the last second, the puck came free and Jeremy shifted. Austin collided against the boards with a force that shook the plexi and made the surrounding crowd go 'oooooh.'

A searing pain tore through his shoulder blade making him see stars. Fuck. He'd landed thousands of checks against dozens of boards and he'd never landed awkwardly. He'd certainly never dislocated his shoulder before. But having seen Linc and Finn both dislocate their shoulders at different times, he was pretty sure his time had come. Flexing his fingers, he attempted to flare his elbow, provoking a sharp stab that sucker punched the air from his lungs.

Not good. As he skated back to the blue line, he dared try to roll his shoulder and almost lost the ability to stand as he did. He'd always had a high pain tolerance, but the slightest movement of his right arm brought stars into his vision.

He hissed a breath through clenched teeth and headed back to base, clutching his bicep and hoping no one came anywhere near him. He managed to stumble off the bench, catching the attention of the team medics as he moved.

Kenzie met him in the tunnel. Someone asked if he wanted meds, but he shook his head. Once they popped his shoulder back in, the immediate red-hot pain would ease and it would be tolerable. He just needed someone to relieve the agony so he could see straight, and think straight, and make his way home so he could take an ice bath and sleep it off.

"C'mon slugger. Let's get you fixed up." Kenzie's voice lacked her usual energy, and her ashen face was creased with frown lines as she pursed her lips and regarded him with sympathy. He didn't want her sympathy. He wanted her expertise so he could get his shit together and get back onto the ice.

"I think I dislocated it."

She nodded and led him to her office. "I think you did, too. Quite a hit on a guy who was struggling to dig the puck out of the corner."

"Were you watching me play, Mackenzie?"

"I watch all my boys play, *Austin*. If I can see the injury as it happens, it's often easier to treat. I can tell ya, about 95% of shoulder dislocations are in the anterior direction, which means the upper arm bone is pushed forward out of its socket. With any luck, you're in the 95%."

"Is this where I slam my shoulder against a wall to put it back in?"

Her laugh wound its way around his throbbing muscles. "You've seen too many Mel Gibson movies. In some cases we need to sedate the patient to relocate the shoulder, but, again, I'm hoping you're a simple case and not going to ruin my Friday night with a trip to the emergency room."

"Hot date?"

She snorted as she led him to the edge of her treatment table. "Wouldn't you like to know?"

He would. Her evasion, while coy and likely a joke, burrowed under his skin like a needle. "Yes ma'am I would."

Her eyes met his and her nostrils flared. "In-a-prop-ri-ate." She dragged the word out longer than any human being had a reason to, and was almost whispering, keeping a shrewd eye over his shoulder toward the door.

"I can ask about your weekend plans."

"And I can ignore your question. I'm going to quietly insist you take the meds, okay? This is gonna hurt like all git out if it doesn't already. I know you're a 'body is a temple' kind of health freak, but right now your body is in pain and you need to take the drugs."

He smiled. "In-a-prop-ri-ate."

Her cheeks flared pink but she didn't back down. He relented and took the meds. She grabbed an ice pack while she waited for the painkillers to kick in and he noted how much he enjoyed seeing her do what she loved doing.

"Do you need me to cut your jersey off or can you manage?"

"I'm good." He wasn't good. It took less than a second to realize he should have swallowed his pride and let her cut the damn thing off, even having taken the meds. But some grunting and swearing later he was naked from the waist up.

He didn't miss the uptick in her pulse, the way her

breathing shifted to quicker little huffs of breath, or the bulge of her eyes as she surveyed his chest. Her hand reached out toward the ink on the left side of his chest over his heart, but she stopped short and yanked her hand back, clenching and flexing her fingers.

"What does it mean?" She slid her thumbnail between her teeth and sucked, as though holding herself back from tracing the lines on his skin.

"It's an Adinkra symbol. They're symbols from Ghana that represent concepts, aphorisms, objects that encapsulate evocative messages conveying traditional wisdom, aspects of life, or the environment."

She spoke around her thumb. "What does it mean?"

"This one is 'Morning Star,' Sesa Wo Suban. It means to change or transform your character. The star means a new start to the day and the wheel represents independent rotation. A vain attempt to remind myself every day that I can choose to be independent of—" He caught himself before he said his father's name. "Never mind."

She pursed her lips and took it in for a moment, tilting her head and narrowing her gaze. "I like it."

"The tattoo as well, right?"

"Aw. You got jokes. It's hella cute. You might want to hold on to that humor, because things are about to get pretty darn painful for you. Just remember not to shoot the messenger, okay? I'm just trying to help."

He smiled. "I can take it."

"I bet you can." She rolled her lips between her teeth and her eyes snapped wide. "Inappropriate!" She shook her head, pink blooming in her cheeks. "You ready?"

"Yes ma'am." He wasn't, but waiting wasn't going to help it either. "Let's get it over with."

❇

It had been a few days since Austin had busted his shoulder against the plexi glass. They'd lost the game, and he'd spent the past few days on the bench during practice and a game. For fans, watching a hockey game was everything. The sound of skates slicing through the ice, the smell of the chilled air, the speed of the game, the thrill of the goals, the camaraderie.

For a player, someone who lived and breathed the game, watching when you should be playing was a special kind of pain.

He'd done his time. He'd worn a sling, iced his aching muscles, and taken over-the-counter meds when the pain got unbearable. For a regular guy on the street, docs suggested two weeks of recovery before starting physical therapy. But he was done. It was time to rehabilitate his body and get the hell back on the ice.

"Austin." Kenzie's smile could light up even the most intense darkness. Her eyes raked over him. "I'm still not convinced this is a good idea. I think it's too soon. But you know your body, so we're going to take it slow, mmkay?"

He didn't answer, but sat on the treatment bed while she crossed the room to pull some loose pages from the top of the printer.

"So, for this type of injury, there are usually three things we want to focus on for recovery." She dragged a stool across the floor to sit in front of him. "Range of motion, stretches, and strength training. We'll go slow at first. We need to find the balance between getting you better and stronger, and pushing you too hard, so I need you to be honest with me or this won't work, okay?"

"Yes, ma'am."

"I mean it."

He glowered, but didn't answer.

"Not used to taking orders, huh?" She rolled her bottom lip between her teeth with her tongue and dropped her eyes to the pages stacked neatly on her thighs.

"No ma'am."

On first-glance the room was like any other clinical space he'd been to. Rehabilitation equipment lined the shelves and floor. A desk with a computer and printer sat off to the side, perpendicular to the treatment bed. The more his eyes roamed the room, the more of Mackenzie he saw scattered around the place. A corkboard hung next to her desk with pictures of her friends and concert tickets pinned to it. Next to it hung a whiteboard, with inspirational quotes scrawled on it, next to a to-do list that included 'making a to do list' as a line item.

The quote said: "She who is not content with what she has, would not be content with what she would like to have."

"You wanna start with some range of motion exercises?"

He nodded once. It was going to hurt like hell. There was no way around it. But he was a college hockey player wanting to make the big leagues, he had no time for injury and needed it to be past-tense.

"Okay then. Bend your arm at a 90-degree angle, then slowly move it back and forth as if you were power walking. Only, hold back on the power." She winked at him.

The first few exercises burned like she'd stabbed him with a red-hot poker. Sweat prickled across his forehead and trickled into the small of his back.

"I know it's hard, Austin. But you'll get there. You don't need to worry. You're not broken forever."

"I'm not. Our bodies are a constant source of feedback on our existence. Our physical, emotional, and spiritual needs. We are all broken in various ways. It's a matter of making sure we learn to listen and respond to what our bodies are telling us."

"You mean as long as it isn't telling you to take two weeks

to heal before starting physical therapy?" She handed him a pillow. "Or to stay on the bench for a while until it improves?"

He grunted. She wasn't wrong. He wasn't used to people calling him on his bullshit, though, and he wasn't quite sure what to do with it. Had anyone ever truly cared what was best for him? Father cared about the family name, and Mamma cared about keeping Father happy.

"Place a pillow between your elbow and torso. Squeeze the pillow with your elbow and hold the position for ten seconds. Repeat the exercise five times."

She walked to her desk and grabbed a Big Gulp sized plastic cup from her desk. Three others stood proudly in a row. Didn't she ever drink water?

He must have positioned the pillow in the wrong place because the scent of lemons wafted up his nose as she gently picked up his arm and readjusted the pillow. She paused, holding his forearm and their eyes met.

Concern swam in her green depths. "I was worried about you."

A moment of vulnerability. So pure, so sweet. "Isn't worrying about me inappropriate?"

She nodded, but her gaze drifted to his lips before fluttering back to his eyes. "Very."

If he angled his head just a little, their lips would meet. They were so close that her breath tickled his face and if he shifted his body forward, he'd end up buried in her chest.

Resisting doing the things he wanted to her was growing harder by the day. Sure, it was inappropriate, but that didn't mean shit. He wanted her. But she'd established a boundary he wouldn't cross, no matter how hard his dick was straining to break free of his sweats.

"You said not in the office."

She nodded and lowered her forehead until it rested against his. "I know."

"Inappropriate."

Her flushed cheeks darkened, and he could feel the thudding of her pulse as it raced. "I know."

She sucked in a breath and angled her head. Her lips closed the gap between them. She was so close he could already feel a ghost of her mouth against his.

"Auzzy, my man. How goes the pain?" Finn O'Brien burst through Kenzie's still part-open office door with the grace of a rhino on roller skates.

She sucked in a gasp that wound up being a squeak and turned toward her computer, angling her face away from Finn.

"Kenz. Loving those llama Toms."

"Hey, Finn." She threw a wave back over her shoulder before grabbing her soda and drinking as if she was sucking oxygen straight into her lungs.

"How goes it, Tin Man? Hurts like fuck, doesn't it?"

He wasn't wrong. But in the moment, his aching shoulder wasn't top of his list of agonies. He shifted on the bed, but that just caused his dick to chafe even more. He swallowed a groan.

"You look green. I'm gonna guess that means no cages tonight." Finn tossed a look at Kenzie's back, then back to Austin.

"Cages?" She angled her head so her chin was parallel with her shoulder.

"Our boy Austin, here, is a cage fighter. Not a bad one, either."

She arched an eyebrow, but not in surprise or approval. That look was nothing but fire. She spun to thrust an accusing finger in his direction. "No fighting. If you want to do this fast, you do it right. Don't be a dummy."

Finn rolled his lips, but couldn't fight the laugh that erupted from him. "A dummy?"

"It's inappropriate to call my patients names. I figured in the grand scheme of things, dummy was pretty benign."

Finn chuckled. "We can take a bit of name calling, Kenz."

She shoved his shoulder with a laugh. "I bet you'd even like it, Finnegan O'Brien."

If Finn wasn't a goner for another woman, the warm interaction between the two would have stirred a bitterness in Austin's chest.

"I gotta jet. But I wanted to make sure you didn't go too easy on him. We need him back on the ice."

"You don't need me to go with you to the cages, Finn. You can fight in your own right."

"I know." Finn pointed finger guns in his direction. "But you make it way more fun. Later gator."

Kenzie didn't move for a long minute after Finn had gone and pulled the door almost-shut behind him. When she finally moved, she walked to the door and opened it, so anyone in the corridor could see inside the room as they walked by.

She wouldn't meet his eyes, but her warm comfort, and easy smile had been replaced by stiff shoulders and silence.

CHAPTER 7
Mackenzie

"Inappropriate." She wasn't sure whether she was repeating the word out loud, or on loop in her head. What she wanted to do was cross the thick tension hanging between them in the treatment room and mount him like a prized stallion.

What she wanted to do was sit in his lap and ride what could only be a quality specimen of peen poorly concealed by his sweats. What she wanted to do was throw her clothes into the air and say "Take me, Austin," like some swoony heroine from a smutty historical romance novel.

She tugged at the collar of her shirt. What the hell had gotten into her? For two years she'd been satisfied with occasional sex and her mediocre toy collection. Last night, she'd found herself scrolling pages of Bellessa's website equal parts enthralled and intimidated by the various offerings.

What was it about Austin Morgan that drove her closer to sexual insanity every time they met? She was pretty sure if he'd told her to take her clothes off and get on her knees her body would obey. Traitorous shit that it was.

"Are you going to stay over there the entire time, Mackenzie?"

She'd backed herself as far away from him as the concrete walls of the building would allow and folded her arms. Her mamma would probably say, "Don't worry about bitin' off more than you can chew. Your mouth is probably a whole lot bigger'n you think." But Austin Morgan definitely felt too big to chew. She almost laughed. From the bulge in his sweat pants he was just about perfect.

"Mackenzie?"

She nodded, but didn't meet his eyes.

"Okay. But could we talk about something while I do these exercises please? I need a distraction from the pain."

He probably wasn't lying. The whole right side of his body probably ached, and she was sure the beads of sweat prickling over his body had beads of sweat of their own. He was pushing himself hard and fast, and it was going to burn.

She bolted forward, arms outstretched like she was going to touch him. "Are you okay? Is it too much?"

"Your concern is moving. But I'm okay."

She nodded but didn't hurry back into the corner, in fact she inched closer. "We can talk about anything?" Her cheeks heated at the question. Anything. Austin Morgan made her think and feel dirty things and what's more, she liked it. It was something she was itching to investigate further, but she had no idea where to even begin.

His chocolate eyes swam with challenge and intensity so strong she could almost feel it yanking the air straight from her lungs.

"Let's do some lateral raises." She grabbed a resistance band from one of the hooks lining the left side of her office wall. "We'll start with five, take a quick break, and do another five. Okay?"

He nodded.

"So... uh... you're really a dominant?" What a great question to start with. A-star grade for creative and wholly inappropriate questions for the workplace went to Mackenzie Abbott.

His lips twitched. "Yes, Mackenzie. I am really a Dominant."

Her heart picked up its pace. What was it about the way his mouth formed words that was so... erotic? "Like..." She threw a glance over her shoulder to check no one was passing her office before dropping her voice. "*Fifty Shades of Grey* kind of Dom?"

He snorted, and somehow the intensity deepened. She shifted her weight.

"Not quite."

Shame. She huffed out a breath as he finished his fifth lateral raise. She walked to her desk to take a drink, and increase the flow of oxygen to parts of her body other than her aching lady bits.

Who knew nipples could tingle so much just from hearing a man's voice? Certainly not her. She would ask her girlfriends if it had ever happened to them – assuming she survived the session and didn't die of sexual frustration first.

"And why is that a shame, Mackenzie?"

She coughed on her tea. She'd said it out loud? Again? For fuck's sake. She really needed to pay more attention to the things that came out of her mouth in his presence. "I mean..." She sucked another mouthful of the ice-cold sweet liquid. "I haven't seen it in a long time..."

She shrugged and forced her brain to search the 'hilarity' portion of her mind. She needed a funny quip that didn't point directly to the fact she wanted him to clip a bar to her ankles and throw her around the bed like an animal. "But I'd kinda love to have a bath with Jamie Dornan."

"Do you remember much else about the movie?" He

started on his second set of lateral raises, and his stare scorched her skin.

She shook her head. When she'd watched it, it had been an under-the-covers sordid affair with her laptop while her parents were out. If they'd caught her watching such '*deviance*,' she'd have been in a world of trouble. It was ingrained in her mind as taboo, untoward, things no sweet southern belle should ever do. Hashtag-mama-says.

Ugh. She eye-rolled so hard she almost dislocated her eyeballs. Hashtag-mama-says had become Paige and Addison's favorite game when they'd first met. Kenzie had done a lot of deprogramming when she'd moved to Minnesota, but considering she still kept every man at arm's length, there was never a real opportunity to explore the things she'd seen on the screen. Until now, at least.

"Mackenzie?"

Her head snapped up, had she said it out loud again? Her entire body flashed hot. "Mhm?"

"You're muttering to yourself, and I am not sure if that cup is deserving of your ire."

The plastic cup of sweet tea buckled in her fist, so she plopped it down onto the table with a nervous laugh. "I remember she used a safe word." She remembered more than just the safe word, she remembered the heroine using it when she'd been denied her release.

She'd never understood the allure of denying yourself the O – wasn't getting to the finish line the whole point? "Does that make you mad?"

He cocked his head and lowered the resistance band. "Does her using her safe word make me mad?"

She nodded. She didn't know much about much, but surely when the submissive reached her limit and tapped out that would at least bug the dominant, right?

"Mackenzie, true dominants appreciate the advocacy of

their submissives. I want nothing more than to see my sub well cared for and her body catered to. A good dominant should never be mad at their submissive for using a safe word. That's a red flag."

Yeah, her clothes were absolutely on fire and she needed to get naked to save herself. Or run. Or get naked and run. Instead, she moved closer to the fire, taking a seat on the stool in front of him once again.

She was caught in his blaze. There was no fighting, no escape, just a burning need between her thighs and the agonizingly long wait for the fire to consume her.

"I desire her curiosity. It is something that fuels me and drives me forward. But, if anything, I may be disappointed in myself if a safe word instance happens when I am not expecting it."

Kenzie swallowed. The man was sucking the oxygen from the room with every word that tumbled from those sinful lips.

"But when a submissive safe words it means a few things. First, that she is aware enough to know her limits and not afraid to speak when she has reached them – that is paramount in the lifestyle. Communication is everything. It's a sign of great strength to know when to use your safe word."

She cleared her throat. "And second?"

The corner of his mouth twitched again. She wanted to bite his full bottom lip and make dirty noises rumble in his chest.

"Second, it means that I pushed her out of her comfort zone."

A shiver pulsed through her. "You must have a very talented d—" Oh shit. Had she really said that? Her 'things you can say out loud' speech filter was clearly all-the-way-broken when she was near the man. "I mean... uh... you must be very talented."

"My dick is not all that talented. Most sexual arousal has

little to nothing to do with the reproductive organs in the first place."

How could he keep such a straight, impassive face, without as much as a muscle twitch, while talking reproductive organs? How could he make something so clinical sound so daggum hot? How could he just come right out and talk about his dick like he was chatting about the weather?

His dick. Sweet God in heavens. She couldn't help but focus on his crotch. "Inappropriate."

He pointed at her and leveled her with a look. The look. The look to end all looks. "You picked this conversation topic, Mackenzie."

He was right, she had. And she wanted more than just the conversation.

"L-let's do some shoulder rolls. Gently roll the shoulders forward for ten reps, then roll them backward for ten." She needed a cold shower.

He did things to her brain. Things that made her mouth say unbecoming words in the workplace. Things that could lose her job. "Why did he deny her an orgasm?" Her voice was barely a whisper. If anyone passing her office heard her talking about orgasms to one of her patients, she was done for. But a growing part of her didn't care.

"With my own submissive it is all about knowing that we are working in tandem to build up to that release." His eyes raked over her face and down her neck. "I have asked her to wait." He pulled in a deep breath. "She has chosen to fulfill that request. It is my duty to make sure the efforts are worth the wait."

Houston. They had a problem. The fire had spread. It had blazed through her clothes and was making a beeline for her core.

"Occasionally it is a punishment." He paused and tilted

his head. "But you should know that in those cases, it is also a punishment for myself."

Punishment? She squeaked. Punishments didn't sound fun, and yet something about how he said it, laced with promise, made her thighs clench.

Five-alarm fire! There was a five-alarm fire in her pants and it didn't matter how many firefighting units dispatch sent, there was apparently only one man who could handle the heat.

She tried to nod, but she wasn't sure her body was processing requests from anywhere other than her pussy at that time. "Lift both arms to the front of your body, then extend the arms above your head. And repeat."

Stick to work. She had to stick to work to let the thick plumes of smoke clear from her mind and allow her lady parts to cool down.

He followed her instructions, lifting both arms to the front of his body, then extending them overhead with a wince.

"You good?"

He nodded and repeated the action.

"What if it doesn't go the way you planned?" Her brain whirred. She just couldn't help herself. Her curiosity and her big mouth often got her into trouble with her parents in Texas. But Austin was so easy to talk to, he didn't make her feel like an idiot for asking stupid questions, and he was open to sharing.

"Mistakes happen. Those missteps are what grow your relationship. It's simply an opportunity to feel closer to one another. Though..." He paused his exercises and there was The Look again. "If you let your submissive lead the way, you'll rarely make a misstep."

She touched his arm. "Let's move to the wall to do some wall push-ups."

He followed her the few feet to the bare wall.

"Make sure your hands are placed slightly wider apart than your shoulders."

He smirked, but stayed quiet. Of course he knew how to do a push-up, he was a college athlete. College. Her stomach dropped. He was younger than her by three years. Maybe even too young. So it wasn't just inappropriate, it was grossly so. She swallowed down her bile.

"Okay, well, of course you know how to do a good push-up. Give me five, we'll take a breath, reset and do another five."

He lined up against the wall and did his first push-up with an almost inaudible grunt.

"Slowly, Austin." She placed her palm on his back. "Don't overdo it. If you exacerbate it, you'll only be stuck with me for longer." She giggled waiting for him to say something, but he remained quiet.

He did a second one. Damnit. Was being in her company so insufferable for him? Then a third. Was he that much of an overachiever?

"Then what kind of journal do submissives keep?" She folded her arm and rolled onto her toes. Nervous energy fizzled through her body and she wasn't sure how to dispel it.

"The things they eat. How much water they drink." He completed a fourth push-up. "Whether they've taken their vitamins, exercise, gratitude... and a record of their edging, plugging, clamping..."

Clamping? Her body froze as he completed his fifth perfect push-up. Sweat beaded across his forehead and his shirt grew damp in spots from exertion.

"You doing okay? Need a break?"

He shook his head. "I'm good for another five."

"Austin, you don't need to push so hard."

Did he snort? She was pretty sure that sound that came from him was a freakin' snort.

After his second set of push-ups, completed in silence

while her brain rolled over everything he'd said to her, he stood upright. Wiping the side of his face on the inside of his left bicep he sniffed. "What's next?"

"We're done for today." If he wasn't going to show himself grace, she'd do it for him. He'd had enough. "You can work on those exercises at home before our next session. There are a few more on the handout, I can email you a copy, too. You don't need to push yourself so hard, Austin."

He smiled and slid his hand through his hair and down the back of his neck, somehow still making the gesture look sexy despite the sweat trickling down his forehead. "Maybe I simply want to extend our time together, Mackenzie."

CHAPTER 8
Austin

"How could you be so careless?" Father's voice echoed around the produce section of the store through the cell phone clenched tightly in Austin's fist against his face. He stood next to his cart, selecting a container of grapes. Frozen grapes were his favorite snack, and he was all out. But talking to his father made his stomach sour.

"I did not do it on purpose."

"It sure looked like a stupid move on my television screen."

And if daddy dearest thought it was a stupid move, then it obviously was.

"You working with the trainer?"

"Yes, sir."

"Back on the ice this weekend?"

Austin winced. While his shoulder had improved over the past three days working with Mackenzie as well as doing the prescribed exercises at home, he wasn't sure he was quite ready for full impact.

"Austin?"

"Yes sir."

"Good. And we need to get a lunch on the calendar, your mother is starting to forget what you look like and she's bending my ear about it almost daily. I'll have Nancy call you to schedule something."

"Yes sir."

"Hogan's daughter is in town, you should call her too."

Austin remained quiet. An arranged marriage with his father's business partner's daughter did not feature on his to-do list. Luckily for him, he'd found out on social media that she was already in a relationship. "She's with someone. And she's not my type."

His protests would fall on deaf ears, but at least he'd made them. Again.

"It's temporary. She's waiting for you to get your shit together and do what's right for both our families. Your type doesn't matter. Keeping the business in the family is important, you know that. Why do you have to be so difficult?"

Why indeed? Maybe because he wanted nothing to do with the family business? It's not like they wanted him to sign his entire life away to a woman he had precisely zero in common with after all.

A door opened in the background, and Nancy, his father's personal assistant's voice came through the line. "Mr. Morgan? Your 1 O'Clock is here."

"Sure. Thank you, Nancy. Make it happen, Austin."

The line went dead. "Make it happen, Austin." Austin mimicked his father's tone and dropped the package of grapes into his cart. "Asshole."

"Austin?"

He'd know that voice anywhere. It had become harder and harder not to pin the lovely Mackenzie Abbott against the wall of her office to discover whether or not she was truly vanilla. But he'd respected her boundary and given her space.

As much space as two people working closely together could manage, anyway. "Mackenzie." He turned to face her.

Her hair hung loose around her face instead of her 'at work' ponytail. She wore oversized, purple-rimmed glasses instead of the contacts that she wore in the office, and a pale blue Snow Pirates hoodie fell almost to her knees. "You look beautiful."

Pink bloomed in her cheeks and she glanced at the ground. "Nothing says height of fashion quite like leggings and a hoodie. I didn't think I'd run into any of the Snow Pirates." She brushed a hand over her shirt. "Obviously."

He smiled. "I think what you mean to say is, 'thank you for the compliment.'"

She pursed her lips and sucked air through her teeth. "You're right. Sorry. I'm not so great at taking compliments." She held her hand up as though to silence him. "And that's not a pathetic, needy request for you to give me more."

Her face grew redder as she spoke. Someone clinked the end of his cart with theirs, pushing it against his back, and sending him a step toward Mackenzie. He reached out and tucked her hair behind her ear, not missing the shiver that passed through her as he cupped her jaw with his hand and tilted her head so he could see her eyes. "Perhaps not, but that doesn't mean that I do not have more to give."

How could she not see how beautiful she was?

She shrugged, her chest rose and fell faster and her eyes flickered down to where his hand touched her face. He stepped forward and she sucked in a breath. They weren't in the office – so far, that was her only rule. Granted, they were in the middle of the produce section – which some might also deem inappropriate – but they were not at their place of work. He lowered his head to hers, their noses touching.

"Austin." It fell from her on a breathy sigh and sounded

somewhere between a plea and a warning as she closed her eyes.

He ran his thumb over the seam of her lips and she parted them. Her eyes fluttered open and searched his, for what, he wasn't sure.

"I'm not kinky, Austin. I don't do the things you do. I don't go the places you go. I'm not the right girl for you."

He captured the other side of her face with his hand and held her gaze for a second before it flickered to his lips. "I'm going to kiss you, Mackenzie. You need to tell me if that's not what you want."

He shifted his palm and she tipped her head. An invitation. Surrender. Submission.

"I'm not what you want, Austin." Her eyes stayed fixed on his lips as he slid his fingers into her hair and tugged gently, so he could see into her eyes. She squeaked, but didn't recoil.

"You don't know what I want."

She tried to turn her head, probably in a bid to look at the passing cart and couple to Austin's left.

"People can see."

"Then let them see." He lowered his mouth to hers, taking his time, and when she rolled forward to meet his lips, he smiled at her impatience. He brushed his lips against hers and her eyes flickered closed.

He brushed against her again, reveling in the soft moan it elicited from her.

"Are you teasing me, Austin?"

"Just making sure you want it, since you were not clear with your words."

She rolled her eyes.

"Careful, Mackenzie. We've talked about your eye rolls before."

"You wouldn't spank me in the middle of the veggie aisle."

When he didn't answer, but tapped her on the ass, she gasped and he seized her mouth with his.

As he kissed her, she softened against him, leaning into his hands. Her lips fell open and his tongue invaded her mouth, sweeping against hers: teasing, exploring, coaxing. She smelled of lemons, she tasted of berries, and she felt right.

Her hand tugged on his balled shirt in her fist, pulling him into her as she met every clash of his tongue with hers. She was the moon, he was the tide. He'd been unable to fight her pull from the moment he'd seen her at the ice rink, and he was done trying.

"Austin..." Her breathy plea between kisses spoke straight to his crotch. He wanted to give her everything.

He pulled back. Desire shone in her eyes and her lips were already puffy from their kiss. She placed an open palm on his chest, for balance or to push him away, he couldn't tell.

Their eyes locked, her nostrils flared, and her brows rose. "Austin..." She touched her fingertips to her lips making him want to grab her and kiss her all over again.

"Excuse me?"

A strange voice pierced the spell like a pin bursting a bubble.

"Excuse me, sir?"

He turned to find an elderly woman with a wicked grin on her face brandishing an eggplant.

"Sir, could you give this a squeeze and tell me if my eggplant is ripe?"

"Bonjour, Maman. Comment vas-tu?"

"Je vais bien, mon chou. Et toi?"

Maman had called him her cabbage since he was a child, and no amount of grumbling about it during his teenage years had deterred her. She'd even saved him in her phone as 'Chou.'

Austin dropped the grocery bags onto the counter and pulled a bottle of water from the fridge.

"Oui, Maman, bien aussi." He unscrewed the cap and chugged half the bottle before he placed it next to the groceries.

"Ton père a dit que tu as appelé."

It was a version of the truth, something Father was very good at telling. He'd called Austin, not the other way around. Truth be told, if he never had to answer another phone call from his father, he wouldn't be mad about it. He didn't reply, Maman knew he wouldn't have called Father. It was the same dance they did every time they talked.

"Il a dit aussi que tu venais déjeuner."

Lunch. Right. He'd been steamrolled into agreeing to meet his parents for lunch. Not that he minded hanging with Maman, he missed her. But he'd rather chew glass than sit at a table with Father and make small talk.

"Oui, Maman. Nancy is supposed to call with a time to set it up." He pulled the grapes out of the paper bag and set about separating them from the stems and into the strainer. "Il m'en veut. Il est fâché après moi. Encore."

A huge sigh echoed down the line followed by a long pause. Not happy with him was an understatement. Father wasn't a subject they agreed on often. He was inflammatory and then some. He'd somehow come up in conversation, Austin would share his displeasure, she'd defend him, Austin would snap, they'd go quiet for a couple days and reset.

The reminder that they needed to stay on more neutral territory always came at a price. His relationship with Maman suffered because of the bully at the head of the table. And he hated it. He rinsed the grapes, dried them on a paper towel, and placed them on a baking tray to go into the freezer.

"Il t'aime, Austin." Her voice was quiet, fragile, like the gentlest breeze could break it. "Il ne sait tout simplement pas comment le montrer."

Damn straight he didn't know how to show his love. Mercifully, Father didn't show his love the way *his* father showed it, with a bottle of scotch and a belt. But he still couldn't find it in himself to excuse the man who used fear and threats of excommunication from the Morgan family to keep him in line.

Austin bit his lip to stop a tirade about the man Maman loved with all her heart.

"C'est difficile pour lui aussi."

Austin snorted, but swallowed it into a cough and washed it down with a few mouthfuls of water. It was hard for Father? Did she have any idea how hard it was for him? To live in his shadow, to strive to meet expectations he was never going to meet?

"I'll see you at lunch." He dropped his voice muttering under his breath. "Je ne serai jamais assez bien pour lui." No matter what he did, he would never be good enough.

Austin had put away the groceries and texted Mackenzie to tell her he wanted to take her out on a date. When she didn't reply right away, he'd gone out for a five mile run in a pointless attempt at sweating out the ire at his parents before showering and settling himself in for a long meditation. His Buddhist faith was yet another disappointment to his Christian father.

His phone chimed, from the kitchen counter and he groaned at how his pulse picked up at the idea she'd replied.

> Mackenzie: We can't be together, Austin. Dating is just delaying the inevitable. We are oil and water.

> Austin: Do you wish to be together, Mackenzie? We can figure the rest out together.

He pulled the tray of frozen grapes from the freezer and dropped a few into a small bowl before bagging the rest up as he waited.

> Mackenzie: How would it even work?

> Austin: We already talked about not doing anything at work.

She didn't reply for a moment so he dropped to the floor to stretch.

> Mackenzie: The kink, Austin. How would the kink work?
>
> Mackenzie: Are you a journal dom? Would you want me to keep a journal? And what? Take a picture of it and send it to you daily?
>
> Mackenzie: Do you want me to hump your shoes?
>
> Mackenzie: Drink milk from a saucer like a cat?
>
> Mackenzie: Wear diapers and suck a pacifier?
>
> Mackenzie: I feel like I need more information before I commit to a date.
>
> Mackenzie: What are the expectations of a Dom on a first date?

> Mackenzie: Whips and chains?

Austin chuckled. Either she'd been doing random searches on the internet, or she had spoken to someone who had whipped her into a frenzy about the kinds of things they knew about the lifestyle.

> Austin: Mackenzie?

> Mackenzie: Yeah?

> Austin: Take a breath.

> Mackenzie: You're not the boss of me.

He wanted to be.

> Mackenzie: But I'll do it anyway.

> Mackenzie: Only because I'm pretty sure I need one.

He waited a few minutes, folding his body forward over his legs and clutching his toes, quietly giving her time to process.

> Mackenzie: There is some wild and scary shit on the internet.

> Mackenzie: I'm not judgy or anything, but… damn. Some of those things… I just wonder how people come up with it to realize it gets them all hot and bothered, y'know?

He snagged a fresh bottle of water and a handful of almonds before moving to the sofa.

> Austin: Would you like to discuss what you found?

> Mackenzie: I'd like to know what I'm getting myself into.

> Austin: Until you tell me you want in, we cannot define the parameters of what it is. This is not a 'me' thing, Mackenzie. It is an 'us' thing.

> Austin: We do this together. We define it together. I am not the boss of kink.

> Austin: You, as my submissive, would hold the power.

After a beat of silence his phone rang.

"Mackenzie."

"Austin." She giggled. "You know, it never sounds as sexy when I say your name as it does when you say mine."

"I beg to differ." He shifted his weight on the cushion underneath him. His dick was already flying at half-mast and all she'd said to him was his name. He was a goner for her.

"So…"

The heavy pause that lingered on the line made him wish she was in front of him to see her eyes. He didn't want her anxious or afraid.

"You'd want me to keep a journal?"

"Eventually. If it's something you're open to."

"And what would I journal?"

He sucked in a breath. Transparency was key in any relationship, not just between a dominant and his submissive. If he held back, she might end up being blindsided in the future. It was best to be up front with his wishes and let her decide whether or not to join him on the journey.

"I believe a fully complete journaling session for you would include water and nutrition, activity tracking – both exercise and edging, plugging, clamping and any other submissive item identified. A counter for days since your last orgasm, an energy level rating, free journaling, maintenance of a list, kind of like a bucket list, affirmation lines, and a goal identified for the next day."

He popped a grape into his mouth and ran through the list again in his head. "Gratitude would be wise as well – with caution to not fill it with fluff. Though please know that this is not something I would propose on day one."

"Good. Because I can barely maintain a grocery list." Another pause and the pop and fizz of a soda can opening met his ears. She took a drink. "What kinds of affirmation lines would I write?"

He smiled, she hadn't called bullshit or said no out of the gate. "Perhaps it would benefit you to start with a reminder that growth and comfort can arise out of communicating when things are difficult?"

She laughed. "Instead of searching things on the internet you mean?"

"Yes ma'am."

"I didn't want you to think I was clueless. And the more I searched the more clueless I felt. And it was just overwhelming. I had no idea..." She slurped at the can and a second later bit into something that crunched. "What about... submissive stuff?"

"We can start with a list of things to talk through together. You can score them on a scale of one to five and we can work from there. Things you're curious about, things you absolutely do not wish to try, things you enjoy. I'd like for you to edge twice a day, and plug and clamp for a minimum of fifteen minutes per day, too."

Something ceramic was put down onto a table. "Hmmm. With this plug you gave me?"

"Yes ma'am. Until you are comfortable leveling up to a bigger one."

Her gasp spoke straight to his crotch. "Bigger."

"Bigger. That's the smallest in a set of three."

"And where is the rest of the set?"

"I kept it. In case you did not enjoy it. Or in case you decided to key my truck with them. Or throw them at my head…"

"Is that a rare moment of insecurity I'm sensing from the great Austin Morgan?"

He chuckled. "It happens more than you might think. Mackenzie, I need you to know that you do not need to be afraid to ask for what you want, much less need. You can tell me 'no' – or 'no sir' depending on the circumstances. I need you to chase your goals and dreams even if that means starting over with something new. I need you to not make yourself small, or hide yourself and your desires and feelings out of an attempt to please me."

A small squeak and a heavy silence.

"Mackenzie?" His heart thumped.

"Yeah?" Her voice was a hoarse whisper.

Was she crying? Had he hurt her? His stomach churned.

"Did I upset you?"

"No sir."

"What is it, Mackenzie?"

"No one has ever told me not to hide before."

CHAPTER 9
Mackenzie

"So hold on a second." Paige lined up the white ball on the pool table and took her shot. The white struck the tip of the triangle of colored balls and scattered them across the table. She spun to point an accusing finger at Kenzie. "You're dating him now?"

Heat prickled across her chest. "I... no. Yes. Maybe?"

"Oh. She's dating him." Adi snorted. "There's no way he gets her this befuddled if there wasn't something there." She picked up her drink and held it high. "And this is where I say, 'called it.'"

"We haven't even been on a date yet. You can't claim 'called it' when you said 'romance of the century.' And don't think I missed that use of befuddled."

"Yet." Paige picked up her drink and took a long gulp as Addison lined up her cue and took a shot. The ball sailed past the pocket and bounced off the green velvet edge. "And I'm with Adi, befuddled is a great word."

Paige rolled her lips, poorly covering a smirk before lining up her next shot. "So you're thinking about dating?"

Mackenzie nodded.

"She's thinking about more than dating. She's thinking about the bow-chica-wow-wow that comes after the date. Am-I-right?"

Mackenzie couldn't deny Addison was in fact right. It had been on her mind since she'd searched for BDSM things on Google. After she'd needed to bleach her eyeballs, anyway. Some looked daunting, even outright agony, but some things teased at her curiosity, coaxing her to take the next step.

"He wants you to keep a journal, with sexy things and not sexy things in, right?" Paige pocketed the ball with ease.

Addison missed another shot. "My competitive streak hates how good you are at this game, Paige. Like what? What kind of things does he want you to journal?"

"You mean your competitive streak hates how shit you are at this game. He wants her to record shit like edging, plugging, nutrition, that kind of thing. Dude probably saw the graveyard of Big Gulp cups in her office and figured she needed a glass of water from time to time."

"Excuse you." Kenzie's indignation was fake, they all knew she had an addiction to sweet tea and no amount of blaming it on her Texan roots made it fly with her friends.

"I'm not wrong." Paige shrugged and leaned on the cue clutched between her hands. "A real dom's entire world revolves around his submissive. Knowing she is properly cared for starts with her caring for herself."

She spun back to the table to take her turn. "If he doesn't know you're well hydrated and well nourished, how is he supposed to tie you up and make you his sexy slave for hours on end?"

Adi whooped and Kenzie smacked Paige's forearm to distract herself from the rush of heat that shot straight to her core. "Would you shut up?" Another thwap. "People might hear you!"

"So what if they do?" Paige took another shot, bagging yet

another ball, and making Addison cuss under her breath. "The dude kissed you in the middle of the grocery store, Kenz. He talked through basic kink with you – and you didn't run away." She gestured her cue at Kenzie. "That means you're in enough to give it a shot."

Addison missed another shot and stamped her foot like a disgruntled threenager. "I feel like the table is uneven or something."

"Here. Let me help you." Thor, the bartender from Protocol, stepped away from a neighboring table and handed his beer to one of the other men standing around it.

"Thor."

Kenzie had never seen Addison's face turn such a dark shade of red in such a short space of time.

"I didn't see you there." She flicked her auburn hair over her shoulder and widened her eyes at Paige and Kenzie.

"If you had you probably wouldn't have thrown that adorable little tantrum you just threw, so I'm okay with that. Can I help?"

Adi folded her arms around the cue. "Depends what your idea of 'help' is. Are you going to mansplain?"

"I figured I'd do the stereotypical guy against your butt helping you aim thing. Skip the mansplaining and go straight to the man-doing."

Adi looked like she wanted the man to do *her*. She pursed her lips and squinted one eye as though giving it real consideration. "I'll allow it."

The bar was mostly empty, save for a few regulars propping it up, and a couple of college kids in the corner. How she hadn't realized Thor and his friends were not only there, but so close, was anyone's guess.

"Your friend is right you know, Kenzie." Thor had Addison bent over the table and his hands clutched over hers on the wooden stick. It seemed almost an intrusion on something intimate to watch them. Addison wiggled her butt against Thor's crotch and a feral growl escaped him as he dropped his forehead into her hair.

"You're making it really hard to remain a gentleman here, Adi."

Addison flashed a wicked grin and wide eyes. "I have no idea what you're talking about." She moved her hips again.

"I bet you don't." He stepped back from Addison's ass and raked his hands through his loose hair. It was about as long as Kenzie's, and in better condition.

She scowled. She hated men with better hair than her own. Jerks. It wasn't bad enough that they got to pee standing up, and could scratch their crotch without judgment, but they also got perfect hair, too? Talk about unfair.

"Can I say something and you don't hold it against me that I maybe, possibly, kinda sorta was eavesdropping on your hard-not-to-hear discussion?"

Adi waved a hand and widened her eyes like he was somehow an idiot for thinking they would judge him for eavesdropping.

"Okay, well, it sounds like Austin is invested in you as a person and he's trying to navigate your..." He waved a hand like the right word he was searching for would fall from the sky into his palm.

"Vanillaness," Paige supplied.

"Exactly. It can be tricky for a dom with a vanilla partner. Educate but don't terrify. Be honest, but not all at once so you don't scare the bejesus out of them. It's a fine balance. But ultimately, the power is all yours. You can submit to him as much or as little as you want. Hell, the way the man looked at you at the bar that night, I'd say he'd agree to no kink at all with you if you said so."

Kenzie planted her hands on her hips. It was an awkward conversation to say the least, and with a stranger no less. Thor had waded into something personal, something private, assuming an intimacy that he hadn't earned. But that didn't make him wrong.

"Please note the grammar police allowed 'bejesus' but flagged 'befuddled.'" Addison shook her head.

"Befuddled. Great word." Thor held out a clenched fist that Addison met with her own.

"Right? That's what I said."

Kenzie held up a hand. "Austin wasn't looking at me in the bar."

Thor scrunched his face up. "Oh. He wasn't? Okay then. Let's swim in this little space called denial." He made breaststroke motions with his arms.

Paige covered her face with her palm, but her shoulders shook with silent laughter. Addison arched an appraising eyebrow.

"Lady, I am an observer of every person in my bar. I see, I listen, I dole out advice... night after night. And that boy was staring. At you. Like it was Christmas morning and you were wrapped in a goddamn bow."

Paige had taken her next shot on the pool table and Thor turned to help Adi once again, getting every bit as close to her ass as he had the first time. Dude wasn't backing down. Adi would like that. Men often found her zero fuck's given attitude intimidating. And the relentless way in which she pursued the things she wanted tended to give them pause as well.

"So what do I do?"

"Figure out what you want and go for it." Adi potted a ball and squealed with delight. She dropped the cue on the table, moving a few of the balls a little when it hit the velvet, and spun to face Thor. She smacked both her palms on his face and jerked him toward her, leading with her lips.

Instead of recoiling, or being caught off guard, Thor slid

his oversized hand from the small of her back up to between her shoulder blades and pulled her to him.

So fucking hot. Kenzie's jaw hung open. She was catchin' flies and she didn't even care. Perhaps all her time spent Googling kinks online had invoked a voyeur kink, because the kiss in front of her was molten lava and she stood downhill, a scorched observer. As Addison hooked her wrists behind Thor's neck, Paige stepped in front of Kenzie and clicked her fingers.

"Control yourself woman, before you turn to a pile of goo on the floor of this dive bar."

Kenzie fanned herself with her hand.

"Look. Ask him for the list of kinky things and go through them one at a time. If you have questions, ask – either him or me, but ask them. Same for any concerns. If you're seriously anxious about the kink element of a relationship, then it's important to draw your boundaries. If you're curious and want to shift them in the future – that's fine."

Thor and Adi still played tonsil tennis behind Paige. Kenzie stroked her throat with her index finger as she recalled what it was like to kiss Austin. How his presence consumed her. He was everywhere as his hands held her face and his tongue explored every crevice of her mouth.

He'd been confident, self-assured, and tasted like nutty dark chocolate. Ugh. She had it bad for the man. And she definitely wanted a repeat of their kiss. "I'm just scared we'll get in too deep and find that we're not compatible."

She wasn't at all scared he'd get too close to her, she was a pro at keeping people at arm's length. What she *was* scared about, was driving him away, when everything in her bones told her he was different.

"If he wants you badly enough, he'll work for it." Paige shrugged and lined up her next shot. "There's a middle ground between him and you. You just have to be patient and find it, or create it."

"And if he doesn't?"

Paige smirked. "Then I'd bet you at least get the best sex of your life from him in the meantime."

Kenzie turned to pick up her drink in time to see a short, golden blonde woman's back as she left the bar in a hurry. Kenzie cocked her head as a strange, familiar feeling rattled through her bones. She'd done everything in her power to forget the fact she'd left her baby sister – who was anything but a baby – back in Texas with their controlling parents. But sometimes a person, a smell, a sound, hauled her ass right back down into the belly of Texas in an instant.

Her sister Bea was an all-star cheerleader, straight-A student, and pageant queen who was engaged to Garrett's much less alphaholey younger brother, Brett. Uh huh. Bea and Brett. With their matching initials that would make the perfect monogrammed towels, sun kissed blonde hair, and wild blue eyes, the army of kids they were bound to have the second they tied the knot had no choice but to be utterly adorable.

An old familiar twist wretched in her chest. As much as she missed Bea, the cost of a relationship with her younger sister was too high. She was in too deep with Garrett's family, and Kenzie couldn't risk being pulled back in on the undertow. There was always an apple who fell further from the tree than the rest and her ass was sore from the crash-landing. She couldn't go back.

That didn't mean she didn't think of her sometimes, though, or relive memories from their childhood. There wasn't anything in the world that Bea wanted that Kenzie wouldn't give her. If Bea over-roasted her marshmallows around an open fire, Kenzie would sacrifice her own.

She ground at her chest with the heel of her hand, but the

hitch in her heart wouldn't relent. She hadn't checked her old Facebook account in over a year. When she first moved to Minnesota, she'd checked it every single day, but the more time went by, the stronger she became and was eventually able to cut ties.

Were Bea and Brett married? Did they already have babies? While the woman in the bar couldn't have been her sister, the visual reminder of a short, blonde woman in a hurried blur smacked the wind out of her like she'd fallen flat on her back on the ice. Grief was a weird fucker like that.

"Kenz?" Addison's warm palm met the small of her back. "You okay? You look kind of green." She spoke in a soothing tone, and concern wrinkled her forehead.

"If you're this bent out of shape about trying kink, you probably shouldn't." Paige drained the rest of her drink and leaned over the pool table. "Just sayin'."

Thor had detached himself from Addison's face, but he'd smudged her lipstick. He hooked a thumb at Paige. "She's not wrong."

"What? Oh. No. No! It's not that, it's just..." She turned back to the door, but the woman was gone. A ghost of her past reminding her that no matter how far she ran, or for how long, it would always be over her shoulder like a marauder, trying to claw her back to a time when she was a ghost of herself.

"Nothing." She shrugged. "I thought I saw... it doesn't matter. I just had a weird..." She waved her hand. "Let's get another drink."

Staring at her social media log in page, Kenzie drummed her fingers rhythmically on the table. It had been over a year since she'd logged in, maybe her log in wouldn't work and it wouldn't be an issue anyway.

She free poured herself a measure of tequila. Okay, so maybe two, and tossed it back like it was a Dr. Pepper on a summer day at the state fair, relishing the comforting burn of the alcohol as it slid down her throat.

What harm would one look do? A quick check on Bea and back out again. No problem.

Her phone chimed and she started, dropping her glass onto her thighs. She picked it up from the table, and smiled.

> Austin: Did you get home safely from your evening out?

> Mackenzie: Yes Sir, I did.

She snapped a selfie of herself in her Sesame Street pajamas, with her sans make up face and wild hair.

> Austin: Well that is certainly an image of perfection.

> Mackenzie: Someone needs to get his eyes checked.

> Austin: I am struggling with how to adequately describe how it feels when you speak ill of yourself.

She stared at the phone. Few people called her on her self-deprecation – Paige and Addison – that was generally it. But something about his words looped around the ice in her chest and pulled it from her heart.

> Austin: Perhaps I'll set you some lines to remind yourself I dislike negative self-talk.

> Mackenzie: And perhaps I'll stick a pen up your ass.

She gasped. Tequila made her sassy. Okay, sassier. She shifted in her chair. She'd read an article on MensHealth.com about being a brat, she was pretty sure her answer would fall under the description.

"A brat is a submissive who loves to playfully push buttons and 'break' rules. They behave this way to deliberately provoke attention from their Dominant..."

Would he think she was being bratty? Well, she kind of was, but would he think she was being deliberately bratty?

> Mackenzie: I take it back. I didn't mean it.

> Austin: That is certainly one way to make my palm tingle.

She shuddered and a pulse flickered at the apex of her thighs. The man would be her undoing.

The log in page taunted her from the screen. She placed her phone on the table next to her empty glass and typed in her credentials. Sliding her thumbnail between her teeth, she bit down. She stood, her dining chair scraping across the kitchen tiles. She paced, she paced back, she paced again.

"Fuck it." She smacked the enter key and the page kicked into action in front of her as she dropped back onto the chair, jiggling her leg as she waited.

The first post that appeared in her feed was a cat meme by someone she barely remembered from high school. What was it about the human condition that drove people to accept friend requests from people they hadn't seen in over a decade? And even when they had seen each other last, they didn't hang out, or even like each other all that much?

She typed Bea's name in the search bar and held her breath. Her heart battered her ribcage as the page loaded and her sister's striking blue eyes on the screen met hers. It had only been two years, but her sister had grown into a beautiful woman. She'd be twenty two, soon to turn twenty three.

Reaching out to touch Bea's flawless cheekbone on the screen, tears trickled down her face. Stupid tequila tears. She wiped them with the back of her hand and scrolled down Bea's profile.

Photos of her with Brett, her sorority sisters, and their family's two handbag pooches – Droolius Caesar and Sherlock Bones filled the screen. A group picture stopped her in her tracks. Mama and daddy, Bea and Brett, Brett's father and Garrett, all dressed up for a charity ball.

Garrett's smug smirk and beady eyes reached through the monitor and grabbed her by the throat. Frost chilled her veins and her pulse raced so fast she was sure her heart would stop from overexertion. Even from thousands of miles away his presence was felt. He hadn't changed a bit. His arrogance dripped down her display, threatening to ooze into her keyboard, and the fact he stood next to her family – the family she'd been forced to leave because of him – as one of them, made her skin crawl.

Her phone made a noise on the table in front of her.

> Austin: Drink some water before you go to sleep, Mackenzie.

His name on the screen poured calm over her frazzled nerves, grounding her in the now. Garrett couldn't hurt her. He was in a whole other state and he'd have to cross Paige and Addison if he wanted to exert his influence over her. They'd eat him alive.

> Mackenzie: I was contemplating being a smart mouth again, but I needed that reminder that someone cared. So thank you.

> Austin: What is going on?

She hadn't meant to be so vulnerable, but despite his cool exterior, she felt comfortable talking to him. It was probably dangerous, but mama always said she was like hellfire and gasoline. Always ready to charge the gates of hell with a gas can in one hand and a lighter in the other.

Kenzie was more partial to thinking of herself as hellfire and holy water: the juxtaposition of naughty and nice, sinful and sweet.

> Mackenzie: Just a little down. It'll pass.

It always passed. Eventually. She just had to plant her feet and scream into the abyss. It got a little easier each time a wave hit, but she couldn't help but wish that just sometimes someone else would step up to save her from the tide.

CHAPTER 10
Austin

Mackenzie: No, sir.

Austin: I'm growling at my phone right now, Mackenzie. The guys are giving me strange looks, they think I'm feral.

Mackenzie: Sounds a lot like a YP not a MP.

Austin: YP?

Mackenzie: You problem.

Austin: MP?

Mackenzie: Me problem.

Austin: So help me Mackenzie Abbot...

Mackenzie: Ah, ah, ah. Doms aren't supposed to act in anger, remember?

Mackenzie: You need to woo-sa your ass down.

> Austin: Bad Boys?

> Mackenzie: Captain ZERO pop-culture references gets Bad Boys?

> Austin: Everyone gets Bad Boys.

> Mackenzie: How are your palms?

> Austin: Itching to spank your pert little ass for being a brat. It's just a date. One date. Say yes.

"Auzzy, you good?" Finn's concern was tangled in a coy smile.

"Why wouldn't I be?"

"You've got 'woman problem' face." Linc pointed his forkful of salad across the table. A few of the team had met for lunch at Applebee's and Austin already regretted agreeing to go out in public.

"They aren't wrong." Will nodded, like his perpetually single self knew exactly what they were talking about.

"Tell Uncle Finny Winny what's wrong, Aus. Let's bag the broad."

Austin pinched the bridge of his nose while Will smacked Finn upside the head. "So many things wrong with that sentence, Uncle Finny Winny." Will tutted.

"It's good. I'm good." Austin pushed the broccoli around his plate.

"This is like when women say they're fine, you know." How Linc had crammed so much food into his mouth and still been able to speak coherently was anyone's guess. "They're never fucking fine. Never. Not ever. They just want you to fall into their web of passive aggression and get eaten alive."

"Where's the lie though?" Finn shook his head. "Spill, Auzzy. Let us save you from the siren's passive aggression."

"You know he won't give in until you tell him what's going on so he can fix you." Will shoveled a slice of grilled chicken into his mouth and washed it down with a gulp of iced water. "It's better for everyone if you just tell him."

Finn kicked back against the booth and spread his arms wide across the back like he was a king holding court.

Austin stared at his phone.

> Mackenzie: My ass ain't so lil, honey.

He gritted his teeth.

> Austin: Self-talk.

> Mackenzie: What are you going to do about it?

The woman would be the death of him.

> Austin: Lines.

> Mackenzie: Don't have a ruler.

He growled. He wasn't used to such a spitfire, not least one who wouldn't even let him take her to dinner.

> Austin: Grab a pen and a notebook.

> Austin: I am worthy. I am beautiful. I am enough.

> Mackenzie: How many times?

> Austin: Generally, I would have a set number for the day and add to it. I have not watched you write to know how to judge. Right now it is in my nature to not push you too hard.

> Mackenzie: …

> Mackenzie: Screw not pushing me too hard.

> > Austin: Twenty per day. Then add ten for the first offense. Twenty for the second (thirty total) and so on.

> Mackenzie: You're kidding?!?!?

> > Austin: I would likely cap it at 100 (total) additional.

> > Austin: And you are lucky I'm not tracking you down at the rink to bend you over your desk and spank the brat out of you.

"Dude. You've got it bad."

"It's family stuff." He grabbed his glass of water and chugged. Stalking her to the rink and spanking her over the desk was not the worst idea he'd ever had.

"No way in hell your family gets you wound tight as a coil like that." Linc shook his head as he spoke.

"Do we need to go punch it out in the cages?" Finn's eyes lit up.

"Maybe later."

"Can I get you guys anything else?" Sabrina, their server and Russ's girlfriend smiled as she stood at the edge of the booth.

"I think we're good, thanks, Sabrina." Linc answered, but Finn gave a salute.

Austin needed to work through his frustrations at home, alone, with his sound bowl and some deep breathing. "I'm out." He tossed a twenty onto the table and stood, pulling his coat from the bench next to him as he did.

"Let me know if you need to punch it out."

"That's the song TaySwift *should* have written." Linc smirked. "We're here if you need us, man."

"I got it."

Did he?

By the time he made his way home, Mackenzie had completed her lines and sent him pictures. She'd written in purple pen, and each line was uniform in neatness and size. The last line, however, was most interesting of them all. In her neat penmanship the words 'I would love to go out with you' stared back at him from the page.

Maybe he did have it.

As much as he enjoyed working with rope, watching Mackenzie craft knots for the first time captivated him. His dick stirred. She was patient, determined, and took instruction well. Everything he thought she would be.

"You're staring again."

"You are easy to stare at." He enjoyed the blush that spread across her cheeks.

She cast a furtive glance over her shoulder. "Why are we here?" She picked up the rope on the table and wiggled it. "Is this a bondage class?"

He chuckled. "Somewhat. Macramé is using knotting techniques to make textiles – rather than weaving or knitting."

"Or restraints." She smirked. "And then you go home and use what you've learned here in class and apply it to the bedroom?" Her arched eyebrow screamed challenge, but her shy smile betrayed her nerves.

"Kind of. It helps to learn to safely and accurately tie knots. But it is Shibari that is a form of rope bondage that originated in Japan. The word literally translates to "to tie" or "to bind." It refers to intricate and beautiful knots and patterns used to restrain and give sensation to the body."

The instructor continued her introduction to macramé but he didn't miss the intrigue that deepened on Mackenzie's face. While her eyes never left the teacher's face and hands as she demonstrated the basics of the square 'reef' knot and half hitches, *his* eyes never left Mackenzie.

He took in her profile as her gaze darkened with intense concentration before she picked up the rope spread on the table in front of them and worked it in her fingers.

"So this is your intro to kink without terrifying me?"

"Something like that."

"What was your intro to kink?"

"Not a macramé class."

She laughed. "Honestly, this is the last place I would have suggested as somewhere for us to go on a date. Color me surprised." She glanced up from the tangle of rope in her hand. "Pleasantly so. But really, what got you into all this?" She gestured around the room like they were in a sex dungeon and it needed explanation, rather than in the public library where they were surrounded by books and middle aged women making pot hangers.

"I knew someone who went to a club one weekend. It sounded intriguing and I was curious. I wanted to see for myself, so I went. I found some friends in the dynamic, people to mentor me."

She paused her knot work and furrowed her brow. "That's it?"

"What were you expecting?"

She placed her work on the table in front of her and took a drink from her water bottle. It was the first time he'd seen her drink anything but ice tea.

"Oh, I dunno. Troubled past, trauma, PTSD, the walking

stereotype for every BDSM book, film, and love story just about ever?"

"Sometimes it's just a normal guy walking into a kink bar." He shrugged. If he needed further proof that the lifestyle often got a bad reputation, or was glorified for all the wrong reasons, Mackenzie just gave it to him. "More often than not, in fact. There are a number of studies that say there is no correlation between past trauma and kink. Most people in the lifestyle just like it."

The instructor appeared behind Mackenzie's shoulder and leaned forward, peering at her work. "That's very nicely done. Even tension, not all clumped together, nice. Very nice indeed, Kenzie."

Despite her smile, stiffness crept into Mackenzie's body at the woman's praise. Her face flushed red, her shoulders and jaw tightened, and a brief flash of panic crossed her face as she looked around the room and discovered ten pairs of eyes on her.

He reached across the table and placed his hand next to hers, stroking her soft skin with the side of his thumb. Her eyes stopped flitting around the room and landed on where their skin touched.

"Is this okay?"

She nodded but didn't speak. Pulling her lip between her teeth, her eyes fluttered closed and he waited for her chest to rise and fall in more equal, measured breaths before he let go.

What was she so afraid of?

Two hours later, they emerged from the library, rope pot hanger in hand. They'd learned how to do half hitch, flat knots, and half knots and Mackenzie had taken to the class with curiosity and an open mind. She'd done well, and every piece of him wanted to reward her for it.

"Hungry?"

She nodded and squinted as they stepped out into the sunlight. "I can't believe it's the middle of the day."

Placing his hand in the small of her back he guided her around the corner of the building to his truck in the parking lot. "You mean you expected a dark and kinky bar late at night for our first date?"

She shrugged. "I wouldn't have said no."

"Perhaps next time."

She paused, arm outstretched toward the handle of the cab door. "Who said there'll be a next time?"

He stepped behind her, pressing her against the truck with his hips, not missing the sharp intake of breath as he trapped her hands between her body and the cool vehicle. He swept her hair from her neck and traced his finger along the curve of her oversized cable knit sweater. He dragged his nose across her skin and up the column of her neck. She sighed, sagging against him.

"Why do you hide your body behind oversized sweaters, Mackenzie?" He slipped his hands under the hem of her sweater, gripping her hips firmly and pressing himself against her ass as he trailed his tongue along the top edge of her shoulder.

The soft whimper that escaped her made his already hard dick throb against his jeans.

"They make me feel comfortable. I don't like people looking at me." She hung her head forward, curling her shoulders. "I guess society kinda tells me I'm not pretty because I'm not skinny anymore. No one wants to see it all hang out."

He let his head fall against the back of hers before slipping her hands from in front of her and holding them at the base of her spine, clasped in one of his. He pulled up the edge of her shirt with his free hand and traced a line across her middle.

"I want to see it." He circled her navel. "All of it. Not just see it, Mackenzie. I want to touch it, lick it, suck it, kiss it, pleasure it..." Dotting light kisses on her neck, he moved his hand higher, slowly savoring the small shivers that passed through her at his touch.

"How did the club make you feel? Seeing bodies of all shapes and sizes on display."

She dropped her head onto his shoulder, opening up the front of her body to him more as his fingers traveled higher. He skimmed the edges of the cup of her bra with the pad of his finger and his name fell from her lips on a sigh. "We're in public."

"Your back is to the road and hidden by me. And only the bushes in front of us can see you. Do you want me to stop?"

She shook her head. He stopped. "Then answer my question, Mackenzie."

She grunted and sucked in two deep breaths before she answered. "I've never been confident about my body. My sister got all the good looks in the family. She may be short, but she's more proportionate... and athletic. After my accident, I piled on a ton of weight and..."

He seized her nipple through the thin fabric of her underwear and squeezed. "Mackenzie?"

"Yeah?"

"Yes Sir."

"Y-yes, Sir."

"I do not wish to hear about your sister at this time." He squeezed harder, eliciting a delicious moan from her that shot straight to his crotch. "I wish to know how it made you feel."

"It made me feel hopeful. That maybe someday I'll be confident enough in myself to do something so bold and daring like stand in front of a room full of people while someone flogs me."

"I would have no problem being that someone. Or helping you find someone." He tightened his grip around her wrists. He released his grip on her nipple and she gasped. "It is often less about the act of clamping and more about the release, letting the blood flow back to places it hasn't been for a little while."

"I like it."

"I know."

She turned her head to the side, dragging her nose along the edge of his jaw as she did. She stared at his lips like she wanted to take a bite out of him, and he was not going to deny her the opportunity.

Hand flat on her stomach, he pulled her so her back was flush against his chest and kissed her, hands still pinned behind her back. She wiggled, jerking her arms as he held firm.

He pulled back, moving his mouth to the length of her neck and trailing his tongue over her racing pulse. "What is the matter, Mackenzie?" His words punctuated the lazy efforts of his tongue along her bare skin.

"I can't touch you."

"You are touching me just fine." He pressed against her for emphasis.

"I want my arms around you."

"And right now I wish to have access to your body that I would not be able to achieve if your arms were around me."

"Yes, Sir."

"Good girl."

A car door slammed behind them and she froze. "Austin."

"Easy, pet. Breathe. They can't see anything." He stroked her stomach but her breathing didn't slow. An engine started and a car drove away, but still her chest rose and fell with quick, short breaths.

"Mackenzie? What is it?"

She twisted in his arms, but gave up after a moment. "I'm not sure what I'm panicking at more, the 'good girl,' or the fact you're calling me a pet."

He chuckled, but released her wrists.

"I feel an overwhelming urge to rub at my arms like they do on TV after being released from handcuffs."

"I didn't call you a pet. I called you 'pet'. It's a common term of endearment."

"And you're endeared to me?"

He reached around her and popped the car door handle. "More than you know, Mackenzie. More than you know."

CHAPTER 11
Mackenzie

> Austin: I'm proud of you for stepping out of your comfort zone.

She'd stared at the message for ten minutes before being able to reply, and even then, it was still doing funny things to her heart. She took a screenshot and sent it to her girlfriend's group chat.

> Kenzie: Why am I so affected by this?

She traced the lines of her lips with her thumb as she waited for Paige and Addison to reply. She could still feel his lips on hers, his dick pressing against her abdomen as he held her against her front door and kissed her like she'd never been kissed in her entire life.

She regretted not grabbing him by the shirt and dragging him inside when he dropped her home after lunch.

Clenching her thighs, she sighed and dropped her head back onto her pillow. She'd been home for an hour and every drop of blood in her body raged so close to the surface of her skin she felt almost sunburned. Everything was hot, aching, pulsing, needy... begging for release.

She'd tried a cold shower and distraction by Bluebell ice cream, but not even Netflix could keep her mind off the throbbing in her pants.

> Paige: Praise kink.
>
> Addison: What she said. I'm hella turned on and it wasn't even my compliment.
>
> Kenzie: A praise kink? Like I get off on getting applauded... complimented... appraised?
>
> Paige: Precisely that. Getting turned on by praise.
>
> Kenzie: It usually just makes me blush, or feel like I'm put on the spot, or – like in class earlier – embarrassed AF.
>
> Paige: And now?

How did she feel? She opened his message again and processed what it did to her.

> Kenzie: I feel a few things.
>
> Addison: List them please.

She tried to start a movie, but she couldn't focus. She stacked the dishwasher but still couldn't keep her mind on task.

> Addison: I said list them please.

> Kenzie: 1. I'm proud of myself. Ugh. That feels so gross to type. I'm proud that I earned that reply from him (and more than a little confused by how sexual this pride feels.)

> Kenzie: 2. Kind of embarrassed that it took so little to put me in a place where I want to do anything he asks me to, to make him say it again.

Paige: That's completely normal. Wait till he says 'good girl'. You'll jizz your pants.

> Kenzie: He said that earlier and I thought I was going to swallow my tongue.

Paige: He did? I guess he recognized your praise kink before you did, girlie.

Addison: And 3?

> Kenzie: How did you know there was a 3rd thing?

Paige: I can think of one you missed. Horny. You're horny AF right?

> Kenzie: I didn't think the good girl thing was a thing. I sure as hell didn't think I'd ever want someone to say it to me.

Addison: And now?

Kenzie thought about it for a moment but her thumbs were typing before her brain had even caught up.

> Kenzie: Now I'd walk over hot coals to make him say it again.

Paige: Such a dirty little sub.

> Addison: Atta girl!
>
> Paige: Go play with your vibrator – it'll take the edge off.
>
> Addison: Pretty sure she's lying, but you know I'm never gonna dissuade you from getting your screaming O.

With an eye roll, she stripped naked and climbed into bed in the middle of a Friday afternoon. She glided her thumb over her nipple, but the sensation wasn't what her aching body sought. She pinched it between her thumb and index finger and squeezed hard. Her hips writhed on the bed as she spread her legs. She put her phone on her chest and slid her hand over the surface of her skin, stopping only when it reached the apex of her thighs. Sliding her fingers into her pussy, she groaned at how wet she was and picked up her phone and opened the chat with Austin.

> Kenzie: I almost replied that I had a great time and would like to see you again. But your words had quite an unexpected impact and I would rather convey that to you.
>
> Kenzie: Communication is everything, right?
>
> Austin: Correct. What impact did my words have on you?

She swallowed, recalling his words from when he had her pressed against his truck. He wanted her.

> Kenzie: My friends say I have a praise kink.
>
> Austin: I suspected as much.
>
> Kenzie: I'm a little wet.

> Austin: Just a little? I will endeavor to try harder next time.

> Kenzie: Okay, fine. More than a little.

> Austin: Where are you, Mackenzie?

She scrunched her eyes shut. She couldn't admit to him that she was in bed with her fingers casually stroking her clit as she texted him. Could she?

Taking momentary leave of her senses, she snapped a selfie of herself, hair splayed out around her head on the pillow like a halo. She pulled the blanket up so it just about covered her nipples, but left enough of her boobs on display that he could not only tell she was shirtless, but with any luck would get him even a fraction of how turned on she was.

The first take was awful, her large boobs pointed to 10AM and 2PM and they were not in any way hot at all. She clenched her biceps, making her titties stand to attention, snapped a series of pictures, chose the best one and sent it to him.

As she waited, her anxiety ratcheted higher and higher, but she kept her fingers on her clit and focused on her breathing as she waited for his reply.

> Austin: Fuck.

> Austin: How can you not see how beautiful you are?

Her breath stuttered and fingers stopped. The last time someone had called her beautiful was at the pageant finals back in Texas when she was a pre-teen. Mama had cupped her cheeks with both hands and told her she was way prettier than Jenabelle freakin' Smith – the girl who'd beaten her. The words had come from a smiling mouth, but the tone Mama had used was anything but warm.

Kenzie shuddered. Austin could have any girl he wanted, any kink-proficient sub from the club that night or any other night for that matter, and yet he was calling *her* beautiful. That landed hard somewhere deep inside her. Tears pricked in her eyes while she typed a reply.

> Mackenzie: I have a lot of baggage.

> Austin: I would like to crack your cases open and learn everything there is to know about you. I want to be a gentleman and take an interest.

> Mackenzie: But?

> Austin: You're naked under that comforter.

> Mackenzie: Yes, Sir. I am. Very naked. And my fingers are very wet.

> Austin: You cannot hear me growling right now, but I most certainly am.

Her slick fingers moved in slow circles over her clit.

> Mackenzie: I'd like to.

She'd barely sent the text when her phone rang. She answered it and hit the speakerphone button.

"Mackenzie."

Yeah. He was growly alright. Was this what his dom-voice sounded like? Every syllable of her name as it came shooting out of his mouth down the phone line lit her up like Galveston pier.

"Austin." Her voice was charged with submission and sex, need throbbed through every inch of her body, and if she had been any less out of her mind with lust she'd probably have felt embarrassed about it. But she wasn't. The desire in his voice met hers. He wanted her every bit as much as she wanted him.

"I'd love to chat but... ahhh..." Her moan slipped out as she cruised closer to the edge. "As you can tell, I'm... oh God... I'm a little busy right now."

"Not. The. Time. For. Jokes." His grunts turned cadenced.

Gasping, she stopped moving her hand. "Are you?" Was he getting off? Fuck. So hot.

"Don't stop."

"But..."

"Don't. Fucking. Stop. Mackenzie."

That did it. It was enough to send her soaring over the edge in a blaze of cuss words and wails the people of Texas could probably hear if they had their windows open.

When she'd finished, he stayed quiet. Her breath returned to normal, but the heavy ache weighing her down all morning was still there. What the hell? Wasn't she supposed to feel better after she'd come?

"Did you enjoy that, Mackenzie?"

"Yes, Sir. I did." Her cheeks burned as realization of what she'd done crashed into her like someone had thrown a glass of water in her face.

"Good. I'm glad. Because it's the last time you come without my express permission."

"B-but you told me to. You said not to stop." Her legs twitched from the aftershocks of her release.

"You're right..." Fabric rustled against his phone. "I did. I told you to come. But you came your way. Not my way. And from now on, you only come my way. Do you understand?"

The ache inside her grew heavier. She was tempted to let her brat answer, to tell him it was her body and she'd do whatever the fuck she wanted to, when she wanted to. He wasn't the boss of her. But the pull at her core flexed, so she pushed the urge to be snarky down.

"Yes, Sir." She had no idea what it meant. Giving control of her orgasms over to the man who could cost her everything if her boss found out. But there was no other answer. The throbbing eased at her compliance.

"Mackenzie?"

"Yes, Sir?"

"Tell me how you're feeling."

"Overwhelmed." Her breath shook as she exhaled. "Confused. I'm not exactly sure what I'm agreeing to, but I trust you."

"Just the orgasms for now. We can explore kink a little until you decide that you're ready to take the next step."

She squirmed against the sweaty sheets clinging to her body. "The next step being?"

"A fully committed relationship with me. As my submissive."

She hissed out a breath at how easily the words came from his mouth. "Are you sure you want me? There are other, far more qualified submissives out there. I have no idea what I'm doing." She sucked in a sharp breath. "I'm so very vanilla, Austin."

"We are all vanilla, until we aren't."

She couldn't argue with that. The only way people became good at anything was if they took the first step to learn, then practiced until they got better.

"Is there anything I can do now?"

He chuckled. "Are you not sated, pet?"

"Can you not call me that please? I don't like it."

He fell quiet for a few moments before he sighed. "My inclination is to call you 'Love', but I do not want to spook you."

Love. It was a term of endearment. It didn't mean he loved

her – that would be crazy, they barely knew each other – there was no way in hell she'd let him call her that any time soon. But it stirred something in her chest.

"Do we have a safe word? 'Cause I'm safe-wording use of the L word for now. For a long now. For maybe ever." Her heart picked up speed.

"Let me know if and when that changes."

"Yes, Sir."

Another silence fell between them, but it wasn't uncomfortable, more charged with promise, anticipation, and desire. "I get the impression you aren't placated either, Sir." She leaned heavily on the last word, not missing the slight hitch in his breathing.

"No, ma'am. I am not."

She pressed the heels of her hands against her eyes. "Tell me what to do."

"Anything?"

His question should probably have scared her, but it didn't. If anything it stoked her fire even more. "Anything. Though..." She twisted a lock of her hair between her fingers.

"Tell me what you need, Mackenzie."

"I liked the idea of trying..." She rolled her eyes back and shook her head. Was she really going to say those things out loud? She huffed out a breath. He wanted communication so that's what she'd give him. "Clamping. But I don't have any clamps. My sex toy collection is as vanilla as my ice cream." She paused and snapped her mouth shut after the torrent of words had rushed from her lips. "Current preferences."

He made a soft 'hm' sound. "That's okay. We can do a little shopping."

She squeezed her nipples enjoying the sharp pinch of sensitive skin.

"Do you have pencils and hair ties?"

"Like... just a regular pencil you write with?"

"Yes, ma'am."

"I'm sure I do, somewhere. How many do I need?" She pulled back the sheets and made her way through the top floor of her house to her small in-home office-gym. She pulled the pencils out of the stationery pot on top of her desk. "I have three pencils."

"You need four. Use a pen as well."

She rolled her eyes. "So bossy."

"I heard that eye roll, Mackenzie. Hair ties."

"How many?"

"Also four. The elastic type. Not the big, scrunched fabric type."

She moved from the office to the bathroom and tugged open the cabinet door. On the top shelf was a container of hair ties. She counted four black ties out and slipped them onto her wrist. "Yes, Sir. What's next on your scavenger hunt list?"

He paused for a moment. "You will need two glasses of water. One with ice, and one without."

"That means going back downstairs."

"Okay?"

"I'm naked."

"Do you live with someone?" His tone shifted, and she smiled.

"I live alone."

"Then I fail to see what your concern is."

She muttered, mostly to herself about not being used to parading around naked and on display. What if the Amazon delivery person came to the door while she was frolicking? She hesitated, but only for a moment. Curiosity trumped embarrassment.

Two glasses of water in hand, pencils braced against the side of one of the glasses, she confirmed he didn't need her to get anything else before going back upstairs to bed.

She settled in with the pencils and hair ties laid out next to her and her water on the nightstand. "Do you want a photo for proof?"

"Not yet. I trust you have everything you need. And you are under no obligation to provide one."

She shuddered. She'd never expected to feel so empowered from a position perceived as one of weakness to his position of power. It was dizzying.

"Are you ready?"

Sucking in a steady breath, she nodded even though he couldn't see her. "I'm ready."

"First things first. What else do you think we might need?"

"A safe word." A thrill shot through her, blazing a trail of nervous energy through her bones.

"Good girl. We do need a safe word. And until we establish one of our own, I am going to say we just use the standard traffic light system, green means you are okay, yellow means you are approaching discomfort or distress, and red means stop right now, I am done. Sound good?"

"Yes, Sir."

She squirmed on the bed. What the hell was he going to make her do with four pencils, hair ties, and two glasses of water?

"It is not a weakness to safe word, Mackenzie."

"I know, Austin."

"Good. Okay. You're going to be using the pencils and hair ties in two sets of two. I'm going to need you to roll one of your nipples until it gets hard for me."

She groaned and covered her face with her forearm, her face burning. "They already are."

"That is nothing to be embarrassed about. Your body being ready for me to do the things I want to do to you is something to be proud of, Mackenzie. It pleases me greatly."

When she'd checked his medical history prior to treating

him, she'd discovered he was a soon-to-be twenty-three year old who had taken a year out of college to travel abroad. That coupled with the fact English wasn't his first language had produced a semi-formal speaking, delicious beast of a man who made her come undone with just a few words.

It pleased him greatly? If any other guy had said those words to her she'd have laughed at him and told him to go shit out the stick up his butt, but with Austin... he owned it. She wanted him to own her, too.

"Let me explain the overall idea first, then I'll tell you how to accomplish it, okay?"

"Okay." Her heart raced and her pussy tingled.

"This isn't a beginner clamp by any means, but I think it's a bit easier than asking you to try bag clips or clothes pegs for your first time."

"Ow!" She winced. "That sounds painful."

His warm chuckle rolled over her like fog on Scottish hills. "It is supposed to be. So you're going to clamp around your nipple between the two pencils. You're going to secure them in place by twisting the hair ties around both pencil ends on each side. And remember what we talked about, it is not about the clamping so much as it is about the blood flow returning after the clamping. You might feel a little discomfort, but not pain. Once you discharge the clamps you will feel the sting of release and a rush of heat to the area."

Her nipples got harder with each word he said. She moved to start but he stopped her.

"Do not put the pencils on your nipples themselves. You want to pull through a good section of skin and clamp that instead."

"Yes, Sir." She picked up two pencils.

"With one hand, pinch your nipple between your fingers and stretch it toward the sky. And with the other, you're going to place a pencil on each side of the nipple."

"But not touching it." She repeated his words back as she lined up the pencils. Pinching together the two ends, she let go of her nipple and slipped her hair tie off her wrist and onto the wood. "This is tricky."

"Like everything, it will take practice. I do not expect you to be perfect the first time. So don't overthink it, okay?"

It wasn't that she was a perfectionist by any means, but she wanted to make him proud. He'd already prodded something within her that made her want to do her best for him.

Praise kink. She almost groaned. The girls would get great mileage from her innate desire to please a man considering she'd spent two years running from them.

"If you keep the hair ties at the ends, that is as loose as the clamp goes. If you slide the ties closer to the center, toward your nipple, it will become tighter."

She had affixed one and worked on the other. Each time her arm touched the clamp on her nipple she shuddered and twitched. It felt strange, but not painful.

"Check in, please. When I say those words I need you to reply with your color of choice. Anything other than a color and I will stop everything until you check in, okay?"

"Yes, Sir. Green."

"Good."

"Austin?" She picked up her phone, squeezed her boobs together, and snapped a picture. "Can you tell me if this is right, please?"

"Yes, ma'am."

She sent it to him, and while she waited for him to reply, she lightly swept her finger over the tip of her still-pebbled nipple. It felt cool to touch, and the sensation was duller, muted by the limited access caused by the pencils.

Heat pooled low in her belly. It was an oddly enjoyable sensation and she found her breathing quicken while she waited.

"Thank you for the picture. Those look perfect."

"They do? I don't need to fix them?"

"No, Mackenzie. You do not need to fix them."

"What next?"

"Are you in a hurry?"

She huffed out a husky laugh. "No, Sir. I just figured there was more to do."

"And there is, but we will get there. Tell me first, how do they feel?"

She ran her fingers over them both at the same time, enjoying the shivers it sent through her. "Cool. Sensitive and yet not. It's like the pencils are stopping some of the sensation."

"Check in."

"Green."

"Good girl. Take an ice cube from the glass of water and trail it over your nipples for me."

Her pussy throbbed, demanding she circle her clit until she screamed his name and the neighbors banged on her door and demanded she shut up. She reached over to the glass and pulled out an ice cube, shivering as droplets of cold water landed on her as she moved toward her nipples.

She gasped. "Oh God." The harsh cold of the ice cube on her clamped skin was a welcome relief.

"Do you know how much I wish I could be there right now? Do you know how hard you are making my cock, Mackenzie?"

"But you just came."

"So did you." Once again, he had a point. Her core ached with a need for release like she had been starved of orgasms for years. The more she got to know Austin, the more she realized she had.

"If you think I'm anything but rock hard and leaking... You. Are. Crazy." He punctuated his words with soft noises like he was stroking himself. Had she ever driven someone to touch themselves over her before? She couldn't recall a time when she had, but every part of her wanted to do it daily. To make him lose his mind over her. Even from a distance over the phone.

The ice melted against her skin and cold water trickled down her breasts and across her chest. The hiss of breath that escaped between her teeth as she trailed the frozen cube over her nipples made him grunt.

"Fuck. I should have arrived at your door and done this myself. Or made you prop your phone up somewhere so I could watch. You're driving me insane."

She wasn't ready for him to watch her. Instead, she walked the fingers of her free hand down her stomach and sank them into her wetness, moaning as they connected with her sensitive clit. "Yes, Sir. You should have."

He moaned and she grinned. She more than liked having that effect on him.

"I'm touching my clit."

A grunt was all she got in reply.

"I'm so wet."

"I can hear how wet you are, Mackenzie."

She paused, heat racing across her skin.

"I do not want you to stop. Do you understand? I don't know who told you that wasn't the most glorious sound in the world, but hearing your girlfriend be so wet and ready for you is the biggest compliment of all."

"Y-your girlfriend?"

"Yes, Mackenzie. *My* girlfriend." His deep voice somehow dropped even lower. "Is that okay with you?"

Her fingers moved quicker between her thighs and the ice in her other hand was almost entirely melted but she swirled the pool of cool liquid around her nipple. "Yes, Sir."

"Check in."

"Green."

"Good girl. How do you feel?"

"Like I might die if I don't orgasm."

"You will not die, but you also will not come."

She squeaked. "What? Why not?"

"This is going to be your first experience with edging. So when you get close, not a little close, but almost the whole way, I want you to stop."

"Stop?" Was he crazy? Who had that much self-control that they could just decide oh hey Mr. Orgasm, you're not needed today, turn around and go back from whence you came?

People couldn't possibly do that, could they?

Except they could and they did. She'd seen it in *Fifty Shades*. He'd edged her and held her at distance from her release. Pressure bubbled in her abdomen, hissing and spitting like lava in a volcano about to erupt. Her toes curled.

"Mackenzie?"

"Yes, Sir?"

"Do not come."

She growled. She could come quietly, he'd never know.

"Right when you get near the edge, I want you to slide off a band from your clamp and release it."

Dear God in heaven the man was a sadist, there was no other explanation. She already knew that the moment she released the clamps around her near-blue, numb nipples that things would get all kinds of sore. There was no way she could simply cut circulation off to a piece of her without it resulting in some form of pain when her body realized it was back in action.

But right when she was cresting into blissful pleasure? He really was intent on ensuring she didn't come.

She gritted her teeth. She'd do it his way, this time. She'd see what he had to offer before deciding whether or not painful boobs and no orgasms was something she could subscribe to beyond once and done.

"Mackenzie?"

"Yes, Sir?"

"Breathe."

"Yes, Sir." She hadn't realized she had been holding her breath, and sucked a ragged intake of air into her lungs.

"When you hold your breath it makes me want to curl my hand around your throat to control your breathing."

Her hips bucked of their own volition. She'd read about breath play, erotic asphyxiation and the idea had been oddly seductive to her. Literally putting your life in someone else's hands was a huge act of trust, and she couldn't lie to herself that the idea sent sparks to her core.

"Check in, Mackenzie."

"What? Oh. Green. Green. I'm fine I'm just... distracted by the idea of breath play and the fact you're about to ruin my orgasm."

"Ruining is something else entirely." The timbre of his voice seemed to be at the same frequency as her clit and she surged closer to her climax.

"I'm going to... I..."

"Release the clamps, Mackenzie."

"Y-y-y... Fuck shit fuck fuck." She was too close, she couldn't possibly stop the freight train headed straight for O-City. She tugged the hair tie, but it didn't come off the first time, making her hiss at the jiggle of her breast. "Fuck."

It wasn't unbearable. Gritting her teeth she pulled again and the clamp released sending a blinding sensation of pleasure-pain rattling through her every cell. She let out a roar which almost drowned out his "Good girl," but she heard it and it did little to pull her back from the cusp of her orgasm.

She stopped playing with her clit and pulled the half-opened clamp from her skin, pulling gently when it stuck. A dark red ring quickly appeared around her nipple and she watched with fascination as her nipple pinked up again as the blood rushed to the surface.

"Another ice cube, Mackenzie."

"Yes, Sir."

"Cool the burn."

"Yes, Sir." She hissed on impact. Her raw and angry skin coming into contact with the cold water and ice was a special kind of bliss that made her rub her thighs together desperate to inch closer to emancipation.

"Check in."

Her chest heaved and her mind thundered, her body was like a console with every light lit up and flickering. "Green."

"Ready for the other one?"

"No." Her word was swallowed by the groan rolling from her body.

He chuckled. "No, Sir."

"Yes, Sir. No, Sir. This is gonna hurt, Sir."

"It is. But it kind of sounds like you like it almost as much as I do."

Another groan. "Okay. Fine." She whistled out a breath. "Let's do it." She tugged on the hair tie, her free nipple still throbbing as the blood rushed to it. The elastic hair tie pinged as it broke free of the pen and pencil clasping her nipple in a vise.

The clasp released, she waited for the sting, then wailed as it rippled through her.

"Good girl, Mackenzie." His words skimmed her already swollen and pulsating clit driving her close to the Promised Land once again. How did three words have such a profound effect on her body? Part of her hated it, and the other part wondered what else he could do to her with minimal effort, and a third kind of hated herself for settling for mediocre, vanilla sex with that selfish a-hole Garrett for so long.

"Ice."

She flailed her hand toward the glass, clipping it with the side of her hand but catching it before it fell over. Grabbing two small ice cubes from the water, she gritted her teeth. Ice meeting her sensitive, pinking skin made her yelp.

He shushed her over the line, but it didn't make a single part of her body shush. Instead, it flared brighter, wilder, and more intense.

"Can I come now?"

"No, ma'am. You may not."

She whimpered.

"Check in."

"Green. Frustrated as all get out, but I'm green."

"Good. Can you sit up a little? The second glass of water is for you to drink."

He'd thought of everything. Well, except for the fact her body might explode from being denied its release, but she suspected that was the desired outcome for him, priming her, making her a needy mess that could erupt with the slightest touch.

She shivered. The man was sinfully alluring and she wanted everything he had to offer her. She wanted his control, his touch, and the best goddamn orgasms of her life. She just had no freakin' clue how to manage that without letting him anywhere near her heart, or her past.

CHAPTER 12
Austin

Austin stood outside the hockey arena, gift bag in one hand and phone in the other. On his screen, a picture of Mackenzie's luscious ass bore into his retinas. She'd not only worn her plug to the office, but she sent him a picture of it – an hour before she was supposed to see him for their session.

She was playing with fire, and if she wasn't careful, he was going to make her feel the burn. Everywhere.

He closed his eyes for a moment and sucked in a few breaths to try to calm the swirl of emotions in his chest. But as soon as the sparkling plug in her ass taunted him from the screen when he opened them again, all control blew away with the gust of cold wind that prickled his cheeks.

"You okay, man?" Linc pushed the double doors to the rink open and stepped outside. "You look like you want to punch puppies. Please don't punch puppies. Am I right? Do you need a trip to the cages?"

His lips twitched. "I am okay, just on my way to see Mackenzie." He rolled his shoulder. "Hoping to get signed off as back to full strength."

He wasn't in fact hoping to get signed off anywhere, but he could only stretch out his treatment for so long. Maybe another week or two at best. She'd denied herself for him on the phone the day before, in a glorious blaze of submission. She handled the pencil clamps perfectly – especially for someone with no experience at all. He wanted more, not less.

It seemed his vanilla girl had some sprinkles. Ha. Sprinkles. Until they were in a position for him to call her "Love" – which he felt in his bones was on the cards for them both – he'd call her sprinkles. It would probably drive her crazy, but he was also sure she'd love it.

"Austin? Now you've got this weird smile on your face. Are you sure everything is okay?"

He nodded.

"Okay, well when you get to Kenzie's office can you tell Finn I'll meet him at the Sugar Bean after his appointment?"

"Finn is with Mackenzie?"

Linc nodded. "I have to pick something up for Cleo on my way, or I'd wait for him. And hey, why do you call her Mackenzie anyway? Everyone else calls her Kenzie. Don't think I haven't noticed." He arched an eyebrow.

"It's her name. And to my knowledge she likes it when I use her given name."

A muscle under Linc's eye twitched and he pursed his lips as though to say something. "As long as you're not tormenting her, it's all good. She's the best trainer I've ever worked with." He jabbed a finger at Austin. "Don't scare her off."

He was literally trying to do the exact opposite, but no one needed to know that. They were used to him keeping his personal shit personal. She was skittish, the last thing he needed was for one of his teammates to open their big mouths about how they knew something was going on between her and Austin. She'd lose her shit. And he'd lose her forever.

He threw Linc a salute. "I won't. She's helped a lot with

my shoulder. I wasn't sure I'd be able to get myself back on the ice so quickly. But she made it happen."

He walked inside the arena, smiling to himself at the thought that Mackenzie was in an appointment with Finn, plugged. It was probably smarting after almost an hour of it inside her. She was also probably going to smack him for bringing the contents of the gift bag in his hand to her at their place of work. Since he hadn't been able to get her to commit to another date yet, he needed to take his opportunities where they presented themselves.

Peering around the doorframe to her office, he knocked his knuckles on the wood. Mackenzie was standing over Finn's half naked body. He lay face down on the treatment table and her elbow was jammed pretty good into his glute.

A lesser man would have been jealous. Beads of sweat glistened on her forehead under the harsh office lighting, her lips were rolled between her teeth and she stared up at the sky as though praying for mercy.

Good. She was feeling her plug. He grinned when she met his gaze. But his smile fell when her eyes widened and panic spread across her beautiful features. "Just a second. I'm just finishing up with Finn."

"Is that Auzzy? Come in, man. I don't mind if he's in here for the last couple minutes."

Mackenzie smiled, or at least attempted to, it was a grimace and her eyes scrunched closed as she silently blew air out of her mouth.

"How's the shoulder?" Finn's voice was muffled by the table.

"Good. Really good. I think Mackenzie must be some kind of miracle worker. I had not expected to recover so quickly." He placed the gift bag on her desk.

Her already pink face darkened and she smiled again. She shifted her weight and mouthed 'fuck.' Whatever was going on with her seemed somewhat bigger than a simple butt plug. She moved again and a faint tinkle met his ear as her eyes rolled back into her head. Her breath caught and her chest heaved.

"She really is amazing, right? My ass was super tight before I came in." He clenched his butt cheeks. "Feels so much better now she's worked me over."

Austin almost snorted.

"Same for my lower back. She has wicked talented hands." Finn was probably not intent on using innuendo, but the more he spoke, the more amused Austin grew. Mackenzie on the other hand, was definitely going through something. He suspected Mackenzie's talents spanned far beyond her hands.

But that was not a woman in distress. That was a woman on her way to climax. And from the muted tinkle he'd just heard, he'd bet his inheritance that she'd tried her hand at Ben Wa balls.

She was so eager to please, and his dick was just that. Pleased. He pulsed in his sweats, wanting to pick Finn up by his shorts and haul his ass out the door so he could bend her over the table and take her from behind.

"O-okay, Finn. You're all done." She plastered a fake smile on her face and tapped his shoulder.

He jumped up and stretched. "Miracle worker, Kenz. I dunno what they're paying you here, but it isn't enough." He filled a cup with water from the new water dispenser in the corner of the room. Twice. Seemingly oblivious to the thickening tension consuming the oxygen in the heavy air.

Her eyes locked on Austin's, her legs trembled as she leaned forward to brace herself on the edge of the treatment table, her face twisted in a mix of pleasure, pain, and desperation.

"Same time next week, Kenz?"

She nodded, but didn't answer.

"You okay? You look like you might be coming down with something."

"I'm f—"

"Linc said he would meet you at the Sugar Bean."

Finn rubbed the back of his neck, eyebrows shooting up in recognition. "Shit. Right. I'd forgotten. I was going to jump in the steam room for a while. Better jet." He turned to leave.

"Finn?" Austin frowned.

"Yeah?"

"Do you not need to get dressed?"

Mackenzie's quiet whimper made Austin's dick twitch.

"Clothes are in the locker room, man." Finn shrugged and left the room, barefoot, bare chested, and whistling something Austin couldn't identify.

"Mackenzie?" Austin didn't turn his head to her, instead kept his gaze on the door Finn had just left through.

"Y-yes, Sir?" She moaned and leaned further forward over the treatment bench.

"Is it possible…?" He dropped his voice. "That you bought yourself a set of Ben Wa balls?"

"Mmhmm." Her inhales were loud and deep, in through her nose and aggressively pushed from her mouth.

"And is it possible that you wore them, and your plug for Finn's appointment today?"

"No, s-s-sir."

"No? It seems that you are in quite a bit of distress right now, Mackenzie. I would bet a substantial amount of money that you did."

He turned to face her, and determination flickered in her pained eyes. "I wore them both to work this morning."

He checked the clock on the wall. It was a few minutes after noon. She'd worn both her plug and the balls for just over three hours. His pulse quickened. "Is this your first time using the balls?"

She bit down on her bottom lip and nodded.

He stepped toward her, and she pushed back from the bed, away from him with a squeak. "Mackenzie, if you've never used Ben Wa balls before, you should start out by keeping them in only around fifteen minutes twice a day, for a total of thirty minutes per day until you get used to them."

She hissed and bared her teeth. "Well, I know that *now*, don't I?"

"You should gradually increase the time you use them until you get to a timeframe that's comfortable for you. Not just jump straight to three hours of use."

How was she still standing? Her strength was impressive, even if her narrowed eyes currently suggested she wanted to maim him where he stood. If she could move without the threat of orgasm, he'd probably be worried she would, too.

"Are you just going to stand there lecturing me for...?" She gestured at her abdomen. "This. Or are you going to help me?"

He backed away from her and swung her door closed, leaning against it until it clicked. Her eyes widened.

"And what kind of help would you like from me, Mackenzie?"

"I..." She worried her lip with her teeth, her chest rising and falling with great effort, and a bead of sweat trickling down her temple. "Fuck." She stepped forward, gripping the edge of the table, knuckles whitening as she clawed at the leather.

Her moan spoke straight to his crotch and he took two steps in her direction. He was still six feet away, and ached to help her, but until she asked him, he was obligated by her boundaries to leave her be.

They were at work. It did not matter that she was moments away from coming undone in front of him. It did not matter that his balls ached with a heavy, desperate need for release. She had drawn her line in the sand and until she begged him to cross it, he had no choice but to suffer with her.

"Please, Austin." Her whimpers drove him forward another few steps. "I can't make it to the bathroom to take them out."

"You want me to take them out for you?"

Indecision colored her every feature. "I need... I... fuck. I can't think straight. I can't..."

"I need you to breathe, Mackenzie. I need you to take a deep breath and tell me what you need so I can help you."

She nodded, licked her bottom lip before pinching it in her teeth and sucking in a cleansing breath. She blew it out with force. "I need to come. I can't think straight. My nipples are chafing against my bra. My butt is aching from the plug, and I'm pretty sure if you just talked to my clit I'd orgasm right now."

"It would be remiss of me not to remind you that we are at work and it is inappropriate."

Her scowl would have been adorable were he not so incredibly turned on.

"You think I don't know that? We can comb over my long list of mistakes for the day once you fix me." She bent over, clutching her knees with her hands. "Fix me, Austin. Please?" She tipped her head back and met his eyes, her bottom lip trembling. "Please?"

The invisible barrier keeping him from closing the distance fell and within seconds her head was cupped in his palm and his tongue was caressing hers. She stood still in his arms, probably afraid to move in case she came.

He skimmed his hand over her chest, stopping to pinch her nipple through her shirt and bra. She leaned into him, gripping his biceps with both hands and deepening their kiss.

He drew his hand lower, gliding over her stomach, and under the band of her scrub pants. Her whole chest rose and fell, and she broke their kiss with a gasp and a whimper as his hand made its way lower.

She nodded her head against his chin. "Please. Please Austin. Please. Fix me."

"Oh, Sprinkles. An orgasm will not fix you."

She searched his eyes. "It won't?"

"No, Mackenzie. It will not fix you because you are not broken. You do not need fixing."

"Sprinkles?"

"Later."

She smacked her hand over her mouth when his fingers slipped into her soaking wet folds and found her clit. She dropped her head to his shoulder, her legs buckling.

He circled once. She mewled.

"This is precisely how I need you to be for me. Wet, aching, eager, ready."

He circled again. Her body trembled.

"Do you understand?"

She nodded.

He circled again. She sank her teeth into his shoulder through his shirt.

"I asked if you understood, Mackenzie."

"Y-y-yes, Sir. I understand. I-i-i… f-f-f-uck." Her head snapped back and her eyes rolled.

He circled again. "Let me take care of you."

She nodded again as his fingers swept over her clit. She curled her fingernails into his bicep and her eyes pleaded with him for release. She was perfect.

"Austin… I can't… I can't hold it…"

Lowering his head to her ear, he brushed his cheek against hers. "What do you need, Mackenzie?"

"I n-n-need… ugh. You know what I need. I need to come, damnit." After a moment her eyes flinched wide. "Please, Austin. Please just let me come."

He dragged his tongue along the shell of her ear. "Yes, Mackenzie. You can come for me."

It didn't happen right away, there was a long moment where her body shook and she said nothing while she held her breath.

"Breathe."

A sharp breath exploded from her mouth as she tensed in his arms and let go in a muffled roar against his shoulder while his fingers swirled her clit.

"Don't stop. Give me everything."

She fisted his shirt and nodded again, clamping her lips shut with her teeth, hips bucking against his. He held her tight against him until the last tremors passed through her body and her muscles softened.

"I-i..."

"Shhhh." He stroked her hair while she recovered. "Easy."

She nodded against his chest. "I think one of the balls popped out."

"Would you like me to take them out for you?"

Another nod, her chest heaved against his and sweat trickled down her face.

"Breathe." He moved his hand from her clit and found the escaped Ben Wa ball. "Let it go, Mackenzie." He tugged it and the balls came free.

Dangling between them they glistened with her creamy cum. Her eyes followed the first ball as he wrapped his lips around it and closed his eyes, savoring her taste.

She gasped his name.

When the first ball was licked clean he moved onto the second, sucking every last drop of her from them before dropping them into her palm and licking his lips. "You taste delicious, Sprinkles."

"I can't believe you just did that."

"And I cannot believe I have the restraint to not drop to my knees and make you come undone on my tongue."

Her jaw dropped open at his announcement.

"I'm proud of you."

A tiny tremor vibrated through her and something warmed in his chest. He could not change who he was, and he did not wish to change her, but perhaps there was a middle ground where they could meet and be happy together.

She tucked the balls into her pocket and took a step back from him. "I'm okay."

He stepped around her, filled two cups of water from the dispenser, and held one out to her. She took it and drank.

"I am still slightly thrown that you ordered Ben Wa balls. I can understand your curiosity, and it does reinforce your need to submit and try things that you were otherwise questioning. I believe you are aware that I am more than happy for you to try those things at your own pace."

She finished the cup of water and he passed her the other.

"I know that your pace is currently an overwhelming desire to be everything I could possibly ever need. But I would be irresponsible to not reinforce with you that you are already enough. Just as you are. My desire to push you is not because I require more from you. It is because I desire you to test your own limits."

Unshed tears filled her eyes. "You're going to ruin me, aren't you?"

"That is certainly not my intention."

"When you say things like that... I..." She covered her face with her palms for a moment before scrubbing them up and through her hair.

"Like what?"

"Like I am enough as I am."

"You are."

Pained eyes met his and something inside him cracked.

Who had hurt this woman so deeply that she questioned her own self-worth?

Her lip trembled and tears spilled over her eyelids leaving tracks down her cheeks. Sniffing, she glanced away and swiped at her face. "Sorry. I don't always cry when I come."

Brushing his thumb over the apple of her cheek, he tilted her head so she would look at him. "Even if you did it would be okay."

Neither of them spoke for a moment, then two. The shrill ringing of her phone startled her out of the post-orgasm bubble and back to reality. She darted across the room to answer and a knock sounded on the door.

Their eyes met. They needed to talk, to discuss whether or not things would progress between them, and how they would navigate the workplace. But it was seemingly not going to be possible right away.

He hooked his thumb toward the door, but she held a finger, telling him to wait. The door opened and Coach poked his head around it. He glanced between Austin and Kenzie, saw she was on the phone and mouthed 'I'll come back.'

Austin nodded as Kenzie continued on her call. Their talk would have to wait, but there was no way in hell he would let her continue to think she wasn't enough. Even if he had to tell her every damn day himself.

"Table for Morgan."

"Yes, sir, Mr. Morgan. The other person in your party has already arrived."

He tugged on his collar. Every time his mentor, Slade, was in town he picked the most ridiculously expensive and exclusive restaurants for them to catch up. He couldn't blame him, the food was good, the ambience relaxed and quiet enough that they could talk among themselves without having to yell.

"You look tired."

Austin's lips twitched. "Tired of these pretentious restaurants you keep choosing for us to meet at."

Slade stood and held out an open hand which Austin gripped in his own and shook.

"You know I enjoy a good steak and a well-aged bourbon."

He rolled his eyes. The guy was marginally older than Austin, but acted like he was in his fifties and ready for retirement. Austin shirked his dinner jacket before they took their seats in a quiet, corner booth and ordered drinks from their server who took a moment to pour glasses of iced water for them.

"So, what's new? How's the shoulder?"

Austin rolled his shoulder in response. "Improving every day."

"Good." Slade sipped his water. "That's it?"

Austin sighed. The man facing him had been more of a father to him than his own, he knew when things were on his mind, he knew when Austin held back, and he knew when he was lying. There was rarely an escape from his inquisition.

"Daddy dearest wants me to marry someone who already has a boyfriend. Someone who isn't right for me."

Slade raised his glass. "For the family, am I right? Do your duty, Austin. Secure the future of the business, Austin."

Austin chuckled. "Something like that."

"Fuck that."

The server returned with their drinks and raised her eyes at Slade's exclamation but didn't comment. "Are you ready to order?"

"Two New York strips, medium rare, asparagus, and au gratin potatoes."

The server picked up both of the unopened menus in

front of them on the table and nodded. "Yes, sir. I'll put that right in for you both."

"She did not even double check that is what I wanted."

Slade picked up his glass and swirled the golden liquid around in it. "What else?" His phone vibrated, and he turned it screen-side-up on the table to see who was calling. "One sec, Austin."

While Slade took his call, he checked his cell.

> Mackenzie: Thank you for my gift bag. It is equal parts exciting and daunting.

He'd left her office earlier that day before she could open her gift. She must have gotten home from work and had dinner before she opened it.

> Austin: Nothing to be scared about. We can go through the contents of the bag together if you would like.

> Mackenzie: Like a kinky show and tell?

> Austin: Precisely.

> Mackenzie: I have a question about punishment.

> Austin: Go ahead. I am at dinner with a friend so my replies may be slow, but I will answer whatever you need to know.

> Mackenzie: A girl friend?

He smirked.

> Austin: No, Mackenzie. The only woman I want to eat is not in attendance this evening. He is my mentor and an old friend.

Slade was still on the phone, but he regarded Austin with a curious expression that said Austin would need to explain himself once he was done.

> Austin: What is your question?

Mackenzie: What would result in a punishment?

Mackenzie: I'm concerned about the punishment thing.

He took a sip of his drink before answering.

> Austin: Refusal to do something. It would depend on what that something was. Most likely that would be a physical punishment until you remembered how to say 'yes sir.'

Mackenzie: Physical how? Like with a cane? Your hand?

> Austin: I am running on the assumption that you were simply being a brat, so it could be any of those.

She didn't miss a beat with her reply.

Mackenzie: Me? A brat? I would never.

> Austin: It would be done safely, never in anger or spite, and we would be very clear about the punishment before we begin: the what and the why. In general, for a physical punishment, you could expect that you will at some point be tied down or otherwise restrained and will be flogged, whipped, caned, paddled, spanked, plugged, and clamped. Maybe gagged.

> Austin: It depends on what your hard limits are. And I also suspect that you'll have experiences where you will either be denied or over indulged in various ways.

> Austin: Coming without permission. Perhaps a rather extended forced orgasm. Hours tied to my bench, no breaks given until you remember why I make you wait until you recover.

> Mackenzie: OMG you'd do that? But I'd die.

> Mackenzie: Wait. What? Your bench?

> Mackenzie: OMG you have a kinky red room in your house, don't you?

"Who is she, Austin?"

"Hm?"

Slade watched him intently from across the table, his phone was back face-down next to his glass of water and his bourbon was empty.

"The woman making your face do things I haven't seen it do before."

"Like what?"

"Grin like a loon."

"If I had something to throw at you right now I would."

"Who is she?"

"She is a trainer for the team."

Slade's eyebrows rose. "Older woman?"

"Not by much."

"In the lifestyle?"

Austin shook his head. "Vanilla."

"Huh." Slade lifted his hand to flag down the server and order another drink. "She must be special."

Austin nodded without hesitation.

"Is she willing to experiment?"

Austin nodded again and took a drink.

"And you're ready to get back into a committed relationship?"

His unspoken ex's name hung heavily over the table between them. She had left Austin for another dom she had been seeing on the side, ripping Austin's heart out of his chest before she left. "I have not felt ready, until Mackenzie."

The server arrived with another drink and a basket of warm bread that Slade tore into with fervor.

Austin punched out a reply as he waited for the next round of questions from his friend.

> Austin: It is often something that is typically in a contract, we would work through it.

> Austin: Ironically you seem to think you are going to die from not having an orgasm. You would know in advance what the possible outcomes were. It is not always a 'this equals that' situation. But you would know what was likely and would flag what your limits were.

> Austin: It varies from dom to dom. Some do enjoy inflicting pain. I find it more rewarding that I am challenging you and teaching you lessons. I do not have an abuse kink, I have a control kink.

"Care to share?" Slade ripped a second piece of bread in two and popped half into his mouth.

"She asked about punishment."

Slade's hand paused on the way to his mouth with another chunk of bread. "Already discussing details. I have to say, Austin, I am both surprised and thrilled. I'm glad to see you're finally getting off the bench." He paused and raised his bread. "And her onto it, I suppose."

> Mackenzie: So the style of the dominant depends on their kinks as much as the style of the submissive depends on theirs?

He turned the phone to Slade.

"She seems intuitive."

"Intuitive, smart, determined, strong—"

His friend held up a hand and laughed. "I get it. She's pretty great."

Heat prickled up Austin's neck. "She is."

"Then I am very happy for you and I look forward to hearing all about her."

Their food arrived and they enjoyed a comfortable quiet where the only sounds to be heard were the scraping of silverware on their plates and the moans of delight from Slade at the melt-in-your-mouth steak he was chowing down on.

"How's Chicago?" Austin paused to take a drink.

"Not Minnesota, but needs must." Slade had moved from Minnesota to Chicago to open a secondary location of his BDSM club, Protocol. "We're in the 'I need to be there to make sure shit gets done' stage. I'm hoping to be more hands off soon. I'm fucking exhausted."

"Thor's doing a great job holding the fort here while you're gone."

"Best thing I ever did was make that Viking-looking-bastard manager of that club." Slade picked up a stalk of asparagus with his fingers and gnawed on the end. "You been in lately?"

Austin nodded. "Ironically that is where I met Mackenzie."

"You met your new vanilla sub at my club?"

Austin chuckled. "I did. She was there with her friends. She had no idea where they were taking her."

"And she didn't run off screaming." He raised his glass in toast. "Good sign."

Two hours later, Austin folded his inebriated friend into the backseat of an Uber and walked home. After a shower and a bottle of water, he settled into bed to finish his discussion with Mackenzie.

> Austin: Yes ma'am. That is correct.

> Mackenzie: How was dinner?

> Austin: Delicious. But not what I truly wanted to eat for dinner.

> Mackenzie: If you keep talking like that I might have to open this gift by myself.

> Mackenzie: How is being flogged, spanked, or any of those other things for punishment different to doing them all for fun?

> Austin: You ask very intuitive questions, Mackenzie. Those things as punishment carry a different tone, a different cadence, and a different message. Often it will be the same pressure, the same process, but it is about how it is approached mentally. Or it may be for a longer period of time.

> Mackenzie: And how do you determine when I need punishment?

> Austin: We can talk more about that later. Most doms, myself included, have a strike counting system that lets a submissive know they will pay for it later in private.

> Mackenzie: Does it still come with aftercare?

> Austin: Always.

> Mackenzie: Even if you're upset with me?

> Austin: If I am well and truly upset with you at my core, it is not something I would be inclined to approach through those activities. True anger does not come with control.

> Mackenzie: So essentially punishment is to maintain discipline?

> Austin: Precisely.

> Mackenzie: To remind me of both of our commitments.

> Austin: Yes ma'am.

She had a way of surprising him with her depth of understanding for someone who had limited exposure to the lifestyle. She seemed to just get it. His phone vibrated on his chest just as he was drifting off to sleep. Mackenzie's name flashed on the screen. His heart raced. No one called anyone after midnight unless something was wrong. He bolted up in the bed.

"Mackenzie? Are you okay?"

"Shhhhhh, crazy boy. I'm fine. I just had something I wanted to tell you that I didn't want to type in a text."

He rubbed his chest over his heart. "And what would that be?"

"I'm ready to be your submissive."

CHAPTER 13
Mackenzie

> Austin: Where is the nearest glass of water?

> Mackenzie: Ugh. Leveling up the sunshine I see. There's a faucet in the bathroom and the kitchen. Glasses are there as well.

It had been a week since she'd agreed to be his submissive. They hadn't yet signed a contract or anything quite so official, but he had definitely leveled up his dom-ness. That was a thing, right?

He was spending the weekend at his parents' house. A bid to keep the dogs at bay – he'd said. Whatever that meant. Apparently his father was pressuring him to make a decision on his future, and Austin felt it would be better to deal with it face-to-face.

Part of Mackenzie also thought he could do with his mom's back up, but she couldn't say for certain.

> Austin: When was the last time you consumed one?

> Mackenzie: Uh when you asked me last time.

> Austin: Until you have a glass in hand and half consumed I will need to pause this conversation.

She rolled her eyes, contemplating her level of brat response. She could joke that she may not even want to talk to him, but she could tell he was still a little insecure. The thought alone made her giggle. Such a strong, confident, handsome specimen of man, insecure in his relationship with her.

But from what she'd heard from her gossipy bestie Paige, his ex-girlfriend, his submissive of a number of years ghosted him for another dom and he was finding his feet after a break from relationships.

> Mackenzie: And how, exactly, do you plan on checking?

> Austin: You wouldn't lie to me, would you?

Her stomach dropped and clenched, but her pussy throbbed. The idea of disappointing him did more to her than she was ready to accept, but she wasn't letting him win quite so easily.

> Mackenzie: There's a first time for everything.

> Austin: Get the water, Sprinkles. It's important.

She smiled at the nickname he'd given her. While her heart ached for him to call her Love, they were a week into something very new for her. It warmed her that he'd maintained that boundary she'd set *and* came up with an alternative that she didn't hate.

Her amusement at a stoic, serious dom calling her sprinkles was not dying down any time soon. He'd told her it was because he didn't think she was all-the-way vanilla, she had some kinky sprinkles through her. He also wasn't wrong.

She got out of bed and made her way to the kitchen.

> Mackenzie: I have the water, stand down.

> Austin: Standing down is not one of the things I am programmed to do.

> Mackenzie: If there was ever a greater understatement spoken, we're yet to discover it.

> Austin: I realize you do not technically owe me any level of compliance since we have not yet signed a contract, but your well-being is still of concern.

> Mackenzie: Is that so?

> Austin: Yes ma'am.

She snapped a picture of herself drinking the glass of water, finished it, refilled it and repeated the photo holding up two fingers to indicate it was her second glass.

> Austin: Good girl.

Her phone rang and she picked it up without a second glance at the screen. "If you're calling to tell me to drink more water I might have to politely decline. I can't keep up with all of this running to the bathroom."

Silence.

She frowned, pulling the phone away from her ear.

832. Sugar Land, Texas.

Home.

Her heart stopped beating. Her mouth ran dry. Her ears rang like someone had used a loud speaker in her ear, and her whole body shook.

"H-hello?" She cleared her throat.

"Abby?"

Someone had pulled the pin from a grenade and shoved it into her chest. She had seconds before she fell apart. "There is no one here by that name." It wouldn't work, she knew it. Her accent, the sound of her voice, her sister, her Bea, knew exactly who she was talking to.

"Please don't hang up."

Kenzie's body ached with tightness and the water in her stomach sloshed, threatening to come back up.

"Can we talk?"

She couldn't form words, her mind raced, and her legs carried her to the front door where she secured the deadbolt she'd had installed when she first moved in but hadn't used for over a year. She turned, pressed her back against the wooden panel of the door and slid to the floor.

"You shouldn't have called."

"But Abby—"

"My name isn't Abby."

"You're right. It's Kenzie now, right? I saw it online." Her sister's voice wavered as she spoke. She sniffed and something brushed against the phone.

"You shouldn't have called, Bea." Her skin felt cold, clammy, and she wasn't sure if her brain was swelling or her skull was shrinking but the increase in pressure in her head made her dizzy and nauseous.

"And *you* should have known I'd never stop looking. Running away isn't the answer."

"It was my answer. And I'm not going back." She pulled the phone from her ear to hang up.

"Wait. Wait! Ab—Kenzie, please? Don't hang up. I just got you back."

She paused, returning the phone to her ear. "I'm not back. You need to leave well enough alone, Bea. Lose this number."

Bea's soft sobs tore at Kenzie's heart. "P-please. They don't know I'm here. I didn't tell them I found you."

Kenzie raked a hand through her hair. "How did you find me?"

"Private investigator. It's easy to siphon off money to pay a professional when everyone thinks you have a wind tunnel between your ears and spend your life at the salon."

Kenzie flinched at her sister's words. She'd been there, too. "You should have let me go."

"You wouldn't have let me go if it was the other way around." Bea's whispered words snaked around her chest. She wasn't wrong. She'd have overturned every rock on the planet if her baby sister had disappeared without a trace.

"What do you want, Bea? I'm not coming back."

"I'm here. In Minnesota. Can we meet?"

A strangled gasp escaped her as she pressed her back against the door to ground herself. "Was it you at the bar? N-no. No, Bea. We can't meet."

The doorbell rang, the shrill sound piercing the final thread of her composure and she shrieked.

"Mackenzie?" Austin switched from the doorbell to knocking on the wood. "Are you okay?"

How had he gotten there so fast? Was he already on his way over while he was texting her?

"I have to go." Kenzie cupped the microphone of the phone in her palm like it would shield her whispered goodbye from Austin. She hung up on Bea's protests and scrunched her eyes shut.

"I heard your scream Mackenzie. I am not leaving until you tell me you are okay." He knocked again on the door.

Sucking in a deep breath, she pressed her palms to the cool floor and pushed to standing. She spun to face the door, squared her shoulders and steeled her spine. Things were too out of hand. She needed to reel herself in. The idea of having a normal relationship with a wonderful man was blissful, but it was a fallacy.

She'd let her guard down and her baby sister had crossed the country to land at her doorstep. It was time to push Austin away, just like the others. She slid open the deadbolt, twisted the two locks, and tugged the door open.

His pale face was etched with lines of worry. "Hey." His eyes searched hers, then her face, then traveled to her toes and back to her head. "Are you okay?"

Her past bubbled up inside her like she was a bottle of Coke and someone had dropped a Mentos into her. She nodded. If she opened her mouth it would all come violently spilling out.

"I brought you a gift." He scrubbed the back of his neck with his palm. "Not a kink gift. A regular gift. An edible gift. To say thank you. I know you were not keen on treating me so soon, or so aggressively after my injury, but I appreciate you working with me and I wanted to say thank you."

He handed over a large cardboard box with a plastic window on top. A dozen cupcakes, perfectly frosted, with the physical therapy icon on top of them made something inside her chest snap.

"You didn't have to do this, Austin. I was just doing my job."

He nodded. "And you did it exceptionally."

She nodded, swallowing down the wad of cotton lodged in the back of her throat.

He tucked his hands into his back pockets and rocked

back on his heels. Every cell in her body yearned to invite him in. To curl into his lap and surround herself with his warmth, his smell, his belief in her strength. But she couldn't.

An awkward silence bloomed between them and she raised the bag in her hand. "Thanks for stopping by."

He hesitated like he was going to say something, then stepped forward. She inched the door closed in response. "I'll see you tomorrow at work?"

Her insides shredded like she'd been put through a blender. Her tone was cold, her muscles taut, and her guts sloshed. She silently begged for him to put his toe into the space, to stop her from closing the door on him, to push into the house and make her spill her truths.

But he didn't. He respected her boundaries, nodded, and gave her a fake smile that didn't hide the hurt in his eyes. "Take care, Mackenzie."

She closed the door with a soft click, keeping her palm flat against the wood as she dropped her forehead onto the back of her hand. How had she let things get this far? Would he even believe her if she came clean about her past? Would he leave because she was too complicated to be with?

He deserved better than the baggage she carried. He deserved more. Her phone vibrated on the floor where she'd left it.

Bea had texted from the same 832 number she had called from.

I miss you.

Kenzie dropped to all fours as oxygen fought around spikes of anguish in her chest. Heavy tears dropped onto the floor beneath her. She'd done everything she could to leave her past behind her, but it still yanked at her chest. She missed her family, she missed her friends, but she didn't miss her life or who she was when she was there. She'd grown. There was no going back.

She was under no illusion that if she'd stayed there, stayed with Garrett, that she would likely either have killed herself out of desperation to escape, or she would be a hollowed out shell of herself. But try as she might, she couldn't seem to break free from the shackles of her past life. Maybe it was time to stop fighting and let it consume her.

CHAPTER 14
Austin

"You've got this, Auzzy. Keep your head in the game and it's an easy win." Finn's grin did little to calm the tornado in his chest as he and his opponent circled each other on the mat.

He had not intended on going to the cages. But seeing Mackenzie so distant, so detached, had driven him to need to hit something, someone. It was not healthy and he knew it. But if he did not open the release valve he stood a real chance of potentially injuring someone on the ice. This way it was at least consensual.

He sure had a knack for picking women. A fist connected with his jaw and he bounced back on the ball of his foot while he recovered. He shook his head. Tonight was not going to be the night where he chalked up his first loss.

Finn's brow furrowed with concern before his eyes widened.

Austin jerked his head again. He was fine. So his new and clearly very upset girlfriend closed the door in his face and did not want to talk to him. He should have stopped and insisted she tell him why, but he hadn't wanted to make a scene. And he wanted to give her space. She'd tell him when she was ready.

It didn't mean anything, right?

His body begged for release. He sprung forward, catching his opponent unaware and striking hard and fast. Jab, jab, cross. Jaw, jaw, body. He could throw combos in his sleep. But something about the look on Mackenzie's face as she closed that door haunted his every breath.

It was his third fight of the night. Finn had bet on each one – and so far, Austin had not failed him. In the corner of the warehouse, two women listened to a police scanner. Four cages had been set up to accommodate the wealth of people willing to fight. And the crowd was feral, hungry for blood.

His opponent advanced but was met with Austin's fist connecting squarely with his face. Something cracked, blood spilled from his nose over his mouth and chin, but it didn't slow him down.

In the underground, there were no rules. No holds barred fighting. A different world than behind the doors of his regular gym where he trained in Krav Maga but an occasionally needed release when the stressors of his life got too much.

He parried a series of punches from his flagging challenger, whose movements were becoming slower, his muscles heavier. And while the bleeding had slowed to a stop, the guy's face probably ached like crazy.

It was time to put him out of his misery. Austin swept his feet out from under him, and followed him to the ground without missing a beat. His rival scrambled to his knees, but Austin didn't give him a second to gain any ground.

In his periphery, Finn nodded, around him, the crowd cheered four simultaneous fights, and the space stank of sweat and cheap beer. He had this. As soon as he won the fight, he could go home, have a cold shower, and sleep off his bad mood.

The challenger in front of him surged forward, knocking Austin onto his back, and he lifted his legs into his guard – a ground grappling position in which one combatant has their back to the ground while attempting to control the other combatant using their legs. The man's knees rested against Austin's ass as his legs were up around the torso of his attacker.

The opponent's weight leaned forward and one of his arms lay exposed. Using both hands, Austin locked the man's arm against his chest, rolled his hips and swung a leg over his head. Tucking his heel tight to his butt, Austin brought the man's elbow above his waistline, rolled him onto the floor until he was perpendicular to Austin and popped his hips upwards to lengthen out the man's arm.

It took less than a second for his rival to tap out from the arm bar. He was three for three, yet did not feel any better for it.

Finn patted him on the back. He gave a short nod and a grunt. "I'm going home." He didn't shower or look back at his friend who was already counting his winnings with a wide smile on his face. At least someone was happy. He grabbed his duffel bag, tossed it in the back seat of his car and took off.

Twenty minutes later he sat outside Mackenzie's house. He had tried to drive to clear his head, he had tried to go home, but something about the look on her face as he had left made him go back to her. She had been afraid.

Running a hand through his sweat-damp hair he tapped his fingers on the steering wheel. Was he overstepping her boundaries? Likely. Was he worried about her? Also true. Was the consequence of overstepping the mark with her less severe than his concern for her?

He popped open the driver's door, locking the car behind him as he walked. He texted her first, telling her he was at the front door, but she did not reply. Her car was in the drive, and a light was on upstairs, so unless she'd taken an Uber somewhere and left a light on, she was home.

One push of the doorbell and two knocks on the wood later she opened the door. Her hair was like a tangled birds nest on top of her head, held back by her glasses. Her skin was pale and dark circles underlined her beautiful eyes. Her hand clasped over her mouth, smothering a screech. What the fuck was going on?

"Austin?"

He did not wait for permission to enter, he did not wait for her to step back from the door, he charged at her like a bull to a red flag and folded her into his arms.

Her body shuddered against his. "What are you doing here?"

He gripped the sides of her head and jerked it from his body to see her face, ignoring her whimper. He crashed his lips against hers as he walked her back two steps into the house and kicked the door closed behind him with a bang.

A frantic need welled inside him as her tongue met his. He turned her so her back was to the door and stepped forward until she was flat against it. Her hands clawed at his chest and biceps, yanking him toward her like she couldn't get close enough to him.

Her fingers snaked up his arms and into his hair, her nails skimming across his scalp, eliciting a growl from him. He pressed her into the wood with his whole body, kissing her like she was his life force, or like he could kiss away whatever was hurting her.

They needed to talk, not kiss. Every piece of him ached to make her his in every sense of the word, but he needed to know what was going on so he could help her face it.

"Mackenzie." He tore his lips from her and leaned his forehead against hers while they caught their breath. "We need to talk. You need to tell me what is wrong. I cannot help you if I do not know what we are fighting."

Her eyes widened. She worried her lip as he stepped back from her, giving them both space to breathe, to think, to come down from their fever pitch. She took his hand and led him into the dimly lit living space.

An oversized leather couch lined the far wall. She sat on one side and he sat on the other, between them lay a neatly folded, handmade, granny square crochet blanket in purples and blues. Had she made it herself?

He ran his fingers over the yarn. "Did you make this?"

She nodded. "My Meemaw taught me how to crochet when I was little. I don't do it a lot these days, but the blankets are pretty."

Turning side on to the couch so she faced him, she tucked her legs up in front of her. "I'm sorry I pushed you away earlier." She wouldn't meet his eyes and played with the edge of the folded blanket with a trembling hand.

"It is okay. I cannot say I enjoy being dismissed, but I know there is something wrong and I tried to give you privacy and space to deal with it by yourself."

She tipped her head back. "But you're here."

He nodded. "I could not stay away."

"Did you have practice? You're sweaty."

"And probably smelly also."

She crinkled her nose. "That's what that smell is."

"You want to tell me what is going on?"

She banded her arms across her chest. "I've just been..." She rolled her eyes. "I feel like someone is following me."

His spine lengthened as he sat up straight. "Have you spoken to law enforcement?"

She shook her head, gnawing on her thumbnail. "I don't have any proof, just a feeling. I was wondering..." Her attention drifted back to the edge of the blanket. "Could you teach me some of the self-defense you do?"

He quirked an eyebrow and she spoke fast, as though hurrying to explain how she knew.

"Finn mentioned something about fighting at the cages. When I prodded he said you were a black belt at some fancy self-defense thingy." She waved an arm. "Not that I should be surprised. Is there anything not god-like about you? Do you steal from old ladies or something? Give me something mere mortal to cling to, Austin."

He chuckled. "I do not steal from old ladies."

"So you fight? Can you teach me?"

"I do and I can. But you need to agree to report anything suspicious to the police."

She nodded but her lip trembled. "I'm sorry. I'm such a hot mess." She slid her fingers into her hair, knocking her glasses off onto the cushion next to her.

"You're my hot mess. And I do not want you any other way. Would you prefer to talk about it more? Or something else?"

The stitch knitting her brows together deepened. "What would you like?"

"To help you find peace."

Her jaw quivered and her eyes filled with tears. "I'd like that too."

He regarded her for a moment, her breathing was shallow, and from the frantic picking she was doing of her cuticles, her mind, chaotic. "Do you like to read?"

She nodded.

"Would you like me to read to you?"

Her eyes popped wider. "Really?"

"Really."

"I think I'd like that. Do you think I could go get ready for bed first? I feel like if you read to me right now I'd fall asleep and my teeth feel weird after I ate an entire box of hot tamales." She arched an eyebrow. "I don't wanna hear any judgment from you, Mr. Health Nut."

He held his hands up. "No judgment."

Ten minutes later she reappeared clutching a book to her chest, wearing Golden Girls pajama bottoms, a "Bless y'all's heart" t-shirt, furry socks and her hair in pigtail braids.

She touched a hand to her hair. "I know. It's like I stepped out of the 90's with these braids, right?"

"That does not cause me to think of the 90's."

She stopped her approach to the sofa. "What does it cause you to think of?"

"Safety first. It means it won't get tangled in any of my toys or play apparatus."

She dipped her head, then her mouth fell open. "I'd say that didn't send a shiver up my spine but I'd be lying, and I'm pretty sure you felt it from three feet away. Do you prefer it this way?"

"I do not really have a strong preference on your hair. Ultimately, I prefer you to wear it in whatever way makes you feel more confident."

She grinned and jerked her chin at him. "It's not my hair that makes me feel confident. It's the look in your eyes telling me you want to wrap it around your fist as you drive into me from behind."

He growled and flexed his hand on top of his thigh. She was incredibly perceptive.

"Precisely why I do not care what style it is in."

"Can you braid hair?"

"Yes ma'am."

"Did you braid your other submissive's hair?"

"No ma'am. Mackenzie?"

"Yes, Sir?"

He patted the sofa next to him. "Come here. Head in my lap. Let us get you relaxed and ready for sleep."

A shy smile tugged at her lips. "Yes, Sir."

She lay with her head in his lap and he covered her with the blanket. Opening the book, he splayed the pages open with his thumb and pinky of his right hand, and with his left he stroked her hair, which she'd taken out of the hair tie and let hang loose.

"You like Formula One Racing?"

She nodded but didn't reply, instead she tucked her thumb in her mouth.

"Mackenzie?"

She glanced up at him. Her no makeup face pale against his dark pants.

"You do not have a daddy kink, right?"

She giggled and spoke around her thumb in her mouth. "Right. I've sucked my thumb forever. I only do it now when I feel sleepy or anxious."

He nodded. "Good, because if that was your kink I am not sure I could get on board with it."

Another giggle and she settled back down on his thigh.

"Friction, by Tracie Delaney. Chapter one, Jared. I cranked open an eye, my sleep interrupted by the unmistakable graze of a nail across my abdomen and the soft moan of a female."

Fifteen minutes later, Mackenzie was still awake on his lap as he read, lifting his hand from her head only to turn the pages. "Check in, please."

"Green. But you feel kind of far away. Can I maybe sit with my back against your chest or something, please?"

He draped the book over the arm of the couch and pulled her up and into his lap. She buried her head into the space between his shoulder and neck and her heels rested against the outer edge of his thigh. Tracing circles over his heart through his shirt she sighed.

"I should have showered, this is not ideal."

"You're not too stinky."

He chuckled. "Thank you for helping ease my self-consciousness."

"I do what I can."

"Is this better?"

She nodded and tucked her thumb into her mouth and he continued reading. A few minutes later, her breathing became heavy and even and her muscles sagged against his body. He tucked her bookmark between the pages and leaned his head back on the couch, stroking the bare skin of her bicep with his thumb.

It was the calm he sought at the cages, from the drive around town trying to quiet his thoughts, from his meditation and breathing exercises. But he'd found it in the woman he was dating, curled up on his knee, who kept a piece of herself back from him. He ran his hands along the curve of her face. "Do you have any idea how insatiable my desire to claim you as mine is?"

CHAPTER 15
Mackenzie

"Do you have any idea how insatiable my desire to claim you as mine is?" She'd heard his almost pained declaration through her sleepy haze, and when she woke up alone in the comfort of her own bed, her core ached. She patted the bed beside her but it was empty and cold. Had he moved her to bed and left?

She'd lied to him, told him she felt like she was being followed, something, anything to deter him from pushing her about her past, from having to open up that piece of herself to him when she was far from ready. Telling him about Garrett, about Texas, would only serve to destroy their relationship before it really even got started.

She'd keep everything locked away inside herself. She'd tell Bea to go back to Texas, and leave the past in the past where it belonged so she could move forward with Austin and her life in Minnesota. Forward was a scary place. Unknown. But she couldn't and wouldn't go back to Texas, even if the scores on her heart twitched at the thought.

She rolled toward her bedside table where a full glass of

water stood with a sticky note attached to it. *Do not panic, I am still in the house. Drink your water.*

She rolled her eyes with a smile at his bossiness, but complied and emptied the glass. She stopped to brush her teeth on her way downstairs, rolling her hair into a top knot and grabbing her glasses from the kitchen as she passed.

She found Austin stretching in her living room. He'd showered and changed into clean sweats and a shirt, he must have had a bag in his car. How heavy did she sleep that she didn't hear him getting up, getting his things from his car, and having a shower?

A better question would probably be how anxious and lightly she had been sleeping for the past two years since moving to Minnesota but she wasn't unpacking that.

"Hey."

"Good morning." He was in pigeon pose – even she knew that one from infrequent attempts at yoga class. He was bent forward at the waist, palms on the floor outstretched in front of him.

That. Ass. Hot freakin' damn.

She did not look that graceful when she did pigeon pose. Or any pose for that matter. She looked like some discombobulated scarecrow, and he looked like Eros. He was the god of love, procreation and sexual desire and she was Patrick from *Spongebob Squarepants*.

Huh. It was a good thing she didn't have to write lines for just negative self-thoughts!

She shook the thought from her brain while she overtly ogled Eros pulling himself out of the stretch and standing upright with a knowing smile teasing his lips.

"Has anyone ever told you, you look good enough to eat?"

"I could say the same about you." He crossed the space between them and lowered his mouth to hers.

How was this real life? The gorgeous man holding her in

his arms like she was precious cargo and it was his mission to protect her, to nurture her, to worship her.

"You didn't sleep in bed with me?"

He shook his head and indicated to the couch. "I was okay here."

Her heart dropped just a little, while he was gallant and noble, she kind of wanted to wake up to him demanding her to come for him. She clenched her pelvic muscles as heat curled around her. "Do you need to leave? Do you have class? I can make something for us for breakfast, or..." She flapped her hands against her thighs. "Something."

"You seem somewhat flushed, Mackenzie. Are you okay?"

Her insides tightened. Would he make her tell him what she was thinking? She was fairly certain he knew. She had a terrible poker face and if he listened hard enough he could probably hear her pussy begging him to touch her clit and make her scream.

"What is making your brain whirr?" His fingers kissed her hair.

"You first. What are you thinking?"

"I am wishing for you to drop calmly on your knees in front of me while I run my fingers along your jawline, slowly shifting to open my hand as I place it across the front of your neck. My thumb and forefinger resting firmly, yet gently, on your pressure points as I raise your chin up, extending your reach as high as you can while remaining on your knees. So I can kiss you to reinforce my needs and desires."

Her heart battered her chest making it hard for her to breathe. "You're playing with fire."

"It is not fire I desire to play with, Sprinkles. But perhaps that could be incorporated."

How did he seem so unflappable? How was he so calm while she was a soaking wet and desperate mess for him?

She dropped to her knees and he groaned. "What would you do next, Austin?"

"You have a proclivity for submission and you are delightfully curious, Sprinkles." He looked at her like she wasn't a disjointed scarecrow but Hemera, Goddess of daylight, and he'd been living in the dark his whole life. Something about him brought out her closet, geeky obsession with ancient Greek gods and goddesses.

"What is your safe word, Sprinkles?"

"Red. Until we decide on a different one."

He nodded. "Good girl. Do you wish to know what I would do next?"

Her chest rose and fell so fast she feared she might pass out from anticipation as she nodded.

"I would place my thumb and fingers on your collarbone. Apply pressure as I slid them up your neck until I was under your jaw line."

She stripped her shirt off, remaining on her knees, then took his hand and placed it on her collarbone as he'd said.

"Then I would shift my pressure to press down, sinking into your chest. The heel of my hand over your heart."

She nodded.

"I would come down to your level, remaining on my feet, knees bent." His body followed his words.

"Locking eyes with you. Kissing you with passion before telling you that you are enough as I am holding your forehead to mine. Eye contact still in place."

His kiss was hard and hungry. She'd never been kissed in such a way before. She felt it everywhere, from the soles of her feet through every bone in her body and when he pressed his forehead to hers she yearned for her whole body to be against his.

"Using the back side of my fingers I'd raise your neck and guide you to stand with me."

She allowed him to help her stand, leaning into his touch as she did.

"I would not tie you to a bench. Or grab a paddle. I would slowly and deliberately remove every article of clothing between us, holding that eye contact as I pull you into me. Kissing you deeply, guiding you to the nearest surface and lying you down gently."

Her breath came in pants and her pebbled nipples tingled with an ache for him to reach out and touch them.

"Yes, Sir."

His eyes swept over hers. "I do not have protection with me, Mackenzie."

"I have an IUD, and I don't have any STIs"

"My last physical was also clear, and I haven't slept with anyone since their last check."

She chewed on the inside of her cheek. "I'm ready." Her hoarse voice came out a whisper. "Please, Austin."

He pulled his shirt over his head by the back collar. "I need to make sure you know that you have been heard and that you are seen. That you are perfect. Exactly as you are. I will remind you that you are perfect for me as I slide inside of you."

She gasped. Slipping her thumbs into the band of her pj bottoms, she leaned forward but his strong hands stopped her.

"Let me."

She nodded. With Garrett she'd have used her arms to hide her breasts and stomach. Even at her slimmest, she was only ever intimate with him in a dark room so he didn't have to see her body. But with Austin, his hunger for her injected a confidence into her she'd never felt before. She wanted him to see her. She wanted him to see what he did to her.

He dropped to his knees, tugging the soft fabric down her legs as he did. "I need you to understand that I do not take you for granted. I need you under my touch." He pressed at the inside of her leg and she widened her stance.

"I need you to feel the energy you ignite within me and feel the way my body responds to touching your skin." He dragged his fingers up her inner thigh making her breath hitch as they climbed higher.

"I need you to feel how much I want to pour my strength into you. For you to feel the way I do. To know how much I believe in you. And how much trust I have in us to be exactly what we need. Both of us. You are perfect for me. I mean that. As you are."

Tears threatened to spill out of her eyes and onto the top of his head, but her quick intake of breath at his fingers gliding through her lips made her moan instead. Winding her fingers through his hair, she allowed her head to tip backwards.

He hooked her leg over his shoulder and slicked his tongue over her clit. There was no way she'd be able to stay standing while he drove her closer to the edge with each swipe.

"I will let you come, Mackenzie. As long as you are a good girl and remain standing for me."

Damnit. He was always one step ahead. "I don't think I can."

"Then I do not think you will come."

She groaned. He slipped two fingers into her, curling them forward, dragging her nearer to ecstasy. "And I really would like for you to come for me this morning, Mackenzie."

The moan that escaped her wasn't ladylike, nor was it quiet. The muffled 'good girl' he spoke on her clit between licks of his tongue against the bundle of nerves at the apex of her thighs had her gripping his hair in a tight fist.

His hand braced her ass cheeks so firmly that she was convinced if she fell back, he'd catch her with ease. Her hips thrust forward against his face, grinding herself against his tongue as he fingered her g-spot. With a slurp, he stopped, pulling his head back.

"N-no. No, please."

"Other than your plug, have you ever had anything in your ass before, Sprinkles?"

Her eyes widened. "W-what? Like…" Her climax threatened to slip away, but he maintained a steady rhythm stroking her clit with his thumb and her g-spot with his fingers, keeping her near the edge.

"Anything. Fingers. Toys. Cock."

Heat flashed across her chest. Was anything more sexy than him being on his knees talking dirty to her while he fingered her? She couldn't imagine it. Rolling her hips to meet his hand she shook her head. "N-no S-sir. Never."

"Where is your gift bag? Did you move it upstairs?"

Her cheeks seared. "At the far side of the couch. They haven't made it upstairs yet."

"Convenient." He hummed approval and placed her hand over his. "Circle your clit. Do not lose my orgasm while I retrieve the bag, do you understand me?"

She nodded.

He clutched her chin between his thumb and forefinger, forcing her to look into his eyes. "Use your words, Mackenzie."

"Yes, Sir." She grunted as her fingers swirled over her clit. "I understand. I won't lose it."

It took him both a lifetime and a moment to make his way back to her with the bag in hand. He reached in and pulled out a small bottle of lubricant. It was lemon scented, she'd opened it to smell it and hadn't been able to resist tasting it to see if it tasted of lemons. It did.

He flipped the cap with his thumb. "You opened it already?"

"Yes, Sir." Her legs trembled as she held off her orgasm with slow, steady circles. "I wanted to see what it smelled like, felt like, tasted like." She expected to feel embarrassed, but the glow of embers in his eyes kept any negative self-talk at bay.

He paused the bottle over his index finger. "Pinky or index?"

She couldn't think straight with the explosion brewing deep inside her, threatening to blow her into a million pieces. "Is it going to hurt?"

"Hurt, no. You will feel some discomfort and stretching. But considering you wore the plug for three hours, I imagine you will only feel pleasure. However, if you do feel pain, use your safe word immediately and we can stop altogether, okay?"

She nodded. As much as she wanted to take the easy route and choose his pinky, something she couldn't explain drove her to make him proud, to push herself, to see what it would be like to have his full finger inside her, or more. More. She shivered.

"Index."

He squeezed a dollop of lube onto his fingertip and settled back between her feet on the floor. "Do not stop circling your clit, okay?"

She nodded before a squeak burst from her as the cold lube came in contact with her ass.

"Check in."

"G-green."

He smeared the lubricant around just a little before slipping his fingertip into her tight hole.

"Check in."

"Green."

Her legs threatened to buckle, but he wrapped his free hand around her, bracing her butt at just the right moment.

"Stand tall, Mackenzie."

She nodded. "Yes, Sir."

His words wove strength into her muscles and while she adjusted her footing, he slipped a little more of his finger into her ass, swirling it gently around while replacing her fingers on her pussy with his. While one hand gently stretched her ass, the other sought out her clit and g-spot, making her quiver.

Fighting the urge to clench around his finger, she breathed deeply. The sensation of being touched in all three places at once almost overwhelmed her.

"Check in, Sprinkles."

"Green."

"Good girl. How does it feel?"

She closed her eyes and focused on her ass. "Not enough." She dropped her weight, pressing herself against his finger.

"So eager to please. Can you take the rest of my finger?"

"Yes, Sir." *And then some.*

As he slid the thickest part of his finger into her ass he lapped at her clit, countering the nip of the stretching at her ass with the warmest pleasure rippling through her core.

Pressing firmer on her g-spot with every thrust. He was relentless in his pursuit of her undoing. And if he didn't give her permission soon, she was going to come on his face, his hand, and she wasn't entirely sure that his finger would come out clean, either.

She clenched. Oh God. What if he got poop on his finger? He would have to, right? That was where the poop lived. Shit. Literally.

A cool breeze wafted between her legs as he pulled back. "Wherever you went to in your head, stop and come back to me. I need your full attention, Sprinkles. I am not taking my mouth off you again until you come for me, so consider this your permission to come."

She groaned again, and he returned his mouth to her pussy in earnest, hands moving in perfect sync like the conductor of an orchestra, drawing her orgasm from somewhere deep within.

Her body trembled and her core ached for release. He pushed his fingers further inside her, pulling a scream from her as current charged through her limbs. Tumbling over the cliff of release she yelled his name over and over until she had nothing left to give him and her voice was hoarse.

He kissed the inside of her thigh, her hip bone, bare stomach, caressed her hard nipple with his tongue as he trailed a path up her chest. Sternum, collar bone, the length of her neck, and along the edge of her jaw.

If her body wasn't in full post-orgasm haze, she'd probably have come from his exploration of her skin alone. A slow shiver traveled through her as he captured her mouth with his. The kiss wasn't urgent, or demanding, it was slow and deep.

It wasn't hard, or sloppy, it was precise, intentional, and as he slipped his palms up the curve of her ass and onto the soft skin of her back, she hooked her arms around his neck, needing him closer.

She needed to get lost in him. To give him every ounce of her anxiety and pain because somewhere deep inside she knew he'd know exactly what to do with it. The more his tongue teased hers the lighter she felt. Like he knew what she needed to set aside her past, the incident with her sister, and just exist for a moment to pull her thoughts together.

As his palms pressed her closer to him her nipples skimmed his chest. He was still half dressed. Her instinct would usually be to hide, cover the pieces of herself she wasn't happy with, the pieces of herself that changed after her injury. The pieces of herself Garrett would have commented on, or poked with his condemnatory finger in some kind of silent act of passive aggressive declaration that she was gaining weight.

But with Austin, she felt beautiful. She felt powerful, capable, and strong. And she wanted him. Her kiss picked up speed like a tropical storm turning into a hurricane. Unadulterated need whipped her into a frenzy. She needed him inside her. She didn't care if he needed to spank her, or string her from the ceiling if it meant she could feel him in places she hadn't felt the presence of a man in a long time – or an attentive and considerate man, ever.

Hooking her thumbs under the band of his sweats she shucked his pants to his knees, his mouth swallowing her cuss when they didn't drop to the floor. Something cold brushed up against her skin and she gasped. Was he...? Did he have a piercing?

Heart racing, she pulled back from the kiss and let her gaze follow the lines of his body until she landed on his hard dick.

Not only did he have a piercing, he had several. A column of four piercings neatly lined one side of his cock.

He kissed at her neck as she took in the sight.

"You're pierced." In fairness, he probably already knew that. But it was all she could think of to say that wasn't: good God in heaven you want to put that inside me?

Except she wanted him to, needed him to.

He nodded against the side of her head. "I am. It's called a Jacob's ladder – for obvious reasons, each piercing is a rung of a ladder. It will not hurt."

She reached out to touch them, sweeping her fingers over the cold, metal balls on each side. "I've never seen a penis I thought was pretty before."

He chuckled. "Thank you, I think."

She needed to stop talking before the man with the beautiful penis tucked it back in his pants and left her and her raging lady boner standing naked in her living room.

He kicked his pants off the rest of the way, stepping out of them with coordination she wouldn't have had at the best of times, let alone when her body was being rampaged by a flurry of electrical charge. Everywhere their skin touched, fizzled and sparked like they could ignite at any moment.

Without a word, or breaking their kiss, Austin softened his knees and picked her up like she weighed no more than a feather pillow. Her forearms braced against the back of his head gripping him to her, fingers forward, splayed into his hair, nails scratching his scalp she moaned his name as he stepped around the loveseat and carried her. Where? She didn't know or care. He could carry her to the devil himself and she'd go willingly.

She locked her legs around his waist and a cold, smooth surface met her back. His piercings brushed against her pussy, the cool metal making her shiver as he settled between her thighs enough for her to grind against him, but she couldn't get him inside her from the angle.

Tipping her head back so it rested against the wall, she sighed. He took the openness of her neck as an invitation and alternated between dotting kisses and nipping at her skin with his teeth.

"What do you need me to do?" Her raspy voice was low and filled with confidence. She was ready for whatever he was going to ask of her.

"Right now? Just take me."

Didn't he want to tie her down and beat her with paddles? To clamp her nipples and leave bruises over her body? Whips and chains – that was the BDSM way, right? But he was just okay for... vanilla? She had to have misheard him. Or maybe he didn't think she was capable of taking what he needed to give.

Like he could hear her thoughts, he stilled, cupping her jaw and turning her head to face him. "There is plenty of time for all of the kink, Mackenzie. But right now I simply need to be inside you."

Her body shuddered in response. She was shamefully wet but felt zero shame. If he had a problem with how wet she was then he should have thought of that before he drove her to insanity. She nodded.

"Vocal consent at every stage, Mackenzie."

She rocked her hips, relishing the bumps of metal rolling

across her lips. "Yes, Sir." She kissed him. "I need you inside me."

Gripping her hip with one hand, he lined up the head of his cock with the other. When he moved his pelvis it was only a fraction, enough for the tip and first piercing to dip into her heat. Sucking in a breath she nodded. She was not only ready for more, she needed it.

Each ridge grazed against her as he pushed himself all the way inside. She'd never felt something so acutely from the inside before.

"If you keep clenching me like that, this is going to be over before it even starts."

She giggled. "Sorry. It just feels nice."

Gripping both her hips, he slid almost all the way out, paused and took his time gliding back in, drawing a low moan from deep inside her chest. With each thrust he somehow felt deeper. He used his hips and one hand to brace her against the wall as his lips and fingers roamed her skin.

She tightened her legs around him, needing every inch of him inside of her. Every press of his hips against hers drove her closer to her release. And when he swept his thumb over her clit and she clamped down hard on his cock, shuddering and screaming like it was her first orgasm, her soul left her body.

He barely let her catch her breath before he placed her on the floor on steady legs, not taking his supportive hands off her. "Grab the gift bag. We're going upstairs."

CHAPTER 16
Mackenzie

Mackenzie's heart raced as Austin plugged in the blue and white wand and methodically placed the rest of the contents of her gift bag in a line on the edge of the bed. After two orgasms her body should have been drained, tired, sated, but as he carefully opened each of the items in front of her, a new wave of desire coursed through her.

He'd blown off classes for the day. She'd rearranged two massages and gave zero fucks. She'd never – in all her twenty seven years on earth – played hooky from adult responsibilities for any reason. But when a naked man looked at you like he wanted to do all manner of dirty things to you – it was definitely the universes' way of telling you to make the damn call and stay home.

A blindfold, two sets of leather handcuffs, metal clamps, a feather on a long stick, a silicone dildo... she shivered. Flames lapped low in her belly as she stood quietly, watching his every move.

He looped a long, black strap with rings and clasps on each end under her bed and draped the ends on top of the quilt, tightening the restraint so the excess strap disappeared and it lay flush on the bed.

"Climb onto the bed, Mackenzie. Facing the foot of it."

She nodded and followed his instruction, kneeling on the soft surface, cradling her hands in her lap. The gift bag in his hand was like Mary Poppins's carpet bag. He pulled a pair of socks, a bottle of water, a bag of almonds and some dark chocolate from it, sitting it on the top of her chest of drawers along with a small first aid kit, two wash cloths, Arnica and a tub of Aleve.

"This is the start of your care-kit. We can add to it as we go."

She nodded, warmth spreading through her chest. The thoughtfulness and kindness contained within the man in front of her was almost overwhelming. He'd thought of everything.

"What is your safe word?"

"Red."

He threaded his fingers into her still-braided hair and tugged her head back. "Good girl. I need you to use it should you feel the need to, okay?"

"Yes, Sir."

His deep, brown eyes swirled with emotion. Intensity, fire, and an affection that set her heart racing and lit up her skin. "You ready?"

"Yes, Sir."

Cupping the back of her neck, he lowered her face down onto the bed, her forearms leaning on the plush blanket, and her ass in the air. His hands skimmed along the curve of her spine before lifting from her skin, and after a beat, both palms connected with her ass cheeks with a light smack.

A blissful sting followed the slap and she threw her head back with a moan. She was hyperaware of every sensation. The thumping of her own heart echoed in her ears. Every nerve ending in her body sparked. The scent of sex mingled with citrus.

Something cold and hard met the warming skin on her ass, making her shiver. He dragged it over the space he'd smacked before taking it away. Spreading her cheeks he gave a hum of approval. "Such a delicious ass, Mackenzie."

A cold drip of liquid onto her tight hole preceded the tip of his finger spreading it around and dipping inside her. She pressed back against his hand, wanting more with a hum of her own. A metal plug pressed against her ass, and she relaxed into it as he slid it inside her.

It wasn't the same size as the one she'd used before, but it also wasn't too big. Her body stretched to accommodate the intrusion and she moaned as he tapped the pink gem on the end once it was in place. She wriggled her hips and he tapped it again.

"I am beginning to think you like having things in your ass, Mackenzie."

She nodded against the blankets and mumbled a 'yes, Sir.' He'd barely started and something was building with urgency inside her. Something potent and fervent.

Tucking himself against her butt, his rigid dick nestled between her cheeks and his hands skimmed across her ass and up her sides before pulling her until her back rested against his chest. He buried his head in her neck, before banding his forearm across the front of her throat. Cupping her breasts from behind with his other hand, he teased at her nipples with pinching fingers.

She felt him everywhere. His warmth captivated her, the strength in his muscles as he held her intoxicated her, and the confidence in his actions as he moved her, caressed her, possessed her, left her dizzy.

"Check in, please."

"Green."

He sighed into her hair and tightened his grip around her before releasing her. "I'm going to cuff you now, okay?"

"Yes, Sir."

While stiff and unyielding, the cuffs weren't uncomfortable. They had a softer lining inside, and a foot-long leather strap linking them together that allowed her to keep her hands shoulder width apart.

"The leather will soften over time. And we can use methods to speed up loosening it if we need to."

She jerked her hands away from each other, testing their limits and enjoying the clink of the metal clasps connecting her hands to the strap.

"The only rule we are going to have for now is that any time you need to come, you must ask prior."

It sounded simple enough. But from the flickering inside her abdomen, it wasn't going to take much for her to be pleading with him for permission.

"Your orgasms are mine."

Fuck. If he kept talking to her like that she was going to come before he did much else to her. "Yes, Sir."

He stood and guided her onto her back, her hands resting on the front of her shoulders, legs up, knees bent, pussy and plug on display to him.

"What a perfectly pink, glistening, and irresistible pussy you have, Mackenzie."

He dragged his cock through her wetness before slipping inside her. Gripping the strap between her handcuffs he used it to brace himself as he plunged deeper. Slow, languid, heavy thrusts that dragged his piercings against her inner wall making tiny tremors ripple through her body.

She heaved out a weighted sigh as he slammed his hips against hers, pressing himself deeper inside her.

"Good girl."

When he withdrew from her, she whimpered. "Please no. Please don't stop. Don't stop, Austin."

She heard the smack before she felt it. Flat fingers meeting her pussy. The burn was almost delicious.

"No topping from the bottom, Mackenzie."

She pursed her lips. "What does that mean?"

"It is when the designated sub in the scene is giving direction to, or making decisions for the dominant in a way that goes against the predetermined power dynamic. You are mine. This is my scene. And you will have me inside you should I decide that is where I need to be. Do you understand?"

The visceral reaction that tore through her body at his words left her breathless. "Yes, Sir."

"Good girl." He unclipped the strap between her cuffs and hooked her cuffs to the clasps on the restraint he'd threaded under her mattress.

A tug of her arms confirmed she wasn't able to move much at all. A thrilling jolt struck her core, and she clenched her muscles to hold onto it. She'd never played with handcuffs before. The closest she'd come was at a *Tingles* party for one of her friends' bachelorette parties back in Texas where she'd run her fingers over the cool cuffs on display.

Austin spread her legs so her hands were cuffed under her thighs. Even if she could lift her forearms, her legs would hold her in place. He checked the cuffs and straps. "Check in."

"Green."

"How does it feel?"

She jerked her hands upward but they didn't give and wiggled her toes. "Like I'm at the mercy of your every whim." She grinned at him. "I feel powerless. And yet..." She tipped her head back. "I kind of feel more in control than I ever have before."

"Good. You're not anxious?"

She'd never felt more certain about anything. "I trust you, Austin. I'm not afraid."

His eyes narrowed, but as much as she trusted him, he needed to trust her as well. Considering what she'd heard about Austin's ex, she could understand his reluctance. She stretched out her toes and stroked the side of his thigh. "I promise I'll use my safe word if I need to."

He nodded. "If I blindfold you, I am going to make sure I have one hand on you at all times to let you know I am here. Okay? If you get uncomfortable or freak out, you need to let me know."

She smiled. The concern on his face, in his eyes, and lacing his speech warmed her insides. "Austin? I understand. I'm not scared. I can take it."

His lazy smile and the twinkle in his eyes were back. She wanted to nibble along his strong jaw, but a thrill buzzed through her at the idea she was helpless, incapable of moving her arms, and her body was his. He grabbed her towel from the chair next to the bed, folded it in half and tucked it under her ass.

He really did think of everything. The clink of metal chain preceded his finger and thumb squeezing her left nipple.

"Adjustable nipple clamp with chain." He held it up so she could see. Squeezing the end of the clamp with one hand, he slipped his finger between the alligator clamps to demonstrate how it worked. "To tighten, I twist these screws."

She remained quiet as he put them on her nipples. The sensation was different to the pencils, a more immediate nip of pain and buildup of pressure. A groan rumbled low in her belly when he rubbed his index finger over her clamped nipples before leaning over her and dragging his tongue along the sensitive pinched skin.

She closed her eyes, enjoying the sensation, wanting to reach out and slide her fingers into his hair and hold him against her chest. She jerked her hand, making the handcuffs clink against the rings on the restraints.

A satisfied 'hm' was all she got from him as he picked up the next toy. "This is a flogger." He pointed to the handle. "This part is called a hilt and this ball, or pommel, separates the handle from the falls." He brushed the strips across her skin and she shivered at the tickle they left in their wake.

"Falls are usually made out of strips of soft material such as leather, nylon, or rubber. This one is suede." He dragged the ends of the fabric up the inside of her thighs, flicked his wrist, smacking the tails against her pussy.

The dull thud of pain that radiated from her core made her grunt. He swished his wrist rhythmically, making the tails dance across her body for a few minutes, kissing her skin with just enough force to sit somewhere between ticklish and tingly. She groaned when the suede connected with her clamped nipples.

"Check in."

"Green." She nodded, urging him on. "Definitely green." Sighing, she dropped her head back onto the pillow and closed her eyes. A soft plop on the bed suggested Austin had thrown the flogger onto the quilt next to her and his weight shifted from the mattress.

Two fingers slid inside her, slowly grazing her g-spot, building speed. Her hips moved of their own volition, meeting every thrust of his hand. His other hand attacked her clit with ferocious speed. She had no time to think or react, her whole body burst into orgasm around his hand. Once she'd finished screaming, she managed a stuttered apology.

"Why are you apologizing, Mackenzie?"

"I forgot to ask permission."

"It's okay." He planted his knees next to her ass and leaned over her body. Stroking her face he kissed her forehead, then her lips. "It's okay."

His reassurance was everything. His fingers slid around the back of her neck as he angled her head to kiss her deeply before trailing a path of kisses down her sternum. He caught her nipple between his lips, making her cry out. As he did the same to the other nipple, he released the clamp on the first.

Pain radiated through her hard, sensitive nipple, stealing her breath and forcing her to grit her teeth as he released the second clamp.

Her back arched as the sting coursed over her skin.

"Good girl, Mackenzie. Check in."

"Green." Her teeth remained gritted, but her body relaxed as the burning pain settled to an almost pleasant throb. She'd never seen her nipples so damn hard before.

He circled them with his tongue before continuing his journey down her stomach and settling on his chest, face level with her pussy.

"Oh, God."

He dragged his tongue through her folds, swirling it over her clit, as a silicone dildo slid inside her. She had never realized just how empty she felt until she was filled with a plug in her ass and a dildo in her pussy.

The sensation was enthralling, and his ability to keep a cadenced pace with both his tongue and the toy would have been impressive if she wasn't so intently focused on chasing the building ripples in her core.

"C-can I come?"

"No." With his no, he picked up the pace, licking faster, sucking harder, and pounding her closer and closer to the edge.

"P-please can I come?"

"No."

Her hips bucked against his face and she growled. She wouldn't make it much longer and she had no idea how to stop the storm brewing inside her. She'd never come as much in her entire life. She was convinced after the last one that she was done. Yet he propelled her forward with each swipe of his tongue. She was fast approaching the point of toothpaste all the way out of the tube with no hope of putting it back.

"P-please, can I come, Sir?"

"Yes ma'am."

He cupped her ass, gripping harder as her orgasm sizzled through her body. When her spasms finally stopped, he made his way over her again and kissed her. His lips were soft and she could taste herself on his tongue. Fuck, she tasted good.

"Good girl, Mackenzie." His mumbled affections between kisses set her soul on fire. "You're doing great. Do you have another one for me?"

Another one? She'd come so hard she'd lost count and he wanted her to come again? Was he crazy?

He skimmed his hand over her nipple. "Mackenzie?"

"I-I could try?" She was pretty convinced her clit was no longer functioning, but if he wanted to keep working her over, to chase another orgasm, who was she to stand in his way?

"All I just heard was 'make me.' Challenge accepted." The grin he tossed her was almost devilish and her stomach clenched. He made his way back down the bed, and after a quick moment something cold pressed against her pussy. One click and a low vibration hummed through her body. He'd turned on the wand.

"This wand has thirty settings and I am intimately familiar with each and every one of them."

She nodded and might have given an 'mmhmm' but her hips were already rearing and her swollen and sensitive clit was letting her know in no uncertain terms that it was not, in fact, broken.

Was this how she died? Strapped to her bed in a blaze of orgasms and kink? There were worse ways to go. After less than a minute, he moved the still-in-her dildo in and out, building up a rhythm. How was she already so close?

Why was he not using her to please him? His dick was still hard, piercings glinting in the sunlight streaming through her window. She was restrained, he could have used her mouth or pussy, even her ass for whatever he wanted. Yet he seemed entirely focused on her pleasure.

He clicked a button and the vibrations intensified making her thighs and calves tense. Yup. Definitely how she died.

When she played with herself she usually stopped at one, sometimes two if she couldn't sleep but it usually took her so long to get herself to number two that she fell asleep before she came again. And there he was, settled between his legs like a maestro of her body.

Closing her eyes, she tipped her head back against her soft pillow and let him have her. She breathed deeply as the vibrations on her clit and lips pushed her further and further. Was her soul leaving her body?

"Check in."

"G-g-g... please let me come, Austin. Please."

"Check in." His calm voice prickled across her skin. She was desperate, needy, soaking and spread for him and he was calm and composed. Did her undoing not affect him?

"Mackenzie, check in." The vibrations on her clit stopped, and her orgasm fizzled just out of her reach.

"Green." Her growl was anything but polite. "Doesn't this bother you at all? I'm lying here, falling apart and you're just... just..."

He put the vibrator back on her clit and pushed the button again. The strong vibrations making her orgasm surge within seconds. "Yes, Mackenzie. You can come for me."

The scream that ripped from her throat left her raw. Limbs shaking, tremors raking through her body, and a growing wet patch under her ass Kenzie finally understood why so many women loved having sex with their partners.

When their partner was invested in their pleasure, everything was different. She blinked back the tears prickling behind her eyelids, not wanting him to see her cry, but being unable to stop as they slid down her temples.

The vibrator clicked off, the dildo was removed, and his presence was over her once again, his warmth encompassing her, his body pressed against hers. She didn't open her eyes, afraid of what he'd see if she let him stare into their depths, but she opened her mouth to him when his tongue roamed the seam of her lips.

He swallowed her moan as he kissed her, deep, passionate, urgent, as though letting her know that her state of submission was indeed impacting him. She felt it through his kiss, through the way he cupped her neck with his strong hand, threading his fingers into her hair. She felt it through his hard dick, pressed against her abdomen and the way his body was poised, ready to be inside her.

"Please, Austin. I need you inside me."

He didn't stop kissing her, but slid down a few inches and lined himself up with her entrance. "Check in." His whispered words glided across her neck as he dotted kisses along her skin.

"Green. But if you don't get inside me soon, I won't be."

His lips curved into a smile against her jaw. "Yes, ma'am."

He sank into her in one motion and thrusted like a man possessed. His balls smacked against her ass as he plunged deeper, her head inching closer to the headboard. His pace slowed for a moment and he lifted his knee, placing it over her thigh, next to her waist. Raising his hips off the bed he drove into her, the shift in his position had deepened his angle and if he wasn't careful, she was going to pee.

"Get. Out. Of. Your. Head." With each word he thrust his hips against hers.

She arched her back off the bed. "You need to stop, I'm going to pee."

"You're not going to pee, and unless you're using your safe word, I am not going to stop." He pounded into her again, driving her closer to another orgasm. The plug in her ass throbbed, he filled her much better than the dildo and the metal ridges of his piercing dragging across her insides made her lose her goddamn mind.

Holy fuck, did she just toot? Her eyes snapped open but his expression only held determination. He rode her with careless abandon. Her fingers scraped against the comforter, and with every rise and fall of her hips the damp patch under her ass grew, but he didn't seem to care. The only thing he was focused on was driving her over the edge yet again.

"Come for me." His low growl in her ear sent shockwaves to her core. He gripped the top of her shoulders and pulled himself deeper inside her. Her release slammed into her after a few thrusts and her whole body went stiff.

Back arched, head tipped back, and his name leaving her body on a scream along with her very essence, she let everything go, convinced he was wrong and she did in fact pee. He lifted himself up onto his toes, arching his back toward her as she came, holding himself right where she needed him to be. "Such a good girl, Mackenzie."

She'd somehow thought with each use of the phrase it would become less; less impactful, less meaningful, just less. But in reality the more he said it to her, the more she yearned to hear it.

He kissed her forehead. "Check in."

"Green." Her chest heaved, her toes were cold, and her clit and ass throbbed.

He nodded against her head, brushing his nose against hers. "Let's get you cleaned up." He unhooked her cuffs from the strap looped under the bed, and removed the leather from her wrists. She rubbed at them, but they weren't painful, just a little stiff.

He cradled each of her legs in turn, brushing the warm palms of his hands along the cool muscles in her thighs and calves. "I'll be right back, okay?" He kissed her so softly her tears threatened to return. She moved to sit up but he pressed her chest back into the mattress.

"Stay here. Do not move."

She frowned, but nodded. Her body wouldn't fight him. Tiredness seeped through her every bone, and every inch of her throbbed. She must have closed her eyes and dozed off for a second because the warm sweep of a damp wash cloth between her legs jolted her awake.

"Easy, Sprinkles. Just relax. I've got you. We can have a shower later, but for now, just let me tend to you, okay?"

She nodded and her head lolled back. He cleaned her up, moved the towel from under her ass and placed it under her legs. He must have re-folded it as she didn't feel any wetness under her. Or maybe he'd grabbed another one from the bathroom?

His palms rubbed together a few times before he picked up her leg. Warm oil coated her foot as he worked her muscles with his hands. She rarely got massages. As a physiotherapist, she was fussy about who she let touch her body, but just like everything else about him, Austin's hands were adept at finding every spot she needed him to.

When he finished with her feet, he slipped on fluffy socks and she wiggled her toes. His hands moved higher up her leg, rubbing warmth back into every muscle.

"Is that lavender?" Her voice sounded far away, and scratchy. She swallowed twice but it did little to ease the burn in her throat.

"Yes, ma'am." He picked her up and tucked another pillow

behind her head. "Here." He gave her an open bottle of water to sip from and returned his attention to her calf.

"I hate lavender."

"Noted for next time." His smile warmed her as much as his skilled hands. "Would you like me to stop using it?"

She shook her head. "It's fine."

He gave her almonds and dark chocolate to snack on while he continued up her left leg and down her right, removing the towel from under her and tucking her legs under the blankets when he had finished. Then he did her arms, rolled her onto her tummy.

"I could get used to this." Her mumbled confession into her pillow sent a shard of panic into her chest.

"You should."

She was already falling for the man, she couldn't deny it to herself. And there was something even more intimate about his tending to her after the fact than letting him have full and total access and control over her body.

A torrent of emotion threatened to overwhelm her. "I've never felt like this before."

"Drained of all orgasms?"

"Taken care of."

He kissed her on the forehead and her heart swelled. Yeah. She definitely felt taken care of.

CHAPTER 17
Austin

Mackenzie's soft little snores as she slept on his chest settled something inside him. She had taken everything he gave her, let him tend to her post-scene, and was currently taking a nap before he took her for a shower.

While she slept, he had pulled up a local grocery delivery service on his phone and ordered a bunch of ingredients for them to bake together when she woke up, as well as ingredients for him to cook her dinner.

Father had called a number of times after Austin had canceled their lunch together, but each one had gone to voicemail. He would have to face him sooner or later, but for the time being he simply wanted to soak up every moment with his girl.

He hesitated to define what he was feeling, but it was already taking root in his chest, burrowing deep. He didn't love often, but he loved hard. He could easily see himself falling in love with the fierce, strong, funny woman whose arm draped over his waist.

"You're staring." Her mumbling against his skin tickled.

"You are easy to stare at. How do you feel?"

She lifted her head up and frowned at him. "All systems have not yet reported in. But I'm pretty sure you broke my clit, bruised my pussy, and stretched my ass hole." She gasped.

"I took out your plug."

"I was worried it came out when I... when... Oh God." She dropped her head back onto him with a light smack.

"Mackenzie?"

She shook her head on his shoulder.

"Everyone passes gas. You can't put things in without expecting things to come out."

Her body tensed against his.

"You also did not pee. But even if you had, I would not have cared."

Her head snapped up again, eyes wide. "Oh my God was there poop on the plug?" She groaned and dropped her head again. She was going to give herself whiplash. "I am so embarrassed."

He squeezed her to him. "You have nothing to be embarrassed about. If I was not prepared to deal with bodily fluids, I should not have provoked them." He shrugged. "And I was raised to clean up my messes."

A delicious shiver passed through her from head to toe. "You're serious, aren't you?"

He nodded, kissing the side of her head through her hair. "I am. And when I come in your ass – and believe me, Mackenzie, I will someday come in your ass – it will be messy. And I would really like it if you grew to be okay with it."

He rubbed her back. "We do not know a lot about each other, but I would be more offended if you didn't make a mess."

She giggled. "So I didn't fart out my plug?"

"No, Mackenzie. You did not fart out your plug. I am not even sure that's possible."

The doorbell chimed. "It's Amazon, just let them dump it on the porch."

He picked the cell phone up from his chest. "No ma'am, it is not Amazon. I ordered some things while you were asleep."

He slipped out from under her, tugged his boxers on, and made his way out of the room.

"Wait, what things?" When he didn't reply she tried again. "Austin? What things?"

He accepted the delivery, tipped the driver, and carried the groceries into the kitchen. "I am making you dinner."

She appeared wearing his t-shirt, hair mussed, sleepy smile on her face. "You're spoiling me, Austin."

"I enjoy cooking." He could not help reaching out to caress her face. "And when you are as amazing as you were, I am going to take care of you." He paused and kissed her forehead. "And I need for you to let me."

A sigh lowered her shoulders from her ears. "Okay."

He jerked his chin at her breakfast bar. "Sit. I will grab you some water and you can watch me until it is time to help."

"Help?" She yawned and dragged her fingers through her hair, pulling it into a ponytail. "Help how? You should know my kitchen skills are questionable at best."

"And yet you have a state of the art kitchen in your home."

"I love being in here, I just don't do so hot at the making of the things."

"That will change. We are making a trifle for dessert."

"A trifle?" She screwed up her face. "Like custard, Jell-O, and fruit kind of trifle? Like the British thing Rachel accidentally made a shepherd's pie trifle?"

Chuckling, he shook his head. "I prefer a light cake, closer to angel food cake with layers of fruit. No jelly. No custard. And a sweetened cream cheese with whipping cream. Almost more like a cheesecake. A trifle is truly layered cake and fruit with some form of cream. My mother's preference is chocolate mousse but she makes a great lemon trifle. Cake, lemon curd, and the cream layer of cream cheese with lemon zest, sugar, and fold in whipped cream. She often included raspberries or blueberries."

"You're making it incredibly hard for me to concentrate on anything other than your mouth tasting of lemon. But it sounds delicious."

"It is only fair, considering you smell of lemons and have been making me literally hard."

Her jaw dropped a little and a blush stained her cheeks.

"You are beautiful."

She pursed her lips as though considering her reply, but shook her head. "Thank you."

"Good girl." He rounded the counter and slipped his arms around her, kissing her forehead. "How do you feel?"

"I'm fine. Better than fine. I feel more relaxed than I have in a long time. I forgot how loose my muscles could get. You don't need to worry about me."

"Mackenzie that is quite literally my job. I do not wish for you to drop after our scene, so I will be keeping a closer than normal eye on you."

"Drop?"

"Sub drop comes in two forms. Physical sub drop which is a reaction by the submissive's body to the strains of a scene, and mental sub drop which is an emotional response that can take place much after the scene is done." He paused. "I'm making pork with apple cream sauce for dinner, is that okay with you? Vegetables and hassleback potatoes. I also bought ingredients for lamb and wine Dijon cream in case you didn't like pork."

She smiled. "Both of those things sound utterly delicious. Chef's choice."

He nodded, placed the meat into the fridge, and moved

the potatoes and vegetables out of the way, leaving only the dessert ingredients in front of him.

"Neither type should be taken as a weakness of the submissive, on the contrary, the occurrence of either usually indicates that the sub has been pushing themselves in the scene to go as far as they can. You did incredibly well in that scene, Mackenzie."

He warmed at her smile. "I am proud of you. But do not be surprised if you begin to feel a little off. And while it is the duty of your dominant to understand and look out for signs of either type of sub drop and cut off the bad effects when possible or at least minimize them, I am going to need you to tell me if you begin to feel out of sorts at all, okay?"

"I feel physically fine. What are the signs of mental sub drop?"

"Emotional sub drop can often manifest itself first as a feeling of detachment and then progresses further from there. The main cause of this is a lack of contact with the dominant of the scene. So I will be in your space a bit more than I have been. Scales?"

She pointed to a cupboard next to him, where he found a myriad of baking equipment. Pulling out a cylindrical, glass salad bowl to use for his trifle, he grabbed the scales and began measuring ingredients for angel food cake.

"Unlike physical sub drop, emotional can happen immediately or days later. I have even seen weeks after the scene."

She paled. "Weeks?"

He nodded. "It is of the utmost importance that you are fully transparent with me, okay?"

"Yes, Sir." She stole a raspberry from one of the boxes on the counter, closed her eyes and moaned.

"Once the detachment starts further lack of contact can bring on feelings of remorse, more guilt, embarrassment, and even in extreme cases self-loathing. We shared a very intense scene. Your first scene and a bond is created there. It doesn't matter if we were *just* friends or if you are *just* playing. The bond it creates is very real in the sub's emotions. When there is no contact following the scene, a submissive can feel rejected like they did something wrong."

He arranged the ingredients in a line in front of him and moved the KitchenAid mixer into the middle of his space. "Even if their conscious mind says "It was just play" the subconscious says "But they would have contacted me unless I did something wrong". This feeling eventually becomes the pervading emotion about the play and often creates a feeling that the sub has done something stupid or wrong or is not good enough to be contacted."

She gasped. "That is so sad, Austin."

He nodded. "I have seen some doms leave their subs in the middle of the floor to fend for themselves. That is a job half done. It is our responsibility as dominants to ensure our submissives are always cared for, not simply in the bedroom."

Tucking the scales away again, he sighed. "Grater?"

"Cupboard to your left."

Pulling out the grater he started zesting the lemons. "So essentially sub drop is what happens to your body after you've drained your brain of all the hormones and chemicals that it releases during the scene or session."

"Do doms drop too?"

The roots deepened in his chest. Her questions were always so astute. "Yes ma'am, they do. Dom Drop is very similar to sub-drop in many respects. When in a scene a Dom is experiencing the very same rush of endorphins just like a sub, add into that a rush of adrenaline as well and you have quite a cocktail. Dom drop can manifest itself in different ways depending on the person and the intensity of the scene or scenes – just like sub drop – and can be either physical or emotional."

He zested another lemon. "When the rush of endorphins and adrenaline is gone there can be a physical reaction, just like coming down off a candy rush. A better way to look at it is if you have ever been in an accident, your senses are heightened, you are dealing with the situation, some people in times like that have even exhibited extreme strength."

She stole another raspberry. "Have you ever dropped?"

He nodded. "Most notably after my former submissive left me."

Sadness flickered across her face. "It doesn't sound fun."

"It was not."

An hour later, the angel food cake was cooling, they'd made lemon curd, whipped the cream and cream cheese together, and the kitchen looked like a small icing sugar bomb had been set off. Kenzie had a smear of flour, or icing sugar on her cheek, and she was flushed from the heat of the oven, but her smile was wide.

"Teamwork makes the dream work, right? Just like a kink relationship." She swiped a finger of the sweetened cream cheese mixture into her mouth and sighed. "And hockey."

He opened his mouth to speak, but her cell rang on the counter in front of them. An out of town number flashed on her screen. She sent it to voicemail, flipped the phone facedown, and slid the button on the side to silence her notifications.

What was going on with her? He did not know a lot about her, her past, her life, but he knew her well enough to know something was wrong. Her entire demeanor shifted, her muscles tensed, and the flicker in her jaw suggested she'd gritted her teeth.

"I had an abusive ex."

He stayed quiet, stacking the dishwasher as she spoke.

"Daddy arranged it." She shrugged. "Good for business."

"I can relate. My father wishes for me to marry the daughter of his business partner."

She gave him a finger gun. "Samesies. The abuse started small. Gaslighting, making me question myself, then it escalated. I found out he was cheating – more than once, but I was trapped. Family, duty, honor."

He had so many questions, but fear of her shutting off from him and not letting him in kept him quiet.

"When he laid hands on me for the first time, I knew I had to leave."

She wouldn't meet his eyes, instead training them on the counter as she dragged her fingers through some spilled flour. Wiping his hands on his thighs, he straightened up tall and walked toward her. Cupping her head, he tipped it back and kissed her deeply. "You are brave and strong." He kissed her again before brushing her tears from her cheeks.

"It was so hard to stand up for myself, Austin."

"You will stand up for yourself again. And again. And every time it will get easier to do, even if it is still laden with fear."

Maybe it was time for him to take his own advice.

CHAPTER 18
Mackenzie

Austin: What is on the table in front of you?

> Kenzie: Full water bottle, laptop, tissues, notebook and pens.

Austin: Push all those things on the table forward so the space in front of you is empty.

> Kenzie: Yes, Sir.

Austin: Feet flat on the ground. That means shifting forward so your knees are at the end of the seat and sitting up tall.

> Kenzie: How do you know my feet aren't touching the ground already?

Austin: Highly unlikely. Tilt your pelvis forward. Bring the curve back into the small of your back. Shoulders over your hips. Ears over your shoulders. Hands on your knees. Deep breaths. I want to imagine that I am there behind you. Keep your pelvis lifted.

> Kenzie: I don't know why you think that would make me relax more. My HR just shot through the roof.

> Austin: I never said anything about relaxing.

Thank fuck for that because she couldn't think about anything other than the heat pooling between her legs.

> Kenzie: Yes, Sir.

> Austin: Pull your belly button into your spine. Imagine I'm breathing next to your ear as you breathe in.

> Kenzie: You're giving me goosebumps.

> Austin: Take a deep breath and listen to the sounds around you.

> Kenzie: Are you outside my office door?

> Austin: Guilty. We're going skating.

Cold hard fear snaked up her spine. While she'd been back on the ice a couple of times since she first met Austin at the rink, the idea still left a lump of lead sitting heavy in her stomach.

"Trust me, Mackenzie. It will be okay." He appeared in her doorway, lopsided smile, beanie hat pulled low down his forehead, hands tucked into the front pockets of his jeans.

"What are you doing here?" She leaned back in her chair to look around him to make sure no one else could see her talking to him.

"Mackenzie, take a breath. I've been seeing you for treatment. There is nothing out of the ordinary about me standing in your doorway to speak with you."

He was right. Of course he was right. She was overreacting. She nodded, and forced confidence she didn't feel into her limbs and voice. "So... You want me to skate? Why? What are we going to do?"

She'd been working on improving the muscle strength and tone in her legs. She'd started low impact exercises, and was already feeling stronger and more capable. But stepping onto the ice with an athlete at the peak of his fitness was daunting AF. That said, Mama raised a woman who always faced a challenge head on.

"We're going to have a little competition."

She arched her eyebrow as a familiar rush passed through her. "Is that so?"

"Yes, Mackenzie. We are going to test who is the superior athlete."

Snorting she shook her head. "I see how it is. You're back to full strength and I am still recovering. Is that the only way you can beat me?"

Fire flashed in his eyes as he grinned. "Let's find out."

Twenty minutes later they stood face to face at center ice having skated a couple laps around the rink to warm up.

"You guys want to tell me what's going on here?" Finn stood between them, waving a whistle back and forth. "I mean, whatever it is, my money's on Kenz." He winked at her with a wide grin on his face. "I gotchu, boo."

"Austin talked trash during one of our sessions. So I've been working to get myself back on the ice."

Finn's brows pinched and he canted his head.

"I used to be a figure skater until an injury ended my potential career." Her chest tightened with every word. It never got easier to say out loud.

"Shut up!" Finn's mouth hung open and his wide eyes shone with something like awe. "I feel like I don't know you at all, Kenzie. I thought we were buddies."

She smiled and sucked in a ragged breath. "I stayed away from the ice for a long time."

Finn pointed the whistle at her. "You mean other than working for a college hockey team, right?"

Laughing, she nodded. "I guess I couldn't stay too far away. Just enough to remind me of my former life and everything I was missing. Some kind of self-punishment for being careless and getting hurt." She shrugged, trying to feign nonchalance on the outside while her insides splintered at the realization that was exactly what she'd done. She'd punished herself for something that wasn't her fault by taking one of her favorite things away from her life. Wow.

"And now?"

"I'm doing better. I've been working off the ice to get some strength back in my leg. I guess we're about to see if it has done any good."

"You know there are these miracle-working people who can help you recover." Finn scratched his chin. "They train in school to help people just like you who injure themselves. We even have a couple of trainers on the team." He gasped and covered his chest. "You might even know one."

She pushed his bicep and groaned. "Shut up. And I tried PT, the next step is surgery and the odds weren't certain enough for success to warrant it. I was never going to be a professional figure skater after the accident. And I was so angry at myself, my circumstances, that I took it out on my love of the ice. But I'm in a better place now. I can skate for fun and not miss my old life *too* much."

Finn wrapped an arm around her shoulders and squeezed. Tears pricked in her eyes at the show of affection from the laid back player who was always smiling and joking. "Good talk, Kenz. I feel like our friendship just leveled up and I'm totally here for it. Next we'll be getting drunk together and painting each other's nails."

Maybe sharing pieces of herself wasn't such a bad thing after all.

"You ready to kick his ass?"

"My current goal is not falling on my ass. We can work up to kicking his." Her muscles were limber despite the extra weight she was carrying. There was no way she was winning any championships, or even beating Austin on their first time out of the gate, but she was in better shape than she'd been in a long time. She was eating better and drinking more water thanks to Austin's influence, and she was even taking a daily multi-vitamin.

Her past self had no idea who this new Kenzie was, but she felt good in herself. "What's first?"

"First, we will skate the width of the rink to see who is fastest."

Electricity thrummed through her as they took up their starting positions. When Finn blew the whistle Austin left her in a spray of ice as he shot away from her. While she surged forward, she had no chance of catching up to him. But her leg also didn't protest against the speed.

"What's next?" It had been such a long time since she'd let her hair down and done something she truly loved. Being back on the ice was as freeing as her submission to Austin. Just existing.

"Skating backward." Austin took up position next to her and smiled. "How was it?"

"Fun? Freeing?"

"Fabulous?" Finn grinned at her again. "You've got game, Kenzie. I gotta say, I'm a little disappointed we're just discovering this side of you now."

She smiled back at him, but it didn't reach all the way inside her to her soul. There was a reason she'd kept herself from the people in her life and that reason was still sending her messages. It had been almost a week since Bea had texted her for the first time. She'd gone back home to Texas but she hadn't given up on the daily assault on the walls Kenzie had managed to build up around her since she'd left her family.

"Ready?" Finn's voice jolted her from her near-spiral and she nodded.

The shrill whistle cut through the silence of the rink and she pushed off. After a few strides, Austin was still in front of her. She was winning. She pushed harder, dug deeper, but after a couple more feet he'd closed the distance between them.

She could still win. Sucking in deep breaths she felt the edge of the arena coming up behind her. When the whistle blew, Austin was beside her. She had no idea if she'd beaten him or not.

Finn announced a tie and Kenzie warmed inside. She'd take it. If nothing else she'd been on par with Austin for one of the rounds. That was everything.

"Do you want to pick what we do next, Mackenzie?"

"Austin, if I pick what we do next I'm going to choose something grossly unfair like doing a spin."

"I have no problems with this." Finn's shoulders shook with laughter. "In fact, I'm totally down with making Austin try to do a spin."

Austin gestured to Kenzie. "You first."

She quietly kicked herself for opening her mouth. She was rusty, she hadn't done a spin in a long time and when she had she was substantially lighter on her feet. She pulled her arms to her chest and pushed off, gaining momentum as she turned.

As she twirled faster she threw her arms above her head and finished with them out at right angles to her body.

"That was pretty freakin' cool, Kenz. Your turn Auzzy." Finn didn't seem to even try to hide the amusement in his voice.

Austin attempted to copy what Kenzie had done, clutching his arms to his chest and stretching them above his head as he turned. But a combination of his much larger frame and his clunky hockey skates resulted in more of a slow motion spin than anything. But another brick came down from the walls protecting her heart at the fact he'd tried.

"Wanna try an easy jump next?" She didn't think he'd back down from her challenge, but his easy 'sure' sent something through her. Would he really try anything for her?

She hopped from one foot to the other, pointing her arms and fingertips when she landed.

Austin smirked, took a few strides and pushed off from the ice. His leg wobbled when he landed so he leaned forward and stretched his arms out to his sides to regain his balance. She couldn't help but applaud. "Nicely done."

"He's such an overachiever." Finn rolled his eyes.

"If you're not careful that could earn you a spanking." She slammed her mouth shut and her eyes popped wide open.

Every ounce of liquid had dried up from her mouth and she couldn't meet either of their eyes. Finn was howling with laughter and she felt Austin's stare melting her clothes from her body.

"Or so I've heard." She shrugged, hoping she could pass off her furious blush as a result of physical exertion.

"True story, Kenz. Our boy does have a thing about spanking." Finn's nod was slow, and his gaze appraising.

Did he suspect something more than friendly rivalry between her and Austin? There were always rumors circulating about every guy on the team. It wasn't a secret that Austin was a Dom. Did she truly care if anyone knew? When she finally met Austin's piercing stare there was no judgment or anger in his chocolate eyes, but she couldn't quite decipher what was there.

"Hold that thought." Finn skated toward the bench and picked up a stick and puck that sat on top of the boards. "Let's see how you handle a stick, Kenzie."

She pushed the outstretched stick toward Austin. "Austin first, so I can see what I'm supposed to do."

Austin skated a couple of strides, passed the puck back and forth between his left side and right side before threading it through his leg and cradling it back around in front of him.

"Show off." Kenzie jerked her chin as he lined up to shoot the puck into the back of the net.

"It is only fair, Mackenzie. I did your figure skating tricks. It is your turn."

She grinned and accepted the stick blade first. She was never someone to back down from a challenge. She circled the puck and moved it with the stick, for a couple of paces before taking a shot on goal, and missing by about three feet.

"I've seen worse." Finn's sympathetic smile made her burst out laughing.

"I can't be wonderful at everything, *Finnegan.*" She dusted her shoulder like she was some kind of superstar. "I have to fit in with you mere mortals sometimes."

"Hashtag facts." Finn offered her his closed fist and she bumped her own against it.

"Perhaps you will do better with a long distance shot." Austin took the stick from her, picked up the puck and skated toward the blue line. He scored again with ease while Mackenzie's shot went embarrassingly wide.

"Perhaps not."

"I feel like that was a pretty even split, you guys. Not bad at all Kenzie. Not bad at all." His pursed lips and approving nod wrapped around her like a blanket. She hadn't sought Finn's approval, but the fact he gave it so readily tugged at her chest.

If she and Austin were going to be a thing, she'd need to get used to the idea of hanging around with his teammates more and she was already friends with Finn. But something about his easy acceptance of her twisted her insides.

"Thank you, Finn. It's definitely nice to be back on the ice."

"Good job, Auzzy. Who knew all it would take to get her back out and fighting fit was some smack talk?"

Austin smirked, making her legs weak. "Who indeed?"

CHAPTER 19
Mackenzie

"Tell. Us. *Everything*." Addison poured from a pitcher of something pink and undoubtedly lethal. "You've been quiet."

They had wanted to go out to a bar, but with the risk of being overheard, Kenzie had requested they have a girl's night in instead. She didn't tell them that she was trying not to be seen out and about just in case Bea made a second surprise trip to Minnesota. She wouldn't put it past her stubborn and persistent younger sister.

"I've been busy."

"Doing the nasty with Hottie McDom." Paige lifted her glass and pointed it at Kenzie.

Kenzie didn't answer, but her thighs clenched to temper the ache in her pussy.

"I feel like you nailed it." Addison took a slurp from her concoction. "Or... rather, he nailed her." She shrugged. "Spill."

Kenzie sighed. "That night we played pool at the bar and Adi sucked face with Thor, I thought I saw someone I recognized. Turns out it was my sister. I haven't seen her and have no intention of doing so, but she found me. So I'm low-key freaking out that someone else from my past life might, too."

"Not where I thought this was going, girl. I'll give you that." Addison blinked, blinked again, then widened her eyes as though processing what Kenzie had just said.

Kenzie flapped her hand. "Stop it. It's not that bad."

Both her friends stayed quiet, peering at her over the top of their glasses.

"It's not."

"I saw new workout gear on the dining room chair." Addison speared her with a hard stare. "If new boxing gloves are 'not that bad' then I don't want to know what 'that bad' actually is."

"Austin is going to do some training with me."

"Let it be noted that I have a myriad of kink jokes about training right now that I am putting a pin in because of the gravity of the situation."

"So noted." Addison clinked her glass against Paige's.

"He's training you in... punching people?"

"Krav Maga."

"I feel like if your asshole ex were to show up on your doorstep tomorrow, one lesson of self-defense isn't going to do much of anything to protect you."

"And while we're being the sensible friends... Kenz... if you're this afraid that he's going to show up and do... whatever it is you're afraid of, don't you think it might be time to talk to a lawyer. Find out where you stand legally?"

She'd already thought about it and had begun a search online to see who the best divorce attorney was in the area. She nodded slowly. "I definitely need to get my ducks in a row."

"No shit. Right now your ducks are well on their way to being drunk."

"They're up the creek without a paddle." Paige mimed

swimming. "But we gotchu, girl. Let the bastard come. We'll face him together."

Despite the cinder block resting on her chest, she couldn't help but smile at their fierce loyalty. If anything would get her through the things she needed to face, it was the strength of her friends.

"Don't negate just how far you have come all by yourself though." Addison topped up her drink from the jug. "You don't need us. We just so happen to have your back."

She gnawed on her lip and nodded. She'd been through the worst of it, right? She'd gotten out from a toxic, abusive relationship with a narcissist. Surely staying out had to be easier than escaping.

"I found a divorce lawyer and sent an email. We have a meeting next week. I don't even know what to expect. I just…" With trembling hands she raked her hair back from her face and blew out a breath. "I'm a grown ass woman afraid that my mama is gonna fly across the country and beat me with her flip flop until I go back to him."

Paige squeezed her hand. "I think you're afraid they're going to still be on his side. That they're not going to have missed you or thought about why you might have left."

She rolled her lips between her teeth, fighting tears. Paige was right. She was afraid her family would want to put the business above her wellbeing.

"If that's the shit they bring to your door, they aren't worthy of you, K-K. You're a fucking queen and you deserve to be treated as one. Garrett can go fuck himself. And if your folks pressure you to go back, they can go fuck themselves too." Paige got increasingly more aggressive with each word.

"I feel like we are getting a little ahead of ourselves. Just because your sister found you, doesn't mean anyone else will. If they do, we'll deal with it. But in the meantime, how about you tell us all about Austin." Addison was like a dog with a bone. She wasn't quitting.

Kenzie pressed her finger and thumb together and dragged it across her lips like a zipper. "I'm not kissing and telling."

"Okay." Paige grabbed a handful of popcorn. "If you're not going to spill your guts about Mr. Pierced Penis – uh huh. I know all about his hardware." She winked. "I hear things. And I've *seen* things. And if you're not going to share things, then you can at least tell us about you. Things you've tried, things you liked, things you didn't."

Heat spread across Kenzie's body. They'd only been together a short time, but her desire to explore kink and his desire to educate was like a spark to kindling.

"We have an Excel spreadsheet. It has a list of over 270 different kink things. We both went through it and rated each on a scale from 'no' or zero, to five. Dislike is one, will tolerate, two, willing to try, three, really turned on and open to push limits is four, and essential is five."

"Fuck." Paige fanned herself. "This is so hot. He's really all in with you isn't he?"

An intimate smile tugged at Kenzie's lips.

"From the look on her face, she's all in with him, too. And he has been all the way inside her, too." Addison snorted and picked up a slice of pizza.

"The list is alphabetical."

"Can I see it?" Adi folded the pizza in half, lengthways, and shoved the tip into her mouth with a groan.

"I can copy and clear it and you can see the empty one."

"Such a fucking buzzkill." Addison rolled her eyes. "We're your friends, we don't judge your kinks."

"I can clear his answers then, and you guys can answer on the same sheet so I know y'all's kinks as well."

"Seems fair to me. What type of things are on it?" Paige

tore chicken meat from a wing with her fingertips and dropped it into her mouth.

"The A's have things like abrasions... anal... pretty... eh, I don't want to say normal kinks, but slightly more mainstream I guess?"

Paige waved her chicken wing. "I'll allow it."

"What off-the-wall ones are on the list?" Addison leaned forward like Kenzie had the key to world peace in her pocket.

"Catheterization?" Kenzie shuddered. She'd been catheterized during the hospital stay for her surgery and could not fathom how anyone would find it a turn on. "Religious scenes," she hissed, dropping her voice in case there was a chance God couldn't hear her.

"You can take the girl out of Sunday school..." Paige grinned.

"There's a TENS unit on the list." She shuddered. "I can't imagine hooking that up to anywhere sensitive. I can tell you there are definitely things on this list I won't be trying."

"And he's totally fine with that, right? If he isn't, I'm gonna have to rip his balls off and feed them to an alligator."

Kenzie and Paige regarded Addison, their jaws dropped open and wide eyes.

"What?" Adi shrugged. "You're telling me you wouldn't help me feed Austin's balls to a gator if he pressured her into doing something she wasn't okay with?"

Paige nodded. "Oh, I absolutely would, it's just the passion with which you seem keen to do it is where my concern lies."

Addison threw a wolfish grin. "I know, right?" She leaned forward and grabbed a slice. "So, he cooked for you? Tell. Us. Everything. For real this time. No cliff notes."

Kenzie smiled. They wouldn't give up without hearing *something* about her overnight with Austin and she wasn't giving up the kink. "He did. He made the most delicious meal.

I sent y'all pictures of the entrée, it was restaurant quality. Let's just say he has *plenty* of attributes."

Paige snorted.

"And the trifle. Guys... I need to get him to teach me how to make the trifle. It was the most blissful thing I've ever had in my mouth."

"That's what she said." Addison crammed the pizza into her mouth. "Isn't trifle that British thing with Jell-O and fruit?"

"Not this one. It was the lightest, most delicious layered eggless angel food cake, with eggless lemon curd, and a mixture of sweetened whipped cream and cream cheese. I thought it couldn't get any better. This delicious man making me food."

"I was totally sure not having eggs would destroy me. I even said it to him. I'd need to really like him to survive without eggs. He replied that a contact allergy probably wouldn't trigger anaphylaxis or anything but if it did it would be worth the epinephrine."

"Ew. Puke bucket. Get back to the down and dirty Dom talk please." Paige rolled her eyes while drumming her fingers on the counter.

"And then he. Ate. It. Do you know how sexy it is to watch a man's lips curl around a spoon to eat a slice of heaven?"

"Oh!" Addison clutched her chest. "Our baby girl's all grown up."

Paige hi-fived Adi before sweeping a fake tear from the apple of her cheek. "It's just so beautiful."

Kenzie was so hung up on the man that she would even suffer her friends poking fun at her. "He used the analogy of the trifle to talk about the layers of a kink relationship."

Paige swooned. She literally freakin' swooned and without

an ounce of sarcasm. "Boy better not break your fucking heart, ZiZi. I'm starting to like him."

"Lies. You're almost as gone for him as I am." Kenzie finished her drink and poured another.

"Hashtag fucking facts. Does he have any single kinky friends?"

"I can ask. I don't know if he has any sub friends, but I know he has this one friend Slade who's a Dom, too. If Austin doesn't know anyone I'm sure he could ask Slade to introduce you to some eligible bachelors next time he's in town."

"Slade? You mean owner of Protocol, Slade? Slade Wilcox, Slade?"

Kenzie blinked. "I uh... I guess so? I didn't ask for a background check. I just know he hung out with him when he was in town."

A fierceness Kenzie had never seen in her friend's eyes before. Was that lust? Desire? What the hell was her deal?

"I don't care if that asshole is on fire and the only available liquid in the world is my piss. I wouldn't save him." She paused, downed her drink and shook her head. "Don't fucking ask, because I'm not fucking telling."

Hatred. It was hot-as-hell hatred. Which suggested something different to the cold-hard-kind. Curious.

Paige shook her head as if to reaffirm her stance. Kenzie and Addison would drag it from her one way or the other, but considering they gave her two years before digging into her past, Kenzie would just have to sit with her burning curiosity for a while.

A text from Austin telling her he was going to bed lit up her screen on the counter in front of the girls. She grinned and bit down on her lip so a dreamy sigh couldn't escape her. But her friends made kissy noises and pretended they were Austin and Kenzie and roleplayed how much they wanted to bang each other.

"You seem so fucking happy, Maxy." Paige raised her glass. "I'm totally here for it."

Addison raised her glass too. "We love seeing you getting pleasured, teased, taken care of, having your experiences – and orifices – expanded. Who knew you were such a kinky bish?" She laughed at her own joke. "And most of all we love watching you being loved."

Her heart stuttered. He couldn't. That kind of thing wasn't a thing outside of romance novels and romcoms. She had thought she loved Garrett but she'd been wrong. While the traitorous organ in her chest wasn't to be trusted, everything with Austin felt different.

"You're going to make me cry, and not just 'cause I had a large butt plug in my ass yesterday and my butthole is aching."

"No tears." Paige refilled their glasses. "Especially butthole tears. No Bueno."

Kenzie burst out laughing, spraying her mouthful of drink across the counter.

Paige pointed at her. "I knew I could make you laugh. Bam!"

"Yeah. That's what my butthole said."

A few hours and many, many drinks later, Mackenzie stumbled upstairs to bed. Austin was busy all weekend – and she found an ache in her chest she wasn't quite expecting. Damn. She was falling too hard, too fast, and her heart wasn't ready for the high-speed impact.

She hadn't replied to his goodnight text as she didn't want to wake him, but lying staring at her ceiling in the darkness she wondered, once again, if she needed to pull back. Somewhere deep inside her a little voice screamed loudly that she needed release. She wasn't even sure what that meant, but if Austin had been local she'd probably have found herself on her knees at his feet, asking for him to quiet the noise so she could simply think.

That only served to scare her even more. What would she want him to do? Spank her? Tie her up and flog her? Curl his hand around her throat and control her very breath?

A shiver passed through her. She wanted all those things. Maybe if he were in the room with her, drawing pleasure from her in all the best ways and controlling her every movement right down to the oxygen circulating her body she could escape the loud thoughts in her head.

Her sister, her ex, the darkness that hung over her while she waited for Mama to come a-knockin', twist her ear, and drag her back to Texas.

She growled. Her life in Minnesota was good, great in fact, but with every step she took toward the life she wanted, the leash around her neck tightened. She rubbed at her throat. Would she ever be free?

The lawyer had given her hope, but she'd seen too many TV shows and heard too many stories about women who never escaped their abusers to dare believe it. And the more she grew to know about Austin, the less convinced she was that she deserved a guy like him.

Her phone chimed beside her on the bed.

> Austin: Please tell me you are okay. I cannot settle.

Was there anything imperfect about him? She hadn't so much as heard the man fart once. Was he even human?

> Kenzie: Just wondering what a guy like you is doing with a girl like me.

> Kenzie: I'm fine, Austin. Go to bed.

He wouldn't like it, but she didn't really care. She was tired, overly emotional and she wasn't getting into it with him.

If he wanted to bend her over something and fuck her mood out of her, she'd let him. But she wasn't spilling her guts to him in the middle of the damn night when he had a game the next day. It wasn't going to land well with him. He was going to be pissed.

The temptation to shut off her phone and ignore him flickered through her mind, but she needed to settle him or he'd probably turn up at her door to make sure she truly was okay.

> Austin: You know I'm not going to take an order from you.

She re-read her message. While it was hard to convey tone, her shitty mood had indeed leaked into her texts. Fine never meant fine. She knew that, he knew that, anyone in the world who had been on the receiving end of "I'm fine," knew it, too.

A shiver passed through her. Would he ever let her assert some form of dominance? Or would he always react from a place of being an alpha.

> Austin: My immediate reaction to that is not one – I believe – you are truly going for.

> Kenzie: What's that?

He stayed quiet for a moment, had he gone to sleep?

> Austin: To be completely honest, my instinctual reaction leaves me concerned for your safety in my presence right now. Emotionally, not physically.

Why did that not scare her? Why was the throbbing between her thighs getting stronger and her pussy getting wetter?

> Kenzie: Tell me what your reaction was.

> Austin: Quite simply? To break you.

She laughed out loud as she typed her response.

> Kenzie: It's flattering you think I'm not already broken, but I'll bite. For what purpose?

> Austin: More like you break a horse, less like you break a lamp. My concern is that my immediate reaction was not to break you of the self-deprecating thoughts. I often want to break those.

Her chest pinched. Every time she thought he couldn't get any sweeter, kinder, more considerate, he opened his mouth and said something that touched her. That made her want to cling to him with both hands and not let go, even if she didn't believe she deserved him.

> Kenzie: Then what?

> Austin: I more desired to put you in your place and ensure you know you do not get to command me in that way. I suspect you knew what buttons you were pushing when you told me to go to bed.

> Kenzie: I might have, yes Sir.

> Austin: My concern is that my initial instinct was to drive home my role as Dominant, not to reinforce your importance.

She was wrong before. This was how she died. Austin Morgan being over-the-top sweet to her because his reaction was more to stick his dick in her smart mouth and fuck it till she shut up than to soothe her emotions.

> Kenzie: Sometimes those things can be the same thing.

> Austin: They do not feel the same.

She pulled up Google Translate and typed the words "my warrior" into the search bar. She could try to kid herself, but she truly was a goner for him and everything he offered her.

> Kenzie: I'm not afraid of you, mon guerrier.

> Austin: That made me smile. But it is not you being afraid of me that has me concerned.

> Kenzie: Explain it to me, please?

> Austin: It's the lack of control on my side. I have time to refocus and redirect over messages. In person I'm not sure how well that reaction would have landed.

> Kenzie: I'd agree if I didn't know my words would have provoked a response. I knew telling you to go to bed wouldn't go well.

She rolled onto her side and propped her head on her hand. She couldn't afford to fall asleep when he was clearly so bent out of shape about the urge to snap at her for being a bitch.

> Austin: Perhaps I would be able to read that better in different circumstances and the concern would be less founded. I should not need to rely on you to know when it is and is not safe to push my buttons. Perhaps it is all moot given you were looking for that reaction.

> Kenzie: I don't weigh up whether it's safe or not to push your buttons. I knew what I was doing and I knew what the consequences would be. Or at least I thought I did. I figured you'd want to fuck my attitude out of me. I trust you. Sure, there is a learning curve, but that trust will only grow – hopefully in both directions.

> Austin: There is no room for error in my estimation of what your intent is and how I should respond.

> Kenzie: Everyone makes mistakes. I'm starting to think that yours was falling for me.

She sucked in a sharp gasp, wondering if she should take it back. She wasn't looking for confirmation that he was falling, she wasn't trying to hurry him along, but the feelings he made her feel... the things he said... it seemed as though he felt everything she did.

> Austin: Not in the slightest. My reaction would have probably been to pin you to the wall by your throat and physically remind you that you are not in a position to call the shots. It is still my job to know when to and when not to push back though.

The throbbing in her pj pants intensified. She slid her hand up around her neck and pressed. What would it feel like if his larger, stronger hand was wrapped around her throat instead of her own? She squeezed her thighs together. Maybe Garrett was right, maybe she was a deviant. But maybe he was wrong that it was a bad thing.

> Kenzie: I'm not sure I should admit it, but I wouldn't have backed down. In fact, I'd have doubled down and I'd probably have laughed around your hand on my throat and made it worse. I imagine I would have ended up beyond frustrated and unable to sit comfortably for a week. It would have been worth it.

> Kenzie: Your reactions don't scare me. It's not the same as with my ex. I feel different with you – stronger, more in control. I know where my limits are and most importantly, I know you'll respect them.

Austin: If your reaction was to fall apart in that moment I would not have handled that well.

> Kenzie: I can promise I wouldn't have fallen apart. Unless you didn't react at all. I think that would have broken me.

> Kenzie: Like a lamp.

Austin: Mackenzie?

Every single time. Whether typed or spoken her name from him sent tingles through her whole body.

> Kenzie: Yes, Sir?

Austin: That is all I needed to know. You pushing back further is what I needed. I should not have questioned myself and my reaction.

> Kenzie: I feel like you need to have more faith in our relationship.

> Austin: The less you have in yourself the harder it is for me to trust myself. I do not say that to simply drive you to self-acceptance. I know it is not that simple.

> Kenzie: Contrary to how it might seem, I'm trying.

> Austin: I do not doubt that.

> Kenzie: I get why you expected me to fall apart. I get why you questioned yourself. It's sweet and comforting and almost charming in a way only you can pull off. I'm sorry I made you question yourself, but I'm not sorry I hit that button. I needed your reaction, I needed the reminder, the clarity, to be anchored.

> For the sake of full transparency, I almost snapped at you earlier to just leave me alone when you kept at me to drink water, but I was too afraid you actually would so I talked myself down.

> My fear isn't how you'll react, or what you'll do to me, it's that you'll leave, either when I push you away or just because I'm too much hassle, and worse still, that it'll be easy.

She'd said it. He'd wanted transparency and good communication, so that's what she was giving him. It was out there now and there was no taking it back. All she could do was scrunch her eyes shut and wait for the chime of his reply. Her heart thrashed. He never took even the smallest quips of self-deprecation but she hoped he'd somehow find a way to ease her raging insecurities.

> Austin: You are not too much hassle. You are perfectly you and I would not ask for you to be any different. There is no right or wrong way for any human being to be. I wish I could teach you to accept that.

> Kenzie: You have a couple of decades of toxicity to compete with, but I'm trying.

For herself as much as anyone else.

CHAPTER 20
Austin

Mackenzie: I woke up with my arousal coating the tops of my thighs, my nipples almost painfully hard they could cut glass. Tread carefully, Love.

He grinned at her use of the L word. Granted it was in warning, and sarcastic, but she'd come around to using it for real sooner or later.

Austin: Careful is something I am capable of.

Mackenzie: Why did that send a shiver to my core?

Austin: I know how to walk a very thin line, Love. Find something for breakfast. I need you to work on building your strength for tonight.

Mackenzie: What happens tonight? Did I miss something? It's Thursday, right? No home game.

> Mackenzie: I just checked the away schedule, no games there either.
>
> Mackenzie: It's not my birthday.
>
> Mackenzie: It's not your birthday.

> Austin: Do you need me for this discussion or should I come back later?

> Mackenzie: Where are we going?

> Austin: I was thinking of taking you to Protocol.

> Mackenzie: You aren't afraid someone might see us?
>
> Mackenzie: I don't have anything to wear.

> Austin: Why can you not wear what you wore the night I saw you there?
>
> Austin: Also, no. I am not.

> Mackenzie: Same club, same outfit? Really?

> Austin: If it is not broken, do not fix it.

He finished his bowl of cashews and almonds, washing it down with the remnants of his protein shake. By the time he had placed his dishes in the sink she had replied.

> Mackenzie: Okay. I'm in. Though I can't say I'm not nervous.

> Austin: Why would you be nervous? I am not signing you up for public flogging or anything.
>
> Austin: Unless that is something you desire.

Her reply took an inordinately long period of time.

> Mackenzie: I'm not saying no.

Every drop of blood in his body rushed to his dick, making it stir in his pants. Her desire to explore her limitations and her sexuality, the things that she had not so much as thought about before, made his chest swell with pride.

The first night he had met her at Protocol he could not have ever imagined her being willing to go back to the club, never mind the idea of stripping off and having someone flog her in front of other people.

His ex had been no stranger to the lifestyle, she was a seasoned submissive who participated in competitions and helped train new dominants and submissives alike. But he'd never felt the dizzying surge of pride welling inside him at anything she did while they were together.

He had deliberately let Mackenzie lead the way, guiding him at her own pace, not wanting to spook her, or pressure her into doing more than she was ready for. But she was ready. And he couldn't wait to give her the world.

Later that night, he leaned over the bar waiting to grab Thor or Melissa's attention to order a drink while he waited for Mackenzie to arrive. She had insisted on meeting him there. She and Paige were going shopping, because contrary to his arguments about her previous outfit being fine, Mackenzie had other ideas.

Thor gave a low whistle at someone over Austin's shoulder before placing a bottle of water onto the counter in front of him. "You are one lucky bastard, Austin."

Before he could turn to face his girl, a hand pressed against the bottom of his spine. "Hey."

A single word was all it took to give him a warm buzz. He really was a lucky bastard. She had walked into the club by herself to meet him – something she probably would not have done before. Her hand slid around his waist and landed on his thigh. He was so fucking proud of her. Picking up her hand, he brought it to his mouth and kissed her knuckles.

As he turned, he kept hold of her arm, keeping her in place so he could take her in. She wore pointed, red stilettos and his dick stirred. Those would be digging into his ass cheeks before the night was out.

She was not tall, but her bare legs seemed never ending as he dragged his eyes up her naked skin. She wore a leather mini skirt that took every ounce of moisture from his mouth. Fuck. It emphasized her sexy curves and showed off a lot of skin.

The skin-tight skirt clung to her like it had been custom made for her hour-glass figure, and the eye-catching transparent net inserts at the sides had small straps with buckles over them. He steadied himself with a breath, clutching his free hand into a fist by his side and reminding himself he couldn't touch her on the bar level. Or at least shouldn't.

Pushing another breath out, he continued his journey up her body. She wore a black, leather gothic corset top that flared over her hips. Between her waist and her hips were three straps with buckles on each side.

Her breasts were cupped by textured leather dipping into a V on her sternum. A large strap and belt buckle led from the top of her left breast to her covered right shoulder – the fabric matching that of the cups for her chest.

A black strap curled around her neck, fastened in place at the hollow of her throat with a large silver stud, reminding him of his desire to collar her someday.

Her hair was braided loosely over her bare shoulder, her lips were coated with a glossy, power red lipstick and an understated smokey eye. What had he done to deserve such an amazing woman and how could he keep doing it so she'd never leave?

"Thor." Mackenzie nodded to the Viking over his shoulder. "Arnold Palmer please."

"Sweet tea and lemonade coming right up for the beautiful lady."

Austin was not a jealous man, but even if he was, he could not be angry at Thor for pointing out the obvious.

"You okay?" Her brows pinched and she cupped his chin with her palm. "You haven't said anything yet and you look kind of pale."

"I'm just..." Words caught in his chest and clearing his throat did little to free them. "You look stunning."

Her cheeks almost matched the color of her plump, shiny lips. Unable to help himself he grazed his thumb over her bottom lip and held it out on display between them. "Just checking I am not going to mess up your lipstick when I kiss you."

She rolled her top lip between her teeth. "I wouldn't care if you did."

"Neither would I." He kissed her until Thor cleared his throat and broke them apart with a grin.

Thor handed her the cocktail, and Austin settled their bill while Mackenzie made small talk with the woman next to her about her outfit. She could make friends with anyone, anywhere, over anything. When they'd finished their drinks she slipped her palm against his and moved closer to him.

"I tried that enema thing earlier." Her eyes sparkled as she spoke. "That was... an experience." She glanced over both shoulders before leaning further in to him. "And, I have my large plug in tonight."

His balls tightened, aching for release. She was intent on killing him. That or making him come in his pants before they even descended the stairs to the dungeon.

Tugging on his hand she led the way to the staircase. "I'll try not to fall this time." Just as she finished tossing her sentence over her shoulder to him with a carefree laugh, she slipped, wobbled, and righted herself. "Totally meant to do that."

He gripped her waist as they made their way downstairs. Sterling, the dungeon master, nodded at Austin as they approached.

"Austin."

"Sterling."

"What does he do?"

Austin gestured to him to explain who he was. "I'm the Dungeon Master." He paused for a moment and pursed his lips like he was thinking of a way to best describe the term. "The BDSM equivalent of a Road Chief: someone who observes at a play party or scene in order to monitor it, and step in if things get out of hand."

"Does that happen often?"

Sterling's narrowed gaze roamed the room as he nodded slowly. "Too often for my liking. Having a Dungeon Master is a way of ensuring that things stay safe, sane, and consensual, especially in large groups. But you're always going to find those who skirt the rules."

Austin nodded. "Just last week Sterling saw a gagged sub was bleeding profusely and seemed to be dazed, so he called out the Safe Word. The Dom didn't listen and Sterling needed to get security to force him away from the sub."

Mackenzie gasped and covered her mouth. "That's awful."

Sterling nodded. "Unfortunately, it happens."

Austin led Mackenzie away from Sterling by the small of her back.

"Is that guy teaching those two women to spank that woman while she gives that other guy a blow job?"

The woman being spanked was restrained to a bench, and the instructor was indeed teaching two newbies how to strike her. The woman on the bench moaned around the dick in her mouth before the guy she was blowing nodded encouragingly at the timid looking woman spanking her. "Slap harder, she enjoys it."

A few feet to the left of the spanking class, three women sat getting eaten out by their respective lovers. Quiet music played in the background and women moaned softly, but no one was screaming loud enough for the neighbors to complain. Yet. The night was still young. Maybe he'd find a way to make Mackenzie bring the roof down.

She stood, rooted in place, watching the women with men between their thighs, lapping at their pussies.

He pulled her close enough to feel his dick straining in his pants. "Would you like me to do that to you, Mackenzie?"

She didn't take her eyes off the scene to answer. "Maybe later."

One of the men paused, turned to Mackenzie and offered his hand in invitation for her to join him and the woman he was going down on. She politely declined, holding up her palm to him in answer, but watched as he brought her to orgasm, coming all over his face.

When they continued their walk around the room, two women had swapped partners and gave head to the men.

Austin guided Mackenzie to the private rooms off to the side of the main play space. On one side of the corridor, were four small rooms with beds and play accessories and on the other, another four rooms with two play spaces contained in each. A room for those performing the scene and a closed room for them to be watched through one-way glass.

In the first room, a man had a woman bound and gagged while he whipped her breasts. Lines of black mascara coursed down her face as she cried, each smack of the whip darkening the bruises on her chest.

Mackenzie shuddered against his chest and shook her head. "Let's try the next one."

In the second room, a woman was being fucked in each of her holes by three men. Mackenzie moved further into the room, not taking her eyes off the woman's face as she sucked on a large cock, pumping the base with her hand. Perhaps she had a touch of the voyeur in her after all.

As Mackenzie's cheeks pinked, she shifted her weight. Austin closed the door to the voyeur room so they had the space to themselves and stepped behind her.

"If I did not know better, I would say you are a little turned on right now, Mackenzie."

She tipped her head back until it rested on his shoulder and moved his hand from her waist to her breast. "Yes, Sir."

He squeezed and she pressed her ass into his crotch, drawing a low moan from him. "You know I would be okay with it, right?"

She gasped. "Okay with what?"

He walked his fingers down her stomach and the front of her miniskirt, trailing his fingertips along the edge of the leather. "Sharing you."

She still hadn't taken her eyes off the men as they took the woman between them. One standing behind her, her hair curled around his fist as he drove into her ass. Another beneath her, arms banded around her lower back as he fucked her, and the third, balls deep, and eyes rolled back as she deep throated him.

"S-sharing me. L-like her?"

He swirled a finger around her clit, enjoying the twitching of her body against him. "Yes, ma'am. If that is something you desire, I can make it happen for you."

She moaned and leaned into his chest as his fingers found her thong. "Austin, please. Touch me."

Her body rose and fell against his. Sliding all four fingers into her damp underwear, he yanked them down her thighs.

She remained quiet, but cupped her breasts with both

hands and squeezed. He pressed her against the glass, mouth on her neck, kissing and nipping at the bare skin on one side. "I am so incredibly glad that you are mine, Mackenzie."

Her knees flexed and he squeezed his chest to her back for support.

"I'm going to slide two fingers inside of you. No more, no less, until you come for me. Hard."

She whimpered, but nodded, her forehead touching the glass. The red-headed woman they were watching screamed around the dick in her mouth as her own orgasm crashed into her.

"As soon as you come I will pull my fingers out, smack that pussy of mine and slide inside you with my cock."

Her breathing quickened.

"Straight fingers, dripping in cum, I will take one lick, before I tell you to taste how delicious you are for me."

Another whimper as she ground against his fingers as they caressed her g-spot.

"I will be able to taste just how much of a good girl you are."

She shook in front of him, the weight of his body holding her steady.

"I need you to feel my body, every muscle tensing as I get closer, and quell it back to relaxation. Feeling how I get harder each time I get close."

Her muscles flexed around his fingers as she got closer. "Austin?"

"Yes, Love?"

"You're serious? You'd... I could... do... that?" Her hips met every thrust of his hand as he chased her release.

"I am serious, yes."

"D-do you... y'know... know people?"

He smiled into her hair. "Yes, Mackenzie, I know people."

"People who would... do that... to me?"

"Yes ma'am."

"Oh God. Austin." Her body clenched. "Please give me permission to come."

He raked his teeth over the bare skin of her shoulder. "Come on my fingers, Mackenzie. I need to be inside you."

She fell apart in seconds with a scream that pierced the air and made the woman in the scene in front of them grin and suck harder on the dick in her mouth. The men had all changed positions, but still fucked her wildly as she grunted and screamed.

He shoved the skirt up over the curve of her ass and pulled her hips back toward him. Placing her hands on the glass in front of her, she based out her feet.

"Is that something you think you might like, Mackenzie? Having all of your beautiful holes filled by my friends and I?"

He tapped the end of the plug in her ass, delighting in the shudder it sent through her. She leaned forward, pressing her hands harder against the glass. "P-please, Sir. Please fuck me."

He rubbed at her ass cheek with his palm, warming the flesh before striking it with his hand. The guttural moan it pulled from Mackenzie was almost enough to make him come over her ass.

"Again. Please. Again."

His girl got hot watching people fucking. Voyeur kink unlocked.

Another smack, a growl, another demand for more. "Harder. Please."

"Check in."

"Smack me."

It was his turn to growl. "Check. In." He unzipped his pants and freed his cock from its prison.

"Green. Now for the love of fucking god smack me."

Not holding back, he did, a loud crack piercing the silence of the room drowned out by her scream. "Yes. Fuck. Yes."

His girl got hot for spanking. And he got hot for watching her body react to the smack of his hand against her ass. Fuck, she was beautiful. He pumped his cock twice, the tip already slick with pre-cum.

"Do you like what you see, Mackenzie? Do you think you might like to be filled in all your holes some day?"

She pushed back against the window. "Please, Austin. Inside me."

He swept his dick through her soaking wet pussy. "It feels as though you might like the idea, Mackenzie."

"You're going to make me say it out loud, aren't you?"

"Yes, ma'am." Another brush through her folds of his dick and she clenched her ass cheeks. He smacked her again. "I am."

"Y-yes. I think I might like to try it. I can't imagine being naked in front of three guys though, they'd... they'd see me..."

He rammed his cock into her without warning, enjoying the yip and squeal that escaped her. "Watch your mouth, Mackenzie. Or you will be writing lines about self-deprecation when you get home."

He pounded her with the same urgency that brewed in his balls, her braid wrapped around his clenched fist. Within minutes the familiar tingle at the base of his spine grew into a blinding release as he came deep inside her.

"Fuck." Her muscles tightened around his semi-hard dick as she broke apart with a wail.

His girl was not quiet, and he loved it. Reaching across to the wall on his left, he pulled some tissues from the clean-up station and handed them to her before he pulled out.

"And they say romance is dead." She grinned as she reached between her legs with the Kleenex. "Nothing says romance like 'here's a tissue to clean up my cum.'"

He chuckled. "I would usually get on my knees and clean you up with my tongue, but—"

A knock on the door interrupted them. "Time." The woman telling them their time was up was a woman of few words, but she rarely needed to use many.

"Thanks, Phoenix. We'll be right out."

"You know everyone here?"

"Almost." He sprayed the glass with Lysol and wiped it clean.

"Phoenix is an odd name for a woman."

"She is an odd woman."

A few minutes later, Mackenzie had righted her skirt, the space was clean, and he had tucked her underwear into his pocket before they made their way into the common area. They watched a male submissive get flogged by a Dom before Austin bought Mackenzie a margarita in the bar.

"Check in." He brushed his lips against her neck.

"Green." She yawned. "But I'm getting sleepy. Can you take me home and read to me until I fall asleep?"

"I would love nothing more."

CHAPTER 21
Mackenzie

Mackenzie sighed as her body relaxed against Austin's chest as they cuddled on her couch. She sat between his legs, her back to his front. He'd read her two chapters of her book while she dozed, but he needed to leave. "You have early practice in the morning, mon guerrier. You should go."

He nuzzled his nose into her hair. "I do not wish to leave."

She could relate. After the intimate experience at the club, she didn't want him out of her sight, not for a single minute, let alone for an entire overnight. She wanted him to lead her to bed, help her change into her pajamas and curl into him while they both fell into a comfortable sleep.

She wanted it all. But she couldn't bring herself to ask for anything.

"But, you are correct, I should leave."

She shifted forward to allow him space to untuck his leg from along the back cushions of the sofa, and stand.

"Would you like for me to tuck you in?"

Yes. Yes she would. She would like for him to climb into bed next to her and hold her until morning. Instead, she shook her head. "No, I'm good, thank you though. I have some things to take care of before I can lie down." She buried her head in his chest as he pulled her in for a hug.

"Can you let me know when you get home okay please?"

He kissed her forehead, rubbed his chin along the bridge of her nose, and nodded. "Yes, Love. I will. I will check in on you again later too, to make sure you're not dropping or having any residual discomfort."

She couldn't pull her arms from his body. She didn't want to let him go, or see just how needy she was. What the hell was wrong with her?

"What is it, Mackenzie?" He pinched her chin and tilted her head.

"I don't know. I feel... I feel clingy. I've never felt clingy like this before. It's kind of pathetic and I don't like it." She sounded like a child who wasn't getting her way and being allowed to eat cake for dinner.

He pulled her even tighter to his chest, his warmth wrapping around her like a weighted blanket. "It is not pathetic. Do not fight it, Mackenzie. It is not going to go away."

"What is it?" She pulled back from him and silently pleaded for answers with her eyes. She knew without him answering that she was falling in love with him. Okay, fine, maybe she was already there. But only a little. She couldn't afford to give him any more than a corner of her heart in case he should break it apart and take pieces of it with him when he left.

She sighed. Lying to herself wasn't going to work. She had already given him more. That's what the feeling growing inside her was. He'd burrowed his way deep into her heart and made it his home.

Maybe she needed assurance that he felt it too, that he felt the draw in his chest to her like she did to him. That he was every bit as reluctant to leave her, that he wanted to stay and take care of her as much as she yearned for him to.

"You know what it is, Love."

She'd always quietly wished for someone to take care of her so she didn't have to be tough – just every now and then – but everyone in her life had conditioned her to take the weight of the world on her shoulders and stand tall with a smile on her face.

For the first time in her life, someone was sharing the burden and he did so without her even having to ask. He stepped into her life, her space, and started taking care of her before she'd even really realized what was happening. It was probably just as well, if she'd realized from the get-go, she'd have put up a lot more of a fight.

But once he was there, she couldn't imagine being without him. Ironically, his presence, his determination to nurture her on every level, made her feel stronger, more capable and calmer – not weaker.

Mama and daddy had it all wrong in telling her she needed to be resilient and fend for herself. As it turned out, she could still fend for herself *and* stay strong. And in taming her to stay strong, to fit into the mold they wanted her to stay in, they'd actually weakened her beyond measure.

Life with Austin brought an inner strength and confidence she'd never felt before, and she didn't want to lose it. It was powerful, intoxicating, and addictive, but a piece of her still didn't think she was worth it, or that someone like him could, or should, love someone like her.

The more she stared into his dark mocha eyes, the more she started to believe. And that was the scariest part of all.

❄

A sharp knock on the door pulled her from a light sleep. The clock on her phone screen told her Austin had only been gone for fifteen minutes. So much for folding laundry. She stood and stretched. Had he left something behind?

Another knock sounded at the same moment she pulled the door open. "Forget something?" Her gasp caught in her throat as an arctic chill doused her entire body.

Garrett. 5ft 10, blond hair, ice blue eyes, and that all too familiar permanent sneer still plastered on his face. He'd found her. Act. Move. Don't let him in. There was no way in hell she was voluntarily letting him into her space. She braced her shoulder against the door and tried to force it closed, but he'd already jammed his foot between the door and the frame and was shuffling it back and forth to open it.

"Awww come now, baby girl. Is that any way to treat your husband?"

She swung the door back and slammed it against him, once, twice, the collision of wood and flesh echoing in soft thuds around the empty house. But instead of relenting, he pushed his way into the foyer and whistled as he turned a slow circle, taking it in. "Though considering I just watched another man leave after taking you home dressed like a slut a few hours ago, I think we're past being a dutiful wife, wouldn't you say?"

She folded her arms across her body like a barrier. She wasn't going to let his words pierce her skin. As far as she was concerned their marriage was over. She wasn't going to let him slut shame her when he'd broken their marriage vows long before she ever had considered it.

"It's time to come home, Abby." He advanced on her and she shrieked, jumping back out of his reach. She collided with a small table, and knocked a glass of water to the tiles.

"Still a stupid bitch, I see." He shook his head and pointed to the shards of glass on the floor. "Clean that up before someone gets hurt."

She shivered. The words said 'do something helpful to avoid injury' but the tone conveyed a much darker sense of danger and urgency.

"You're coming home with me."

She was not fucking going anywhere with him. "No."

He laughed and cupped his ear. "What was that?"

She cleared her throat and straightened her spine. This was when she needed to be truly strong. "Your hearing has never been all that good, has it, Garrett? I said, no. I'm not going anywhere with you. We're done. I want a divorce. It's over. Do you understand?"

"Do... I understand?" He hooked a thumb at his chest, his voice incredulous. "You think you can just up and leave me in the middle of the night without consequence?" He shook his head. "You embarrassed me, Abby. But..." He stepped forward, reaching out to touch her face.

She side stepped out of his way, smacking his arm from her space and he reached again.

"I'm willing to overlook your... whoreish transgressions... if you come home like a good girl and put all of this behind us."

Good girl. Bile rose in her throat. When Austin said it she felt powerful, capable, and confident. When Garrett said it, it made her skin crawl.

"The longer you stay here, the worse your life is going to get, so just come back with me. It'll be easier on both of us."

Making it sound like he was negotiating and doing her a favor was one of his specialties, but she had become more aware of his toxic behavior since getting out from underneath it. Narcissists gonna narcissist. It was what they did. But she wasn't falling for it this time.

"Kenzie?" Clare, Kenzie's unassuming, divorced, single mom next door neighbor stood in her doorway, hands behind her back. She had a tendency to spend her free time peering out into the street between her blinds. She'd probably clocked Garrett's rental car outside Kenzie's and gone outside to investigate. "Is everything okay in here?"

"Yes." Garrett answered at the same time as Kenzie said, "No."

"He was just leaving, Clare. I'm so sorry he woke you."

He jabbed a finger in Kenzie's face, closing the distance between them. "You don't get to just fucking dismiss me, Abby." Spittle sprayed from his mouth as he spat every word at her.

Clare crossed the space, seemingly deaf to Kenzie's protests and pleading for her to leave. If it wasn't the middle of the night and Garrett wasn't such a psychopath, Clare's 4ft 11 stature next to Garrett's 6ft 4 height would have been comical.

He gripped Kenzie's wrist with frightening strength sending shooting pains up her arm and into her shoulder. "You're coming back with me, now."

Clare tapped him on the shoulder. "Excuse me, sir?"

He half-spun to face her. "What?"

She didn't blink, she didn't seem in any way phased or afraid of the raging lunatic in Kenzie's living room. From behind her back she produced a can of pepper spray. "If you don't take your fucking hand off her and get out of this house, I'm going to burn your eyes out, motherfucker."

"I like her." He smirked. "She's got spunk for a little thing, hasn't she?" He jerked Kenzie's arm, making her yelp. "Sorry, lady, but she's coming with me, and you can't stop me."

Clare grinned. "You know what I hate about assholes like you? You assume the world owes you something. A hot flash woke me up. I'm of that tender age now where I'm a little more sensitive to temperature. But you know what else comes with age?"

Garrett remained quiet but didn't drop Kenzie's arm.

"Zero fucks." She pressed the button, releasing the pepper spray into his face. He squealed like a pig at the slaughter.

He dropped Kenzie's arm and rubbed at his eyes. Clare kneed him in the balls like the badass bitch she was and when he doubled over at the waist, she grabbed him by the collar and led him to the door.

"Get – and I cannot stress this enough – the fuck out. And don't come back. I'm calling the cops right now, asshole. Be a dear, and save them a trip."

He turned back to the house, wildly pointing a finger in Kenzie's general direction. "This isn't over, *Kenzie*. I know where you are now. That makes it easier to make your life a living hell."

Lifting her head over the parapet she'd hidden behind for two years was bringing danger to her door. She had no idea what his next move would be, but Garrett wouldn't give up just because the middle aged woman next door threw him out.

If she knew Garrett as well as she thought she did, it would only serve to add fuel to his rage-fire. Which meant only one thing: she needed to run. Again.

"Don't be fucking stupid." Addison slammed the suitcase shut for the third time. "You're not leaving."

It was the second time she'd been called stupid in less than two days, she wasn't enjoying it much at all. "What other choice do I have?"

"You could stand your ground and fight that pussy ass

bitch Garrett like the badass you are." Paige pressed the other side of the suitcase lid closed so Kenzie couldn't open it.

"He won't stop."

"He will if you let Austin kick his ass and send him back from whence he came." Adi sing-songed her sentence like it was the most obvious answer in the world, but Kenzie's stomach swished. She was not bringing her shit to Austin's door.

"Agreed. I know he's a cinnamon roll for you, but man." Paige fanned herself. "Dude's a scary motherfucker and I wouldn't want to meet him in a dark alley."

"Mostly because he has the skills to back up his threats." Adi laughed.

"That's what she said." Paige reached out and fist bumped Addison.

"Absolutely not." Kenzie raked her hands over her face. "I'm not getting him involved."

"Girl. Denial is not just a river in Egypt. That boy is already involved. He loves you." Adi reached forward and poked Kenzie's bicep.

"You know that, right? He's head over his fancy-ass heels for you."

Both her friends regarded her for a moment before their eyebrows pinched and their jaws dropped open.

"Fuck. You have no idea, do you?" Paige slapped Addison's arm. "She has no fucking idea."

"Oh honey. You know *you* love *him*, right? You know that much?"

Her skin sizzled. She did in fact, know that.

"The pink color of her face says yes, she at least knows that she loves him." Paige swiped at her forehead. "Phew. I thought we were gonna have to have a come to Jesus meeting."

"So..." Adi assessed her with a wagging finger. "Is it that

you don't feel like he loves you? Or that you're just not ready to accept that he does?"

Something constricted in her chest, but she tried not to react.

"Ah ha. The latter. I see. Well, you need to accept it, *Sprinkles*. That man is cray-cray for you. And Adi is right, he's already involved."

Her friends had taken to using Austin's nickname for her to get a rise from her. It was kinda gross to use a romantic pet name for your friend but they just wouldn't quit. Bitches.

Addison's finger stopped wagging, but remained pointed at Kenzie's face. "He's also going to be awfully pissed that you didn't go to him with this."

"I don't want violence to be the answer." She cringed. Garrett's backhand ghosted her cheek in her mind more often than she cared to admit. "More violence."

"Fuck that shit." Paige's eyebrows rose. "Some fuckers only speak violence. Garrett isn't a 'no means no' kinda guy, Kenz. You're going to need to bring out the big guns."

She tried to find the flaw in her friend's argument. Running would work, but only for so long. Staying in Minnesota required a plan, support, and a shit-ton of strength she wasn't sure she had. It was only a matter of time before her parents found her and added to the cacophony of noise demanding she return to Texas.

She needed to get her shit together and find her spine so they didn't break her all over again.

"Mackenzie?" Austin pulled the door to his apartment open and scratched his jaw.

All of the words that had bubbled up inside her chest to spill to him evaporated as she took him in. Shirtless. Perfectly sculpted abs. An Adonis belt of dreams leading to the Promised Land. Very visible outline of a semi erect penis through his gray sweats.

Did she do that to him?

God bless the inventor of gray sweat pants, whomever she was. It had to have been a woman, right?

She'd come to talk to him, to speak her truth and tell him she was married to an asshole that showed up at her door, grabbed her arm and threatened to ruin her. But all she wanted to do was to drop to her knees and suck him until he came so hard he bruised the back of her throat.

"Austin." Her breathy voice shook like her hands. She couldn't do it. She couldn't risk losing him by confessing the truth. She cleared her throat. "Austin."

"Mackenzie? What is wrong?"

She shook her head. "Nothing. I was just... in the area. I thought I'd stop by and say 'hi.'" She tossed a pathetic wave. "Hi." She turned to leave but he grabbed her wrist, making her hiss.

"Mackenzie? What happened to your arm?"

Bruises darkened the skin of her wrist. "I fell. No big deal. I iced it and it's totally fine."

He cradled her hand like it was made of fragile bone china as he looked her over. But from the pursed lips and suspicion in his eyes, he didn't believe her for a single second. Though after a moment, he nodded. "Come in."

"What? No. It's okay. I just..." She just what? Freaked the hell out at the idea of telling him the truth about her past? Wanted a booty call? What could she say to get herself out of the stupid situation she'd managed to put herself into?

"Please, come in."

When he closed the door behind her, she dropped to her knees, bringing his pants and boxers down with her in one seamless motion. He groaned as she took him into her mouth.

Bracing a hand on the door behind her, he slipped the other one into her hair and yanked so her head fell back.

"Whatever is bothering you Mackenzie, this is not the answer."

But she so wanted it to be. She jerked her head free and took him back in her mouth. She sucked and pumped on his dick, waiting for him to stop her again, or cry out in pain. When he did neither, she tightened her fist and pumped harder.

He grunted. "Mackenzie." His voice was thick with lust and warning. His hand tautened in her hair. "You do not have to do this."

But she did. Reaching her free hand between his legs she cupped his balls and squeezed, before moving her fingers back toward his ass.

"Mackenzie." He spoke through gritted teeth and his knees buckled as she pressed her knuckle against his taint.

"Hmmmm." She hummed around his cock. Her assumption had been correct. She knew he'd worn a plug before, so maybe he'd like a little ass play while she blew him. She circled his tight hole with her index finger and he thumped once the door over her head with a grunt.

"Mackenzie, you need to stop. We need to talk about whatever is going on."

When she slipped her finger into his ass and swirled it around he gripped her arm. Eyes wide, she met his. Dark, intense, concerned. "Not like this."

He pulled her hand from between his legs and she released his cock.

"Do I want for you to play with my ass while you suck my dick? Yes, I do. Do I want it like this? When you are visibly upset and deflecting by escaping into it? No, I do not."

Her heart stung. "You don't want me?"

"I believe I just finished telling you how much I *do* want

you." He cupped her neck and helped her stand. "But not like this. Never like this. If you do not want to tell me what is wrong, that's one thing. This is not okay. It's my job to learn the difference and protect you, even from yourself."

Heavy tears slid down her face, but she still couldn't bring herself to tell him anything.

After a moment of weighted silence hanging between them, he brushed her tears away with the pad of his thumb. "Do you need to hit something?"

She canted her head. "Why do you think that?"

"Restless energy, you are fidgeting. And you look like you might murder me with your eyes alone if I am not careful."

She laughed. "You mean I get to level up from footwork for our next lesson?" Their first lesson had been a solid hour of practicing her maneuvering. Keeping one heel off the ground for a full hour had left her with a sore calf for days, but he insisted it was building a foundation that would serve her well.

It just wasn't a fast enough foundation for her to defend herself against Garrett. She kicked herself for not having started lessons the moment she moved to Minnesota. She knew better. Hope that he wouldn't chase after her, that she was free to live her own life, had kept her from taking every precaution she could and should have.

Austin had told her that if she trained frequently and focused on the basics, she could be ready for her first belt test in a few months – if that was what she wanted to do. Which served only to remind her that she could have accomplished numerous belts over the two years she'd been in the city.

"I don't think that's a great idea. I think I should probably take classes from someone else."

His gaze bounced off her bruised arm before landing on her face. "If you are going to train I would prefer you train with me."

"So arrogant, Love. You don't think there is someone else,

someone who might be better suited to train me, anywhere at all in Minnesota?"

"I do not." His intensity somehow intensified to the point of maximum intensity. Christ, he was so fucking intense.

"Y-you're the best fighter in the city?"

He remained quiet, but confidence rolled off him in intoxicating waves that made her want to drop back onto her knees.

"Wow. That's..." So fucking hot.

Without another word, she nodded. If she couldn't escape into sex, maybe an injection of endorphins would help her feel better about everything. And if Austin truly was the best, she wanted him teaching her.

Training with him could be fun, too. And by fun she meant sexual torment and insanely long sessions of foreplay. Same difference.

He led her into a home gym. A black heavy bag with a red X on the side hung over a weighted stand. Pads and gloves were lined up neatly on a rack next to a weight rack. Various gym equipment sat in one third of the room, while a mirrored wall faced an open expanse of red matting on the floor.

"The mirrors are to watch your form. It is easy to get into the habit of doing something wrong, watching yourself while you practice helps ensure that does not happen."

He picked up a pair of black, red, and white pads and slipped them onto his hands. "You remember your stance?"

She nodded and moved her legs until they were shoulder width apart. Picking up her heel, she winced. Her calf had not yet forgiven her for their first lesson. Was he smirking at her? Oh, yeah. She totally wanted to wipe the smugness off his smug AF face.

"Make two fists."

She did.

"Thumb on the outside of your fist, not inside."

"Won't it get broken out there?"

He shook his head and tapped her closed hand. "It will get broken in there."

"Yes, Sir."

"Do not clench too tightly. Same result."

She loosened her hands.

"Hold them up to your face. They need to hover between your cheek bone and your jaw bone."

She did as he asked, remaining quiet.

"When you extend your arm to strike, your fist must rotate to a forty-five degree angle on impact. The rotation must come up from the floor." He touched her knee. "This is where your force comes from. Rotate your foot, knee, hip, shoulder and fist. Under rotation and you'll miss your target, over rotation and you'll lose power from the strike."

Her head was already swimming. But she nodded.

"When you release your arm for your strike, use your shoulder from the striking arm to protect your jaw on that side. And make sure you keep your jaw protected with your other hand up high on your right. Understood?"

Sure, she understood he was punking her and it was going to go terribly. What had possessed her to think she could learn something like Krav Maga? Was he laughing on the inside?

There was no trace of humor in his eyes, only resolute determination. But she wasn't a fighter, she was a physio.

"Do you trust me, Mackenzie?"

"Yes, Sir. Implicitly."

"Then get out of your own head." He raised the pads. "Focus on your form, and hit me."

She nodded, pictured Garrett's arrogant face on the pad in Austin's left hand, and started punching.

CHAPTER 22
Austin

"Putain." He swung his fist at Finn's face, but the slippery bastard evaded him.

"Did you just call me a ho, Austin?" He winked and took a swing of his own. "You know I love it when you get down and dirty in French. You're off your game."

Finn was right, every muscle in his body had been tense since she'd left his house. Something was off with her, something had scared her and left her out of sorts and off balance. Something she did not even wish to discuss with him. And because something was off with her, something was off with him.

"Say it again, Auzzy. Talk dirty to me."

Austin snarled. "Ta gueule."

Finn fanned himself with one of his gloves. "I know that one too. But I'm not shutting up. You're on edge today and I'm going to land a solid hit. I can feel it in my loins."

He did not like it. While he was her dominant, he was not naïve enough to think he had learned everything about her in such a short space of time. Was it him?

Finn swung and Austin blocked. Did he push her too far too fast? Was this her withdrawing from him?

Finn swung again and he took a step back. Was she going to leave him like his last submissive?

Another swing, another step back. Should he even have ventured into another serious relationship?

His back met a cold, hard surface. "Merde."

"Yeah, shit." Finn rained a shower of playful hits on him as he protected his face. "Where the fuck's your head at, Auzzy? It sure as shit ain't here."

"Raclure de bidet." Austin growled and shunted Finn back with a hard shove.

Finn frowned and pointed a golden boxing glove at him. "That's one I don't know. What does it mean? You're such a sexy beast Finny? You're the superior fighter, Finn? That's it, right?" He winked and Austin snarled.

"Dude. What the hell is going on with you?"

He shook his head and grabbed a water bottle from a few feet behind him. "Nothing."

Finn gave a comical wide-eyed, downturn lipped face while he drew the word 'okay' out to reach fifteen syllables.

"The literal translation is bidet scum."

Finn scrunched up his face.

"It is the closest we have to douchebag."

"Ouch. I prefer douchebag."

Austin smirked and took a drink.

"How do you say motherfucker?"

"Enculé de ta mère."

Finn scrunched his face up again. "Doesn't quite roll off the tongue as easily as motherfucker." He took a drink of his own. "You're really not going to tell me what's going on with you? Is it your dad?"

He shook his head. "It is not. For once I stood up to him

and he is not currently speaking to me. I am enjoying the quiet."

Finn smacked his back. "I knew you had it in you, Auzzy. Boundaries are important, man."

Boundaries were important, it was true, but the number of boundaries Mackenzie seemed to be creating, instead of pulling down, between them was increasing. And he had no idea how to stop it.

Arms banded around his biceps and hauled him back from the curled up body on the ice. Linc on one side, and that smug fucker Jeremy Lewis on the other.

"You doing 'roids, Auzzy? If you are, the first step is admitting you have a problem."

Austin growled and faked a surge at him, making him stagger back two feet.

"Whatever the fuck your deal is, it doesn't belong here. Keep that shit off the ice and away from my team, are we clear?"

The guy wasn't small, but he also wasn't their team's enforcer. He should be having this discussion with Alabama's enforcer, AJ Williams. Not their mouthy sniper.

Austin turned to skate to the penalty box, he was undoubtedly about to be smacked with a misconduct for dropping gloves and railing on the guy who ran Sébastien over like he wasn't even there.

Lewis skated by his side like they were in Madison Square Gardens at Christmas for a leisurely turn about the rink. "You should be going that way." He pointed to the tunnel. "You got a game for that."

His blood bubbled and hissed under his skin. He hadn't

got thrown out of a game in years, not since high school. Changing direction, he skated toward the tunnel, not making eye contact with his teammates, nor reveling in the cheers of the bloodthirsty crowd for throwing down.

Mackenzie had not returned any of his texts or answered his calls for a day and a half. When she had seen him walking toward her in the rink when he arrived for the game, she had ducked into another trainer's office and closed the door.

Were they over? He had no idea. It sure felt like he was being ghosted. If she needed space, that was one thing, but the lack of communication was grating on his raw nerves like acid. They had spoken about the importance of open channels of communication.

"Je m'en fous."

"Oh, it kinda feels like you give a lot of fucks right now, Auzzy. Whatever the bug up your ass is about..." Jeremy jerked his chin at the Snow Pirate's bench. "Talk it through with your team. I don't know much about you, but I know this isn't you."

"You speak French?"

"Just the cuss words. Spanish too. I feel it's important to know how to insult someone in their own language." Lewis winked and skated away.

As soon as Austin stepped off the ice he felt her eyes on him. But he would not meet them. Shame curdled in his stomach with his pre-game meal of chicken and veggies.

He showered, dressed in his suit, and waited for Coach Swift to tear him a new butthole at the period break. The urge to punch things had all but passed, but the ache in his chest at her dismissal of him pulsed every time his heart beat.

❄

> Mackenzie: Are you okay?

He had stared at her message for six minutes, unsure of what to reply. In a way it was better than staring at the ceiling of his living room from the couch as he had been doing for the three hours he'd been home since the game ended.

> Mackenzie: Austin? I know we have some things to talk about, but please, just let me know you're safe.

> Austin: I am safe. I am not happy, but I am safe.

> Mackenzie: How are your knuckles?

He assessed them, flexing and rotating his hand.

> Austin: They are bruised, but otherwise undamaged.

> Mackenzie: Do you want to talk about it?

A grumble rolled low in his chest. He wanted to strap her to his bench and remind her of her place.

> Austin: I do not believe that has served us well over the past few days.

> Mackenzie: I'm sorry I pushed you away. I don't like this space between us.

> Mackenzie: I'm just not ready to share right now, is that okay? I will, just… not yet, please?

> Austin: It is more than okay. I just wish you had found your voice to explain as much before you pushed back so hard.

> Mackenzie: I really am sorry.

> Mackenzie: Tu me manques.

He smiled at her use of French.

> Austin: I miss you also.

> Mackenzie: I'd suggest make up phone sex, but I have my period so… no dice.

> Mackenzie: But, for the record? I feel like I'm burning from the inside out and I might die if I don't come.

The draw to give her what she needed pulled at him. She'd tell him what she needed to tell in her own time. But this, her orgasm, that was something he could control, something that would make them both feel better, and perhaps close some of the distance stretching out between them.

> Austin: It is as though you have forgotten who I am over the past few days. Blood is not a deterrent for me.

> Mackenzie: I've never… uh… my ex always made me feel like a leper when I had my period.

The overwhelming dislike he had for her ex was growing with every day he got to know her.

> Austin: Your ex is a dick. Go get a spoon.

> Austin: And a glass of ice water.

He freed his cock from his dress pants and gave it a lazy pump. His cock was already hard and a bead of pre-cum was nestled in the slit at its head.

> Mackenzie: You say 'get a spoon' like it's enough to cure this ache.

> Austin: Cure some, cause others.

Another pump of his dick, gliding his thumb up the ladder of piercings.

> Mackenzie: Just go about your business. It's fine. If you need me I'll be here dying of sexual frustration and grumbling about it.

> Austin: You will not be dying. And grumbling will be the least of the sounds you will be making.

It took her a long moment to reply.

> Mackenzie: Always so sure of yourself, mon Guerrier.

> Austin: I have good reason to be, Love.

> Mackenzie: Why's that?

> Austin: I have never struggled to know what you need.

> Mackenzie: Fuck. I'm straight up going to die.

> Austin: I would truly rather if that did not happen.

> Mackenzie: Mackenzie can't come to the phone right now. She died of sexual frustration.

> Austin: Wondering who set that automatic reply.

> Austin: Do you have iced water and a spoon?

> Mackenzie: No, Sir.

He rolled his eyes. While he did not want to make her feel uncomfortable, he also did not want her to deny herself pleasure because of a little blood.

> Austin: Get the damn spoon, Sprinkles.

Mackenzie

> Austin: And make it fast, or you will not orgasm this evening.

She blinked at the words on her screen. While her period definitely made her feel icky, her pulsating pussy demanded she submit to Austin's wishes. Plus, she couldn't help but be curious. A spoon and iced water?

Was he planning on asking her to suck the spoon while she fingered herself? Smacking it off her nipples? Or... oh, wow, was he going to ask her to use the spoon on her pussy?

As she made her way into the kitchen, she pulled up a web browser on her phone and typed, *is it normal to masturbate while on your period?*

Why she needed validation that other people did it was anyone's guess, but she did.

Masturbating during a period is normal, and it may have some health benefits.

Well, if she was doing it for the good of her health, who was she to say no to her dominant?

She picked up a spoon, filled a glass with ice water, and texted him to see if he wanted the spoon *in* the glass of iced water.

> Austin: Yes, ma'am. And you might wish to place a towel under you in bed if you are uncomfortable about making a mess.

He always thought of everything.

> Austin: You know there are benefits to masturbating while on your period, right?
>
> Austin: Endorphins are released which help with the pain, and it can help improve your mood and sleep.
>
> Austin: Not to mention: it is just blood and tissue.

She smiled. Garrett wouldn't even have picked her up a box of tampons from the drug store if she needed them. The phrase, 'it's just blood' would never have crossed his lips.

> Mackenzie: If I asked you to grab me a box of tampons, would you?
>
> Austin: Is there another condition to that question?
>
> Mackenzie: Like what?
>
> Austin: Like, would you grab me a box of tampons if you were being chased by zombies? Or if the store was on fire?

> Austin: I am failing to find a reason for not being okay with it.

> Austin: If you do not give me specifics I may end up bringing back multiple boxes in a moment of panic buying to make sure I get the right ones, but of course I would buy them for you.

Her face hurt from grinning at the screen and grew wider when another message appeared from him.

> Austin: Your ex really was an asshole.

She climbed the stairs to her room, kicked off her slippers and placed the glass of iced water next to the bottle of water on her nightstand. Dropping the spoon into the glass, she shivered. Wherever that spoon was intended to go was going to be cold AF.

Her poor, unsuspecting clit was probably the intended target and she clenched. Was he punishing her for her behavior over the past couple of days? While she wouldn't blame him – she had been a raging bitch by ignoring him – she wondered how he came up with such a unique form of torture. Or was she about to embark on the best thing since spicy chicken nuggets?

> Austin: Are you lying down?

> Mackenzie: Yes, Sir.

> Austin: Audio call?

> Austin: You do not have to put your video on, but it would be easier for you to play if you were not typing responses. And I need to hear your breathing.

She burst out laughing.

> Mackenzie: That sounds so stalkerish. "I need to hear your breathing." You're lucky I already know you're a weirdo.

> Austin: I am your weirdo.

> Mackenzie: Hashtag Facts.

Austin's name flashed on her screen, she hit the answer button, dropped the phone onto the bed next to her, and yanked off her shirt. Her puckered nipples were already standing to attention. Guilt swirled with the lust deep in her belly, but she swallowed it down.

She'd tell him. She just needed a few more days to come up with a plan to get rid of her shitty ex so she could move forward, then she'd come clean to Austin. Everything would be fine.

"Austin?"

"Yes, ma'am?"

"Is this freezing cold metal spoon about to go on my clit?"

"Yes, ma'am."

She sucked in a breath as a shiver rippled through her. "Yes, Sir."

"But first, I need you to tilt your head back and close your eyes for a second."

She followed his instruction.

"Take a deep breath. Imagine my palm is flat in the small of your back and I ask you to breathe into it."

She focused on breathing into his phantom palm, which somehow felt heavier the more she sucked in air.

"I know you have been conditioned to believe that what you are about to do is gross and shameful, but it is not. There is no reason you should not be able to derive pleasure while on your period."

Her muscles softened, and the knot in her chest flexed as heat crept along her body. The tension held in her body continued to fizzle out of her on each deep and even breath.

"Are you ready, Love?"

"Yes, Sir."

"Check in."

"Green."

"Good girl. Pick up the spoon. Move it over your body quickly. Allow the droplets of cold water to drip onto your nipples."

She did as she was told. The tiny splashes of water made a series of gasps escape her as they sent tiny chills through her breasts. Austin made a satisfied sound on the other side of the line.

"You really do enjoy hearing my breathing, don't you?"

"I enjoy all of your reactions, Mackenzie. But yes, hearing your breathing tells me more than you might think about how you are enjoying something, or how close you may be to release. In the absence of you under my fingertips, I at least need to hear how your body is reacting."

She moaned. How did he make everything sound so goddamn romantic? She was about to accost her clit with an ice cold spoon, and he was making her body flare like a sunset after a 100 degree day.

"You know where to put the spoon, Mackenzie."

"Bowl of the spoon on my clit, right?"

"Yes, Love. And once the metal warms up, I want you to put it back into the glass."

She groused but followed orders. The cold metal slid between her wet folds and she shrieked, hissing as she waited for her body to adjust to the bite. Using the handle of the spoon she moved it up and down against her clit, savoring the cool more and more. She'd never realized just how hot her pussy got during her period, the cold was quite a relief.

Her moans built with the slick friction brewing a frenzy at the apex of her thighs.

"Back in the glass, Love. And dry off your clit while you are waiting for it to cool."

Dry off? Wasn't everything being wet the whole goal?

As if reading her thoughts yet again, he answered her unasked question. "You will feel the sensations better if you are not too wet."

Huh. She called BS, but she'd try his way at least once. Despite the odd masturbation implement, he had been right about everything she'd tried so far. She dried off with a washcloth, repositioned the newly cold spoon, and got back to chasing her orgasm.

It only took a few minutes before the tingle building in her toes and low in her spine crackled through her body like the snap of a whip. She cried out as she came, squeezing her bare nipple with her free hand as she humped the spoon through her release.

When she'd recovered and cleaned up, she draped her forearm over her head. "I should probably be ashamed of myself for riding a spoon to orgasm, shouldn't I? Wait. Don't answer that. You're not the right person to ask."

"You should not be ashamed of enjoying that which brings you pleasure."

Swoon.

"Check in, Love."

"Green." Her voice was heavy with sleep and satisfaction.

"Close your eyes, relax."

As she rolled to her side to sleep, her phone chimed. Ignoring her better instinct to let it lie until morning, she unlocked her phone. A message from an unknown number waited for her in her inbox. A series of photos of her and Austin from the night at the club lit up her screen with one word of text *Slut*.

Bile rose in her throat, suffocating her body, stealing her blissful calm. A picture of her kissing him when she arrived at the bar, another of them leaving Protocol, another of Kenzie leading Austin into her home – thankfully there were none from inside the dungeon.

They had strict rules about locking up your phone on entry to the dungeon and while she knew little about Thor, she *did* know he'd lose his shit if someone's privacy had been breached.

"Mackenzie?"

"I'm fine," she croaked her answer, not at all expecting him to buy it.

"Your breathing shifted. You are no longer relaxed and lying down."

She flopped back onto the bed, dropped the phone to her chest, and willed her body to find the peace she'd had post-orgasm.

It was one thing for Garrett to threaten her life, her future, but those pictures threatened Austin's life, his career, *his* future. And while he didn't seem to want to work with his father in that future, an incident such as that could do damage to the Morgan family name.

Her stomach clenched. Garrett wasn't an empty threat kind of guy, either. He had taken the photos with intent, and he'd use them to get what he wanted. She was going to have to find a way to come clean with Austin, fast, and hope that somehow he wouldn't break up with her for sitting on this big-ass piece of her past for so long, or for the fact her ex now had ammunition to use to destroy them both.

CHAPTER 23
Austin

"That was a fun run." Will chugged water from his water bottle at their usual table in Applebee's.

Finn picked his head up from the table, he sucked in ragged, fragmented breaths and his pasty-Irish skin was bright red from exertion. "I don't think that word means what you think it means."

Linc snorted. "Yeah. Even I'm with Finnegan." He leaned forward and patted Finn's head like he was a Doberman.

"Was someone chasing us?" Russ shook his head and tiny beads of sweat sprayed the table from the ends of his wet hair. "Did we steal something and I didn't know about it?"

"I think Will is just a sadist." Finn dropped his head onto the table with such a clang, Will flinched.

"Nope. I'm pretty sure that's Austin." Linc pointed his glass of water across the table.

Austin smirked but did not answer. Movement outside the window pulled his attention from the conversation. Across the parking lot, Mackenzie stood next to a man, in front of a silver Dodge Charger. He was way too close to her for Austin's comfort. Digging his nails into his thighs he reminded himself that she was perfectly capable of handling herself.

"I thought he was just a masochist. Which is the one that gets sexual pleasure from their own pain and humiliation?" Finn's voice was mumbled by the table pressed against his face.

The man's hand snaked around Kenzie's neck and he leaned forward as though to kiss her. She turned her head and he brushed his nose and lips across her cheek before nipping at her earlobe.

"Masochist. Sadists enjoys inflicting pain and humiliation on others." Will sat his empty bottle onto the table and started drinking his glass of water.

He bit down on the inside of his cheek as the stranger placed his hands on her hips and jerked her toward him. He could not see Kenzie's face, but she did not attempt to stop him. She clearly knew the man.

"Yeah. I'm pretty sure he's a masochist."

Was that why she had not answered him for a couple of days? She was dating someone else and had come back to him when she needed an orgasm. And now she had been sated, she returned to the douche canoe with the flashy car?

He steadied himself with a breath. That wasn't Mackenzie. He wasn't going to let what he was seeing in front of him color his judgment of the woman he loved. There had to be a rational explanation.

"Lighten up, Auzzy. It's just a joke." Finn had pulled himself upright and elbowed him as he spoke.

Austin faked a smile, and schooled his face. He did not need his teammates to see him upset at Mackenzie being touched by another man in the street. While he did not mind sharing her from time to time, he minded her seeing someone without his agreement, and behind his back.

The man dragged his tongue along the curve of her jaw, and Austin's urge to spring from his seat and demand answers returned with gusto. When the stranger drove off, Mackenzie stood for a moment, watching the car leave the parking lot.

Only when he had left did she heave a breath. When she turned to walk into the Ulta store she stood in front of, Austin could finally see her face.

She rubbed at her red-rimmed eyes and cheeks with a Kleenex. Her eyes flicked back and forth, as though she somehow expected him to return, and her shoulders rolled forward, closing around herself like she needed protection.

That was not the face of a happy woman. Was she upset for cheating on him? Or was the asshole the problem? His stomach sank, maybe he should have gone outside and intervened.

His insecurity made him question. But deep down he knew something was not right. Mackenzie did not strike him as the cheating kind. And the fact that he'd jumped straight to cheating was something he would need to work through later, but for the moment, every fiber of his being wanted to pick her up and take care of her.

"Austin?" Sabrina stood, pen on pad, ready to take his order while his teammates stared at him, impatience clear across their faces.

"Chicken salad, please, Sabrina."

She nodded, scribbled on her pad, and turned to leave. "I'll bring you guys another jug of water in just a sec."

He pulled his phone out of the pile in the middle of the table. He'd suck up the penalty of having to pay for everyone's lunch if it meant he could talk to his girl.

"Holy fuck." Finn's jaw dropped. "If I had put money on someone pulling their phone it would *not* have been Austin."

The impatience on his friend's faces had been replaced by questioning and curious stares. "Who is she?" Lincoln jerked his chin at the phone in his hand.

Austin ignored him and typed out a message.

> Austin: Are you okay, Love? You have been quiet this morning.

Mackenzie pulled the phone out of her jeans, still standing outside Ulta as though waiting for a bus. Her shoulders shook harder as she read his message. What the fuck was going on?

"Whoever she is, he must think she's worth paying for lunch for everyone to talk to." Russ shrugged. "She's important."

> Mackenzie: Yes, Sir. I'm okay. I knew you were out running, then lunch with the guys. I didn't want to interrupt.

> Austin: You are always a welcome interruption. What are you up to?

> Mackenzie: Just a little shopping.

> Austin: Are you sure you are okay?

"And I can't help but notice, he isn't denying that he's talking to a woman." Finn's grin almost earned him a smack.

"Connard."

"Call me an asshole all you like, that's still not a denial." Finn's grin widened.

Maybe he'd hit Finn yet. Mackenzie turned and walked inside the store. It was a couple of minutes before she replied again.

Sabrina appeared with plates, handing out food to his starving teammates which got them off his back in an instant. But as soon as their plates were cleared they would be back asking who she was and why she was worth covering the check to talk to.

She was by no means ready to reveal their relationship to his teammates, and he was not going to force her. He respected her too much to compromise her position with the team in any way.

> Mackenzie: I'm fine. Tired. Okay, kind of exhausted. I haven't been sleeping well. I could probably do with some water, too. Some vegetables wouldn't hurt. Are you okay? You feel... off somehow? Do you need something?

He almost laughed out loud at the deflection.

> Austin: My needs right now are to care for you. That would include guiding you to the shower and helping work through some of the tension trapped in your shoulders using the warmth of the water to my aid. I would stretch out every muscle one by one, starting at the center. I would let the warm water help release the tension and encourage the blood flow, using my breath to ease and release the acidic build up from stress.

> Mackenzie: That sounds pretty perfect TBH. I can shower when I get home from the store if that would make you happy. But how do you know I'm tense?

> Austin: I can feel it, Love.

He cringed at his own lie, but he could not tell her he could see waves of tension radiating from her every pore, it would send her further from him and he was not prepared to let her flee when fear was the driving force.

> Austin: As much as I know you want to care for me, the best way you can do that is letting me work throughout every inch of your being. I cannot ask for more of you until your body is in a safe state to take more. Your physical state is a direct result of your mind's attempt at protection. Take care of your body and your mind will follow.

> Mackenzie: You're telling me that letting you rub me from head to toe is going to help me relax my brain to sleep better?

> Austin: Something like that.

He needed to figure out how to find out what the hell was going on with her, and fast, before he lost her without ever understanding why.

A knock on his apartment door pulled Austin from his battered and worn copy of *Creating True Peace*. He opened it to find Finn, holding a bag of take-out food in one hand and a six-pack of beer in the other.

"Finn?"

"I am taking it upon myself to be a good friend right now."

"Did you lose a bet?" Austin jerked his head to indicate Finn should come in and closed the door behind him.

"Something like that. We played 'rock, paper, scissors' and I lost, so here I am." Finn winked. "But you know I love you, Auzzy. I never need a reason to bring Vietnamese food to my favorite dark horse."

Austin led the way into the kitchen and pulled out plates while Finn put the bag of food onto the table, then five of his six beers into the fridge. "You want one?"

"I'm good with water, thank you."

Finn nodded, popped the cap, and sat at the table. He took a long drink before he began taking boxes of food out and placing them between them. "It's time to talk, Auzzy. And if you don't talk to me, the others are going to keep coming at you until you do."

Despite the invasion into his quiet time, warmth bloomed in his chest. Knowing his teammates were there for him, especially when his father – and possibly even Maman depending on how the chips fell – were not, suddenly made a world of difference. "Thank you."

Finn nodded before dipping a summer roll into peanut sauce and taking a bite. "You've been there for so many of us over the years, it's just nice that we get to have a chance at giving something back for a change." He clutched the summer roll and pointed the half-eaten appetizer at Austin.

"Okay, process of elimination." Another dip into the sauce. "First things first: Is it your shoulder? Is it worse than expected? Do you need surgery? Are you hooked on meds?"

"No." Austin lifted a summer roll and dipped it into the sauce. "None of those things."

"Good. Cool. I know how important physical activity is to you. And we didn't want to have to strap you to a chair for a couple days detox, and clean up your puke. I mean, we would, don't get me wrong, it just wasn't our first choice."

Austin chuckled. "I am glad to be of service."

"Is it your dad? Look, I know he's a hard ass. I mean…" He chewed and swallowed his mouthful before continuing. "You don't talk about him much, but we all know he's a jackass. If that's what it is, if you're afraid of losing your inheritance – we've got you. Russ can stay at his mom's and you can bunk with Linc if you need to. I'm sure we can find you a job, too. If not one of us, you could maybe tend bar at your friend's club. There are options. We won't let you go hungry or homeless."

A smile pulled at the corners of his mouth as he finished his roll and cracked open a tub of stir fried broccoli in garlic. "You have put a great deal of thought into this."

Finn nodded. "I didn't want to come to you with 'there, there, it'll all be fine.' You're a solution orientated friend, so I needed potential solutions."

"You guys had a meeting about this, didn't you?" He was not even mad about it, in fact, he was mostly touched at how intuitive his friends had been and how much they cared.

"Kinda, sorta. More like a 'someone needs to make sure he's really okay,' kind of meeting."

Austin had been part of many such meetings over his time as a Snow Pirate, he'd never thought his team would need to have one on his behalf.

Finn unwrapped his banh mi sandwich and took an oversized bite before moaning like he was about to have an orgasm. "Fuckin' love this place. There's no egg in that pho by the way. Or any of the sides. I made sure."

Austin nodded. "Thank you."

An expectant silence fell over them as they ate. "You don't need to confess your sins to me or anything. But we're worried and we want to help if we can. If you tell me shit's good, I'll believe you." He took another bite. "Well, I won't believe you. But I'll back off and let you handle your business. We just needed you to know we are here for you."

Shit was certainly not good. Austin sighed. "This needs to stay between us. No one else, not yet." If Mackenzie became the subject of team gossip she would leave him in a heartbeat for breaking her trust, and rightly so. Trust was the very cornerstone of every relationship, but more so for a couple in the kink lifestyle.

"You might want to swallow your bite before I tell you."

Finn's eyebrows shot up and he placed the remainder of

his sandwich on the table before wiping his hands on a beige napkin. "Oh, this is going to be good. I'm all ears."

Austin lowered his spoon to the table. "Mackenzie and I are dating." He waited for Finn's outburst, but it didn't come. His nostrils flared and his cheeks flexed as he clenched his jaw.

"Mackenzie who?" He frowned and canted his head. "Wait." His mouth fell open. "*Our* Mackenzie? Trainer from *work* Mackenzie? Forbidden because she's a Snow Pirate's employee Mackenzie?" His voice rose higher with every question. "You and... Kenzie? Holy fuck."

Finn picked up his beer and took a long pull from the cold bottle. "I'm gonna need a minute. Shit. I had no idea."

While he came to terms with Austin's revelation, Austin continued to eat his soup, filling Finn in on some of the details of their relationship, including the stranger in the parking lot. "He was in her space. I let jealousy and assumption cloud my judgment and assumed it was consensual, but when he walked away her whole demeanor suggested otherwise."

"And you asked her about it?"

Austin shook his head. "Kind of, I texted and asked how she was, but she said she was fine. I am not sure how to proceed. I was thinking of hiring a PI to dig around and figure out what the fuck is going on with her."

"Wait." Finn dropped his sandwich again. Austin had never seen him take so long to complete a meal before. "A PI? Dude. Are you listening to yourself? That's fucking insane."

"How else am I supposed to find out what is going on with her and that asshole? I should have taken his license plate or something." Austin's spoon hit the bowl with a clang and he raked his hands through his hair.

"Austin?"

He jerked his head up, meeting Finn's wrinkled brow and concerned eyes. "Or – and hang in there with me for this one. You could just go and talk to your fucking girlfriend."

"She will not be happy."

"And you think she's going to be thrilled if she finds out you sent a PI into her closet to look for skeletons?"

He had a point.

"You love her, right? There's literally no way on earth you get this out of whack about a woman you don't love. I mean, I can see why, Kenzie's great. Better than great. But, Jesus. Stop and take a breath before you do something that will lose her. And that would absolutely lose her. A PI is an extreme invasion of her privacy. That's not you, that's not what you want."

Austin grunted, tightness in his shoulders and neck increasing with every word out of his friend's mouth.

"You know I'm not wrong. From the murderous look on your face right now you want to kill dead things." He took a drink of beer and smacked his lips. "And that's fine, that's what's supposed to happen for those we love. You'd walk through hell for her. You'd go to jail for murder for her. All totally normal responses to someone you love being upset, or – based on what you've said about this douche nozzle in the Charger – maybe even threatened."

"I sense a 'but' coming."

"Smart man." Finn tipped the end of his sandwich at Austin before shoving it in his face and washing it down with a generous mouthful of beer. "But you can't be a raging asshole. Especially if she's having issues with a man who invades her space and licks her face in public and makes her cry. Because that sounds like she's already dealing with a flaming douchebag."

Finn shook his head. "I can only imagine how pissed you feel right now. Hell, *I'm* pissed right now and want to run him down with his own fucking car. But you need to do what's best for Kenzie. And poking around in her life? Not it. Not even close. And I think you know that."

He stewed in silence, stirring his soup, while Finn dipped

two cauliflower wings into sriracha mayo. "I definitely asked for chicken wings, not cauliflower." He popped the second one in his mouth. "But they aren't bad at all."

"You are right." Austin heaved out a sigh. Every breath weighed his already heavy body down further.

"Happens sometimes, man. Don't let it get to ya." Finn smirked. "I knew something was off when your head was out of the fight. I suspected a woman at lunch when you picked up your phone, but Kenzie... wow." He went quiet, as though working through things in his head.

"Is she kinky or are you going vanilla?" He frowned and shook his head. "Know what? Never mind. Forget I asked. It's none of my goddamned business."

He was right, it was not, and he was quietly happy that Finn reminded himself of his boundaries without Austin having to say anything.

"So." Finn smacked the empty glass bottle on the dining table with a tad too much force. "What are you going to do?"

After a long pause, staring into the pho broth at the bottom of his bowl, he rolled his neck. "I'm going to go talk to her."

CHAPTER 24
Mackenzie

Kenzie raked her hands through her hair and pushed Garrett back by his shoulders, but he didn't budge. She'd stupidly opened the door thinking he was the takeout guy and he'd muscled his way in. They'd spent the last ten minutes in a standoff and he refused to leave.

"You need to leave." She wouldn't give him the satisfaction of seeing her cry, but dangit, she was close. A pounding at the door made her start. Fuck.

"Mackenzie, open the door." Austin's usually calm voice was strained, she could tell he was struggling to stay calm.

Double fuck.

"Get rid of him."

She wanted to punch Garrett's snarl off his face, but violence really wasn't the answer, even if she wanted to beat him repeatedly with a hockey stick, then shove it up his ass and wave him around like a fucking flag.

She cracked the door, bracing her foot against the bottom so Austin couldn't force it open. Though she knew if he wanted to get into her house she was pretty powerless to stop him.

"Let me in, Mackenzie."

"It's not a good time, Austin."

"I heard you yelling. I know he is there, let me in." His sad and pleading eyes almost broke her.

The door came loose from her hands as Garrett swung it open. "My wife and I are having a discussion, so if you'd kindly fuck off, that'd be peachy."

Her stomach dropped through her body and crashed onto the floor. Wife. He'd said the word, out loud, to Austin. She couldn't bring herself to meet his eyes.

"I am not going anywhere. Especially not based on how you address your *wife*." Austin's voice was now freakishly calm, cold, hard, and heavy with unspoken threat. "It is time for you to leave."

He sounded like an animal, growling at Garrett with menace, and his towering presence was impressive. How Garrett wasn't already shitting his pants was anyone's guess. "This is your one and only warning. Do not come back here. Leave Mackenzie alone. Move on and forget you ever knew her."

Her heart squeezed. He was probably breaking inside at the revelation that she was married, and had kept it from him, but he was holding himself together enough to take care of her. Doing what he did best.

Garrett's answering laugh was hollow. "Who the fuck do you think you are?"

Austin surged forward, stepping into the house and not stopping until the arm of the couch met Garrett's legs and he fell backward onto the sofa. Scrambling to stand in a blur of curse words and limbs, he squared off with Austin.

She'd never seen Austin so angry. His brows hung low, his nostrils flared, and his jaw twitched as he clenched his teeth. Rage radiated from him, as he stood tall, not backing down from Garrett's advances.

"I think I am the person to tell you to pick on someone your own size." Without looking at Kenzie, Austin reached out and picked up her arm. She'd worn a long sleeve shirt, but he slipped the sleeve up to display her bruises. "Because any man who does this to a woman, has no place in Mackenzie's life. So you need to leave. And I am happy to help you get to whatever rock you fucking crawled out from under if I need to."

She shouldn't be turned on by the brazen display of machismo, but try telling that to her aching clit. Angry Austin was hot. Angry Austin laying down the law to her shitty ex? Suffice to say her panties were on fire.

Garrett shoved Austin, but it was as though he'd shoved a solid brick wall, Austin didn't move. Instead he smirked and a cruel grin appeared on his face as though he was toying with his prey.

Garret shoved again, harder, leaning into it, but Austin still didn't move.

"Garrett..." His name was barely a whisper from her lips. But with how skilled Austin was, she felt as though she should at least warn him.

Austin's head turned toward her voice, and Garrett's fist swung, striking Austin's chin with a dull crack. Shit.

Austin stepped back, his glare intensified, but Garrett was already throwing a second punch, and a third. Austin kept his arms up, letting Garrett swing. Kenzie swallowed. She hadn't ever seen Austin fight before, but she knew Garrett was playing with fire and was about to get his ass handed to him.

She reached out to stop him, clutching his forearm. "Austin, don't. He's not worth it."

Garrett swung again. "She's my wife, asshole."

"That does not mean anything when you treat her like shit." Austin deflected the next couple of punches easily, she wasn't sure whether he was waiting for Garrett to tire himself out, or if her plea not to strike him had worked.

"Some people only understand violence, Mackenzie." Austin's words echoed those of her best friends. Garrett wasn't relenting, he continued his assault, even though he was barely landing any punches at all.

Before she could take a full breath, Austin swung his fist and on impact, broke Garrett's nose with a sharp crack. Blood streamed down his face onto his shirt as he howled in pain and blinked back tears. "I'll fucking kill you."

He rushed toward Austin, but Austin held him in place with the side of his forearm against Garret's shoulder. "I do not believe you are understanding me. You need to hear the words coming from my mouth. Leave and never come back, before I throw you out."

"Abby tell him."

"He's right Garrett, we're done." She crossed the room and pulled a manila envelope containing divorce papers she'd already signed from behind the couch cushion. "Sign these and send them back to me."

Austin shook his head. "Get him a pen. He'll sign them right now."

Kenzie darted into the kitchen, hoping Austin wouldn't commit murder in her living room. She loved her house, she had gotten lucky on a foreclosure, and she didn't want it to be commandeered by the police to investigate her shitty ex's murder. Blood was a bitch to get out of carpets.

Striding back into the living room brandishing a pen, she struggled not to grin. Austin stood, arms folded, scowling at Garrett, who'd grabbed a fistful of tissues and stood with them pressed against his still-bleeding nose.

"Sign them." Austin's voice was still emotionless, and his laser focus bore into Garrett's head.

"I need to take them home and have my lawyer look them over."

Austin shook his head. "Sign. Them."

"You have no right to do this. Abby, tell him. Be reasonable. Your parents are going to be so disappointed in you."

Austin held up a hand. "Do not gaslight her." He sucked in an audible breath. "This is not the first time you laid hands on her."

Fuck. Austin remembered her telling him about her ex. He'd obviously put two and two together, which explained the throbbing vein in both his temple and down the side of his throat and the reddening in his face. He was going to kill Garrett.

"The statute of limitations in Texas for assault and battery is two years. Is that why you are back? Because she can no longer report you in your home state?" Austin laughed, but it was humorless. "You grabbed her here, in Minnesota. And left marks. She could go to the police if she so desired."

Even a whisper of a domestic violence scandal would not reflect well on Garrett's family, his father, their business... She silently sent up a prayer that the threat of law enforcement would be enough to get him the fuck out of her house so she could talk to Austin. Her neighbor had threatened it but not actually called. Austin would likely not back down and use every weapon at his disposal to get Garrett away from her door.

Austin. Her nickname of 'mon guerrier' for him grew more and more apropos with every day she knew him. She just had to hold out hope that he wouldn't walk away, that he'd listen to her, hear why she didn't tell him about her past, and still love her every bit as fiercely.

"I will end you. Both of you." Garrett jabbed a finger at Austin and swung it toward Kenzie.

"You could try, but you would fail. Be smart. Sign the

papers. Get the fuck out of here and do not ever contact her again. Are we clear?"

Garrett seethed, hissing breath through his mouth, his bright red face glaring at Austin. "This isn't over."

"Yes, it is. You do not wish to cross me, or my family." He paused, shifted his stance, and sneered, arrogance hanging on his every word. "I am sure you have already looked us up."

That did something to Garrett, he flinched. The Morgan name wasn't a global brand by any means, but Garrett would have looked up who he thought of as his competition the minute he arrived in town. He wasn't an idiot. Even he knew better than to pick a fight with a Morgan. His father had been on the cover of Time magazine only a few months prior, they'd recently acquired two smaller aviation firms and were quickly becoming the fastest growing aviation company in the country and a recognizable name.

Using his family name wasn't something she imagined he did freely, or without some form of suffering given the strained relationship between him and his father. She wanted to throw herself at him and hug him for hours. She'd never be able to repay him for standing his ground and chasing away her demons.

While she'd done the groundwork herself, spoken to a lawyer, filled in the papers, and had made the decision to proceed with divorcing that part of her past, it was Austin helping her slam the door on it.

Garrett opened his mouth, but seemed to rethink his decision to speak. He simply nodded, snatched the pen from Kenzie, slipped the papers out of the envelope and signed where she had left sticky notes flagging the spaces that needed his signature. "So this is it Abby? We're done?"

Kenzie nodded. "I told you, my name is Kenzie now. Abby died the night you raised your hand to her. The first time."

It was her last chance to say something to him. To give him

a piece of her mind. To let her know that he did not, nor would not, destroy her.

"And yes, Garrett, we're done. You robbed me of enough of my life that I am not letting you have a single minute more. While we're at it..." She pointed a finger at him. "If anything should happen to Bea, I will go to the media and tell them everything. So while we are outside the limits of the law, the court of public approval is still in session."

Garrett's jaw dropped. "You wouldn't destroy your father's business with such a scandal, Abby."

She narrowed her gaze and tipped her chin. "Try me."

Fear flickered in his eyes as he searched her face. Whatever he found there must have been enough. He turned and left without so much as another word or a backward glance.

"Austin—" She stepped forward to touch his arm, but he stepped back. "Austin, please."

When she pulled her eyes from his feet to his face, what she found splintered her heart into pieces. Pure, unadulterated pain across his beautiful features.

"Please let me explain."

He raised both palms to her. "I am giving him enough time to leave the area and I am leaving also."

Her breath caught, her heart raced so fast it felt like it was trying to escape her body and got stuck in her throat. He was leaving. She was losing him. "Austin, please?" Her ragged, broken voice, reflected the pain traveling through her nervous system.

The tears she'd fought while Garrett was yelling at her fell freely down her face and dripped onto her shirt. "Let me explain."

He shook his head. "There is nothing else to explain, Mackenzie."

Her lip quivered as streams of tears trickled down her

nose, cold droplets falling onto her mouth and chin. "There is. Please. Don't leave like this."

"We talked about the importance of being honest. Of trusting each other. Trust is what the BDSM lifestyle is based on. Without it, a relationship can turn destructive."

She stepped forward, but his eyes darkened and she stepped back. She wasn't afraid of him, but she also didn't want to crowd him. He was trying to establish a boundary and no matter how agonizing it was for her, she needed to respect it.

She rubbed at her chest with her fingertips, and her shallow breaths grew more rapid. "I was going to tell you."

His eyebrow quirked. He didn't believe her. She couldn't blame him, but it was the truth. "I mean it. I was going to tell you."

"You gave me the selective truth about your ex. Did you think I would judge you for still being married to an abuser? I am honestly not sure what impression I have given you that made you think I would be anything but supportive." Even his voice was pained, charged with hurt, and the accusation that she should have known him better.

He scraped his palm over his jaw, his eyes frantically flickering back and forth between hers, like he was looking for the answer to appear on her face. "No matter what kind of relationship you are in, trust is paramount in order for the relationship to work for both sides."

He reached out and brushed her tears away with the back of his knuckles. She closed her eyes, savoring the touch.

"Since bodily harm and mental health are at stake in some BDSM relationships, trust is not just something to discuss, it's something to hold dear and take seriously."

He had said it all to her before, but in the context of what had just happened, it all landed differently. This wasn't an introduction to kink, it was an ending.

"Countless submissives and even Dominants are both physically and emotionally hurt by actively playing with someone they didn't trust. BDSM is not about having new experiences with someone you don't fully trust."

She nodded, gnawing on the inside of her cheeks. "I know. I'm sorry. Austin, please. I'll do better. We can fix this."

His frustrating calm grated on her every inflamed nerve. Didn't he feel what she felt? Wasn't he torn the fuck apart by what was happening between them? Did walking away from her truly come so easily for him?

His knuckles grazed her cheek. "BDSM is about having experiences and pushing your boundaries with someone who you can trust to have your best interests at heart. Someone who respects you enough to stop when you want to. Someone who respects you enough to let you in and share their innermost thoughts and desires."

"Austin." Her heart was shattering and a heaviness snaked into her muscles.

"I need time to process this. To meditate. To think about what happened and figure out if there is enough trust here to repair things, or if we would be better to part ways. It would be different if the trust was lost in the bedroom. If I pushed you too far, too fast. Or if you should have safe worded but said you were okay. Those things we could work on, come back from, but this..."

He pulled back from her, leaving a coldness that went straight into her chest.

"This is not that." He shook his head, his piercing stare searing her skin.

Was he trying to decide then and there whether she was worth another shot? Or was he truly done?

"I need space."

She nodded, but no words came, only more tears. Sliding his hand around her neck he pulled her close and kissed her forehead. Her body itched for his arms to wrap around her and make everything stop hurting, but he pulled back and left.

Dropping to her knees she hung her head in her hands and cried. She'd managed to mess up the best thing to have ever happened to her, someone who saw her for what she was and loved her for it. Who didn't make excuses for her, or criticize her. She'd broken the most precious thing she'd ever found and in turn it was breaking her.

He'd said he needed space, but the look in his eyes, the rounded shoulders, the sadness that seeped through his clothes, she knew he was done.

Pulling her phone out of her back pocket, she sniffed and wiped her nose with the back of her hand. She needed her friends.

> Kenzie: 9-1-1.

Addison: Fuck. What happened? Leaving work now. I'll fake an aneurysm if I have to.

Paige: There in twenty. I'll bring tequila.

CHAPTER 25
Austin

"Are you dropping?" Slade's voice boomed through Austin's apartment.

He groaned. He had not moved from the couch for the past two days, maybe even three, he had no idea for certain. Once he had left Mackenzie's house and made his way home, he crumbled and had not found a way to get off the sofa since.

"Why are you here?"

Slade appeared in front of him, his knees at Austin's eye level, before crouching down and meeting his stare. "One of your teammates activated the phone tree. I'd have brought cookies but I don't bake, and you don't poison your body with that shit, so I'd have had to eat them all myself." He swept a hand over his belly. "And this body didn't get this way by eating pans of cookies by myself."

"How did you get in?"

Slade beamed like he was James-fucking-Bond. "I won't ever reveal my secret."

"Will gave you the spare key, didn't he?"

He dropped to the floor and crossed his legs. "Again, I ask: are you dropping? I mean..." He gestured at Austin. "The answer is pretty obvious to me, but I want to hear your own self-awareness answer."

"I have dropped, yes."

"Wanna talk about it?" Slade reached into a bag at his side and pulled out a can of Pepsi Zero. He cracked it and took a long sip.

"She kept something from me. Our trust is fragmented."

Slade's eyes narrowed. "Must be something big. Did she go beyond her safe word?"

He snorted. "If only. She kept an abusive, psychopathic husband in Texas a secret."

"Kenzie is married?" Finn's voice sounded from behind the couch.

Fuck.

"You couldn't have told me he was there? That does not go beyond these four walls, Finn. Do you understand?"

"I-I would never, Austin. I just... shit. She's married."

Slade's eyes flexed wide for a beat. "I admit, that's not at all what I expected. Not good, either. Definitely harder to fix than fractured bedroom trust."

"What are you doing here?" His question was directed at Finn who answered almost instantly.

"The agreement was he'd come break in, but one of us would go with him to make sure you were okay. Turns out I really suck at 'rock, paper, scissors.'"

If every part of him was not hurting, he would have laughed. "I appreciate you coming, but I am okay."

Finn guffawed. "And I'm the queen of England. I might act a jester sometimes, Auzzy, but I'm not fucking stupid."

Slade reached back into his bag and pulled out a bottle of Gatorade. "Hydrate."

He took the bottle but did not open it.

"Does someone want to explain to me why this is such a big deal? I mean, I get that it's a big deal but..." Finn circled the couch and dropped onto the floor next to Slade. "Not my life is over, I'm on the couch for days and ignoring life outside the walls, kind of big deal."

He swung his legs over the edge of the sofa and pulled himself to a seated position. He cracked open the bottle and drank, giving Slade a nod to explain the situation to Finn.

"You know that Austin is in the BDSM lifestyle, right?"

Finn nodded.

"Okay, well the entire time during a scene a good Dom will be aware of the possibility of someone getting hurt. It does not go away, it is not swept under a rug. A misplaced smack, an unsteady hand with a whip, a rope tie that is too tight causing blood flow to be cut off... the possibility is always there. That is just another aspect of what a Dom bears in his mind, the weight he carries."

Finn nodded again. "That's why I won't ever venture beyond light kink. I couldn't handle that kind of responsibility."

"When trust is broken in the bedroom between two people in a kink lifestyle, it is severe, but not irredeemable. You talk things through and figure out how to move forward. But this wasn't a kink breach of trust. This was external. This was something about her life that has now impacted them both. The breach of trust is every bit as grave, and even harder to fix. You know that submissives can drop after a scene, right?"

"Yeah, it's like a depressive episode. I've heard about it, but never seen it."

"Dom drop can also happen. It's far less talked about, but every bit as dangerous."

Austin continued to drain his drink while Slade gave Finn a BDSM 101 lesson in his living room.

"Think of it like an accident, your senses are heightened,

you are dealing with the situation, some people in times like that have even exhibited extreme strength. But once the emergency is over, the endorphin and adrenaline rush is gone and you crash. You feel every muscle in your body, any injuries you didn't feel before will now be felt. It sounds a lot like BDSM-drop and in a sense it is."

Finn's frown deepened, like he couldn't figure out the connections in his mind.

"The emotional side of Dom Drop is more treacherous. This hits you and you may well feel like you are experiencing a deep melancholy, self-doubt, lethargy, listlessness, and in some cases guilt. Spanking, flogging, and causing harm to someone goes against the norms of society."

"The lessons we're raised with to not hit women."

"Exactly. And even with consent, that is what we do in the lifestyle – and what's more, we even enjoy it. There is a fine line. And while BDSM is not abuse there can still be that hint of guilt that can creep in."

Finn's eyes drifted to Austin's face and he looked anywhere but at his friend's eyes. His chest constricted and the Gatorade he'd just swallowed turned to sand in his throat.

"I still don't get it, Kenzie consented, right? So I get some low-level guilt over hitting her – or whatever her kink is – but I still don't..."

He cleared his throat. "She came from an abusive relationship that was not over. She lived with the constant threat of her ex hunting her down and finding her. That fear is embedded deep inside someone. She did not disclose the depth of her trauma, the fact that she was still married, the fact that he was still an issue..."

"So you feel like you might have inadvertently exacerbated her trauma through your kink time with her."

"I am concerned I might have triggered her and she kept it from me. I... I have concerns, yes. And I came from a relationship in which my ex cheated on me with another Dom and eventually left me – another severe breach of trust that left me feeling inadequate and broken."

He had never been so open with his non-kink friends before, but if he was to get through the situation, he needed to be honest with both himself and those closest to him.

Finn's slow nod seemed to release the frown on his face. "I get it now. How do we fix this?" He waved his hand in front of Austin's face. "Is there a cure for Dom drop?"

"The amount of time that it can last or take to manifest varies from Dom to Dom and from incident to incident." Slade took over again as Austin drained the end of his drink.

"When this happens there are a number of things you can do. First is to recognize it for what it is. Sometimes taking some "me time" can be helpful, going somewhere quiet and just relaxing, listening to music, reading a book. Do something that challenges you, engaging in a hobby you like. Clearly we aren't there yet. I don't think he's even changed his clothes in days."

Finn sniffed and scrunched up his face. "Can confirm."

"It is kind of like riding a horse, if you fall off you get right back on. The same thing here, don't stop being a Dom."

"I cannot dominate her when things are this shattered."

Slade nodded his agreement. "I know. I'm not telling you to, I'm simply educating." He gestured at Finn. "You know I love an attentive audience, Austin."

"It's kind of fascinating." Finn shook his head. "I totally have a newfound respect for your level of badass right now, Auzzy."

He did not feel like a badass. He felt as though he had let both himself, and Mackenzie down. He should have been more thorough, he should have pushed her for more information about her past, her ex, and the marks on her arm.

"Communication is the next thing on the list. Talk to your

sub about what is happening, yes you are the Dominant and are supposed to be strong but there comes a point where the trust and communication aspect steps in if it gets too bad."

Finn hung on Slade's every word. "I mean, some of this is just common sense, right?"

"You would be surprised at how uncommon common sense can be in BDSM relationships. Some people watch a kinky movie on TV and think it gives them free rein to beat the shit out of their girlfriends. It does not end well." He screwed the top back on the bottle and accepted the protein bar Slade shoved at him.

"Sometimes all it takes is for your sub to tell you that they love you, that they enjoyed what you did during a scene. Telling your Dom what they did was what you needed that can go a long way to pulling them out of Dom Drop. Even as Doms we need that gentle reassurance." Slade offered a bar to Finn who declined.

"Wow. You're way deeper than I expected, Auzzy. And... dare I say it without having my face broken, softer. I would never have guessed you needed reassurance of any kind, you're always so confident, sometimes even arrogant." He shook his head like it was all some kind of magical realization to him. "So none of what you have listed there is possible, what else can we do?"

We. Finn's blind loyalty to him warmed his cold chest. He was luckier than he realized to have such good friends, and he suspected had Finn let them, some of the others on the team would be breaking his door down to talk to him as well.

Austin extended a finger. If he was going to be quizzed on being a Dom and how to navigate difficult waters, he at least owed it to both his mentor and his friend to answer the questions. "Vitamin B and Fish Oil. This will help replace many of the minerals that will be lost from your adrenaline and endorphin highs to decrease the potential for drop, and mitigate its effects."

"I think we're past that too, Auzzy."

He shook the empty bottle at Finn and swallowed another bite of his protein bar. "Good nutrition and hydration. Talking to Mackenzie, seeing her, even meeting for coffee would probably help."

"I don't think we're there yet either." Apparently Finn was a master of stating the obvious.

"Sunshine, a natural vitamin D boost contained within sunlight, can be a great aid to help battle drop."

Finn gestured to the door. "Cats and dogs out there. Zero out of ten. Do not recommend."

Slade grinned. "Mild exercise such as a light jog, yoga, aerobics and similar can help release endorphins if you have many left in your body which will help mitigate the experience of drop. Basically he needs to drag his ass off the couch, have a shower, a home cooked meal, and get himself outside for a run."

Finn held his hands up. "I'm willing to take a beating if it gets you out of this funk. You wanna grab an arm? I'll grab the other. We can haul his ass to the bathroom and dump him in the shower."

"Cold water, fully clothed?" Slade offered Finn a fist bump. "I'm in."

He grunted. "No way you can both take me. It's okay, I'll go take a shower." He couldn't rely on Mackenzie to help pull him out of this one, he needed to muster up some strength and figure his shit out by himself. Yet again.

"Are you prepared to lose everything by crossing me?" Father's threatening tone was laced with challenge. No one said no to Malcolm Edward Morgan, those that dared, were decimated, teaching others not to try. Thankfully, Austin's paternal grandfather, Edward, had ensured Austin's inheritance had gone into a trust fund he gained access to when he turned twenty five.

Three more years.

He did not want to open his mouth to remind Father of the fact, he knew it all too well. It would serve only to add fuel to his rampage. And while getting cut off from his father would result in an urgent need for him to find a job and pay his own way through the remainder of the school year, he had faith he could figure it out by himself if he needed to.

"Yes, sir. I am."

Father slammed his open palms on the cherry wood desk sitting between them before jabbing a finger at Austin. "You'll marry that woman, Austin. So help me fucking God, you will."

"No, sir. I will not."

Maman hurried across the room and patted Austin's bicep. "Ce que ton père veut dire…"

It was the same line he'd heard a thousand times before, 'what he meant to say…' She was always defending him, explaining his words, apologizing for him.

"No, Maman. Il a dit ce qu'il avait l'intention de dire."

He always said what he meant to say.

"Malcolm…" Maman's face paled and her eyes turned sad. "Let us not argue over such things."

Father picked up his tumbler of scotch and knocked it back, banging the empty glass against the wood when he was done. "Who is she?"

"Who?"

"The piece of ass keeping you from your destiny." Father raised his brows like Austin was asking the dumbest question in the world.

"The family business is your destiny, Father. Not mine. I do not wish to work with you, or take over when you retire." He had never said it out loud for both of his parents to hear before, and once the words were out of his mouth the silence engulfing the room swallowed them whole.

"Qu'est-ce que tu veux faire?"

"I do not know what I want to do past college, Maman. But I do know it is not to work with Father, or marry someone I do not love." The bands across his chest tightened with every word he spoke.

Father's glare intensified, his brows pulled low over his eyes. "You're being a goddamn idiot. This is your future you're talking about."

"Yes, Father, it is my future. If it is a mistake, it is my mistake to make. But I will not marry her, I will not do that to either her, or me. I will not step up into the family business, and I will not be bullied into doing something I do not want to, simply because my choices displease you."

Maman squeezed his hand on his thigh in silent support. It was the first time he'd stood up to Father and while his insides were slop, he was confident in drawing his line in the sand. He needed to live his own life, make his own choices. No matter the cost. His stomach tightened.

Even if it meant Maman stopped speaking to him. He had thought his delayed start to college would quell his yearning to step out from Father's shadow, but it had not. He had also thought that perhaps his time away would be enough for Father to realize that Austin was not destined for the family business, but it seemed to only fuel Father's determination to bring him in all the more.

Father wagged his finger, took a breath like he was going to speak, but glanced at Maman who shook her head. Father said nothing, instead he growled, turned, and left his study, slamming the door behind him.

"Tout ira bien, mon Chou."

And for once Austin was starting to believe that everything might be well after all.

CHAPTER 26
Mackenzie

Kenzie had read and re-read Austin's letter so many times the folds in the page were already well-worn. She'd woken up the day after Garrett had left and a cream envelope had been waiting for her in her mailbox. It broke her heart all over again.

My dearest Mackenzie,

It occurs to me that no matter what happens between us in the future, you are about to embark on something you were not prepared for. Your ex is more than likely going to tell your family where you are and things might get messy.

As such, I needed you to know some things. And I wanted them in writing so when you need a reminder, you have it at hand.

You are an incredibly strong and resilient woman. I know this because you have already overcome more than I believe even you know. You paint yourself into a small box in the corner, because that is what you were taught to do your entire life. But you are not meant to be small, Mackenzie. When you allow yourself to believe in what you are capable of, you are a force to be reckoned with. I have seen it. I have seen you shift from "I can't" to "I can" more times than I think you realize.

Plugging, ruining/denying an orgasm, sleeping when stressed, getting back on the ice, leaving your toxic marriage and family, krav training with me... and those are only a few off the top of my head.

There are many big and small things and I would really like you to spend some time sitting down one of these days to think about all the times you believed you could not and then you did.

You could not ever set boundaries with your family, it is why you left, but you have done so now. I understand those things take strength along the way, but they should also build your resilience. They can only do that if you give yourself credit for them.

You are notorious for not celebrating the good. Not celebrating your accomplishments. I can only do so much to celebrate them with you, especially when I know there are small moments every day where you overcome those obstacles.

The things you focus on are the things that will consume you. I know you have a lot of tough things in your life. I know you are bombarded with it on a daily basis. If you are running out of ways to find the good in life, we either need to find more ways for you to find them, or to change your circumstances. Changing is not as simple as snapping your fingers – but you changed your circumstances. You did that. By yourself.

Someone asked me if I was really the problem, or if it was possible I was dealt a shit hand. I was quick to answer it was me. But it was enough to make me question. Would things be different in a different place with different people?

Nothing is off the table when it comes to starting new. We always have a choice, we just often do not like the choices that are in front of us. You have always been able to figure things out.

This time will be no different as long as you remember who you are and what you are capable of.

When the voices of others in your head tell you that you are not strong enough, remember that you are one of the strongest individuals I know. I have witnessed it firsthand. It is not just something I made up. I also know that there are a lot of voices that lead you to believe you have reached the bottom when in reality there is still plenty of space left.

You can choose not to believe me, but I have not yet been wrong about you and what you are capable of – despite you trying to protest. The universe guides us places, but we are never without our free will to make the choices that determine our outcomes. Life is just one long series of choices. Sometimes we simply have to choose to get through to the next moment.

You can do this.

J'taime, Mackenzie.

- Austin

Seven days.

It had been Seven days since the showdown between Garrett and Austin in her living room.

Seven days since she called an emergency sisterhood meeting where her friends turned up at the door with enough snacks and liquor to sink the Titanic.

Seven days since Austin kissed her on the forehead and left.

Seven days since her heart had shattered.

She hadn't heard a single word from him. And while she'd seen him at the rink for games and practices, it hadn't done much to soothe the ache in her chest. In fact, she wasn't feeling any better at all. She'd done some intense drinking, then even more intense drunk-thinking on the issue and decided that Austin wasn't okay with any of it either.

He'd been shit on by his ex, Kenzie had kept the extent of her abusive husband from him, and he was going through shit with his parents, everything was likely compounding, and despite his frustrating AF calm exterior, she knew him better.

She did. Deep down she knew he was hurting inside which in turn only made her hurt even more. Her family had always made her feel like she was too much, that giving herself to someone in her entirety would be too much. Austin had found out about her past, about her ex, about her darkness, and he'd left her too.

She was too dramatic, too over the top, too much. Too much for her family, too much for Austin, and, given enough time, she'd probably end up being too much for her friends as well. UGH.

She was in her dining room, feet crossed on her table, leaning back in the dining chair with her laptop resting on her thighs searching about how to fix things when they were broken with your Dom.

She had to try. She had to give it her all. She wasn't prepared to lose him, to lose them, and potentially lose the pieces of herself she'd just gotten back or discovered for the first time. Despite feeling like she was falling apart, she needed to make him see her, hear her, and to find a way to bring their broken hearts back together in sync as one.

Double ugh. She barely recognized herself. Two years spent running from men, keeping safe distance for her own good replaced by something out of a chick flick on Netflix.

She found a blog post about something called Dom-drop. While she knew what sub-drop was and how to look for signs that she was dropping, she hadn't ever thought to look up how to know if he was dropping too.

There are a few things that you can do to help them with their drop. The first is touch. Touch him in a way that works for your dynamic. Perhaps that means you put your head in his lap. Maybe you lay with your head on his chest and cuddle, wrap-

ping yourself around him. You could give them a massage to help ease any muscle tension that they have.

She'd give anything to be able to touch him, to rest her hand over his heart and feel the fluttering, steady beat under the warmth of her palm.

Not all touch has to be sexual. It simply needs to be comforting.

That had been the thing which most surprised her about their dynamic. He had showed her that passive touching, being tactile and showing affection did not always lead to, or mean sex. She missed his physical presence: the kisses on the forehead, the brushes of his knuckles on her face, the squeezes of her hand, the stroking of her hair.

The knot in her chest grew tighter as tears slid down her cheeks.

You can also try words and phrases to reassure your Dom.

She would if he would fucking talk to her.

Let your Dom care for you. Allowing him to feel needed and provide loving and tender care can remind him how much you want him to be the one to care for you. Let him provide for you.

It was just getting cruel. She wanted all those things. Specifically to curl herself into his lap and tell him she was sorry.

Be willing to break the rules or protocols set between you and your Dom.

Huh. Say what now? Wasn't the entire foundation of kink about respecting the rules and protocols?

This could be staying when you are supposed to leave. Stand your ground, and make sure that he knows that he means enough to you that you are willing to break the rules.

Game. Changer. She sniffed and wiped her nose with the heel of her hand. She loved him, enough to break their rules to fix things.

Another suggestion is to reach out to another Dom to help

talk your Dom through the drop and help bring him out. This is risky, and for extreme cases of drop. You will need to share with someone outside of your Dom/sub relationship what is going on. Your Dom takes this as a breach of trust and there are consequences for breaking trust.

Consequences for breaking trust. Understatement of the century. Would it be worth an additional breach of trust to fix the first breach of trust? She wasn't sure. But he wasn't talking to her and she was pretty sure they were done. Would talking to someone really make things any worse than they already were?

She picked up her phone and typed out a message to Paige.

> Kenzie: Question.

> Paige: I'll try to answer, shoot.

> Kenzie: Is Thor a Dom?

> Paige: I'm not sure. It wouldn't surprise me. Why?

> Kenzie: I need to talk to a Dom to try to fix things between me and Austin.

> Paige: Not to tell you what to do or anything, but that could go REALLY fucking wrong.

> Kenzie: More wrong than him not speaking to me?

> Paige: He might never speak to you again level of wrong. Going to another Dom about your own Dom is a big fuck-off deal, K-K.

> Paige: I'll ask Thor, if not... If you don't want my advice as a part-time Domme... and would prefer someone with a penis, I have... ugh. I have another contact. I'd rather not use it if I don't have to, but I can. For you.

> Paige: But I need you to think it over for a while first, okay? Actions have consequences.

She nodded, though Paige couldn't see her.

> Kenzie: Thanks. I'll think on it.

A knock at the door made her put her laptop and phone on the table. Maybe it was her new tortilla blanket she'd ordered while she was feeding her feelings tequila, or the cereal dispenser her Facebook ads told her she couldn't live another second without.

She pulled the door open and came face to face with Mama, Daddy, and Bea. Holy shit.

Bea put her hands up. "Not it. Garrett sang like a choir boy at Christmas." She pushed her way into the house and made a beeline for the kitchen, but Kenzie was rooted to the spot.

She'd expected that if her parents were to show up at her door they'd arrive in a blaze of 'get the fuck home,' and spitting fire hotter'n a summer in San Antonio. But the two people in front of her were anything but confrontational.

They'd aged a decade in only two short years, the lines on their foreheads and around their eyes and mouth had deepened, and there was a sadness in their eyes she never recalled having seen before.

"Can we come in, Kenzie? We aren't here to cause trouble." Daddy spoke, imploring her with his eyes.

Wordlessly, she stood aside and let her parents cross the threshold, closing the door behind them with a quiet 'snick.'

Mama pulled her into a hug and burst out crying. "I thought you were dead, Abby. I mean..." She sniffed. "Kenzie." She squeezed hard, before pushing back and wiping her eyes like she hadn't just exploded into tears.

Bea had pulled out four shot glasses and a bottle of the good tequila. She gestured at a chair with the neck of the bottle. "Sit."

She hesitated, only sitting when Mama and Daddy had taken up seats. Bea handed her a shot of tequila, which she swirled around the glass. An awkward silence held the room hostage and she had no idea where to start, what to say, or even why they were there.

Bea threw back her shot, seemingly giving zero fucks it wasn't even noon. "This is awkward." She refilled the glass and took another shot.

Kenzie cleared her throat, placed her shot on the table, and folded her arms. "I'm not going back to Texas."

Mama reached across the table and squeezed her hand. "We aren't here to fight or drag you home Ab—Kenzie."

"I'm not really sure why y'all are here." Her voice softened, but she was still wary. She wouldn't be manipulated into going back to Texas. "Garrett and I are getting a divorce." She picked up the shot and tossed it back.

"We know. He told us." Mama sipped at her tequila.

"Said something about you having a man threatening to kick his ass all the way back to Texas." Daddy's chuckle engulfed her like stepping outside into the humidity, stealing her breath away. "Sounds like you found yourself a keeper."

Bea leaned forward to refill Kenzie's glass. "Is it true you're dating a Morgan? *The* Morgan. He's the sole heir to the kingdom, right? No other siblings?" Her eyes were alight with excitement.

"What are y'all doing here?" She wasn't giving them an inch. They arrived on her doorstep unannounced, and she refused to play happy families and share girl talk like they hadn't spoken since last week and needed to catch up. Anxiety stabbed at her temples and shoulders and she wasn't going to relax until she either knew what the hell they were doing in her space, or they were gone.

"We just wanted to see you." Mama took another sip. "When Garrett came home madder'n a wet hen saying he found you and you were divorcing him, and Beatrice said she'd been to visit but you wouldn't see her…"

"We miss you, Kenzie. I know we have a lot to talk about, and your mama and me, we have a hellova lot of things to say sorry for, but we're just here to see you. No tricks. No fights. We've missed you like all get out and we just wanted to see that you're okay, and tell you that we love you. And if you're ever ready, we're waiting."

Tears streamed down her face. Mama and Bea both sniffled and wiped their cheeks as well.

Bea flapped her fingers close to her eyes and blinked frantically. "Okay, enough of this emotional shit, can we please hear about your boyfriend now? And your life here, what's it like to work for a college hockey team?"

"Are you back on the ice?" Mama's voice was quiet and she wrung her hands on the table in front of her.

She had no idea where to even begin. She opened her mouth, not sure of what was going to come out when her front door swung open with a bang as it collided with the wall behind it.

"Right, K-K. We love you, but it's time. You gotta get out of your sweatpants, take a shower, and go out into the world for a little while." Paige's voice echoed around the foyer. "It's still spinning you know."

"She's right, Kenz. We do love you, but you smell. And if

Austin-fucking-Morgan is dumb enough to let you go, then we'll find someone who isn't. Get up, bish. We're going shopping." Addison stepped into the kitchen and stopped, making Paige crash into her back. "Fuck. Sorry. We didn't... uh..."

"You have guests." Paige's eyes were as wide as Adi's.

Addison elbowed Paige in the ribs. "Way to state the obvious." She stepped forward, hand outstretched toward Mama. "Even a blind person could see the family resemblance. Ma'am." She shook Mama's hand. "Sir." Then shook Daddy's. "It's nice to meet you, but all due respect, Kenzie isn't going back with you. She's staying here, where she belongs."

A fresh wave of tears tracked down her cheeks. Paige nodded and planted her hands on her hips. "That asshole will never lay a finger on her again."

"Hell, he doesn't deserve to breathe the same oxygen as her." Addison pursed her lips. Both fiercely loyal women stood behind Kenzie like some kind of badass bodyguards.

"Stand down, crazies. They aren't here to take me back. Even if they were, they know I'm not going. They're just visiting." She wiped her cheeks with the heel of her hand.

"Oh!" Adi took a step back.

"Well in that case." Paige extended her hand. "It's nice to meet you all. We're Kenzie's besties. And we were just leaving."

Bea laughed. "You don't have to leave. In fact, it's kind of awkward AF right now so it might help if you stayed." She stood and got two more shot glasses from the cupboard. "And it sounds like we need a game plan to win our girl back her man."

Addison accepted the shot from Bea and clinked their glasses together. "Day drinking and man scheming? Count us in."

Later that night, Kenzie had said goodbye to her parents, they were going to stay across town in a hotel for a couple of nights so they could spend more time together before returning to Texas. Bea wanted tickets to see the Snow Pirates play before going back home, and Mama and Daddy were keen to meet Austin, no matter how many times Kenzie insisted they were taking a break, or whatever the hell it was.

Bea was spending the night sharing the guest bedroom with Addison, while Paige bunked in with Kenzie.

"You really love him, don't you?" Paige pushed Kenzie's hair back from her eyes as they lay face to face in bed.

"I do."

"And you wanna live his kinky life with him?"

She nodded. "I do. I wanna be choked, pounded into the mattress, spanked and called a good girl. Then I want him to take me for milkshakes and burgers, hold my hand, kiss my forehead, and read to me from my favorite book."

"Now *that's* romance."

She laughed, but it didn't warm her all the way through.

"Have you given much thought to fixing things between you? Are you going to talk to another Dom?"

She shook her head in the darkness. "No other Doms. I don't think that's what we need. I read something earlier though, it said to stand your ground. To let him know that he means enough to you that you're willing to break the rules."

"So... what are you going to do?"

She grinned. "Break the rules. Will you help me?"

CHAPTER 27
Austin

Kenzie stood in front of him outside the locker room at the arena. He had just come off the ice from practice and found her waiting for him, piece of paper clutched in hand. When she'd seen him, she'd brandished it at him, a small smile playing on her lips.

"What is this?"

"I'm breaking your rules."

"You are... breaking my rules?"

"Yes, Sir. I know I was wrong to keep what I did from you. I know I should have come clean about my past and I know it was damaging to our relationship. But I miss you. And I don't accept that we're finished. So I'm breaking your rule, shitting on your boundary, and giving you this."

DOMINANT/SUBMISSIVE CONTRACT

"Mackenzie, I'm not sure you understand the gravity of what this is."

She swallowed, then sucked her cheek between her teeth and nodded. "I do, Austin. I understand exactly what it is and what it means."

I, Mackenzie Abbott (The Submissive), with a free mind

and open heart request of Austin Morgan (The Dominant/Sir) that he accept my submission unto him. I ask that as my Dominant, Sir, takes me into his care and guidance and encourages growth together in care, trust, and mutual respect. It is my desire as his submissive to satisfy his needs and desires whenever possible, and I offer him the use of my body, abilities, and purpose.

His heart quickened. He had previously been the one to broach the subject of contracts with his former submissives. This was new ground for him and he was somewhat overwhelmed by the weight of what he held in his hand.

Further, I ask that as my Dominant will accept the responsibility of using my body for the fulfillment and enhancement of both of our sexual, spiritual, emotional, and intellectual needs. In order to achieve this, he has unrestricted use of my body any time, any place, and in front of anyone as he determines appropriate.

He cocked an eyebrow. "In front of anyone?"

She nodded, the apples of her cheeks darkening. "Can we build up to it first though, please?" She glanced over her shoulder at the hive of activity behind the locker room door. "And our workplace is still off the table."

He nodded and continued reading.

As a submissive, I will show an attitude of respect at all times.

Including: manner of speech, promptness, kneeling to serve (when able), proper answers, obedience, and wholehearted honesty.

Disrespect is a serious offense and will be punished.

His heart twitched. He knew that one would be hard for his sassy, spunky Texan, but the fact she was willing to try meant everything to him. The sincerity waiting for him when he met her gaze shot to his soul like an archer with astounding precision.

"I'm sorry I didn't tell you the full truth about my past.

But I promise never to be anything less than truthful with you going forward." She paused and brushed her hair from her face. "Unless it's like a birthday surprise or something. That I can tell a small white lie over. But that's it. Nothing else. Cross my heart."

She made an X over her heart.

Training activities will include: Offering of self every evening (where possible). Proper answers, orgasm control, anal training to increase my ability to offer every hole as he wishes. Learning to present myself as a submissive full of poise, grace, and beauty in public and private. Learning protocols and rituals throughout this contract on an as-needed basis; any other training activities as Sir deems fit.

"Mackenzie... This..." The tightness in his chest began to untangle.

"Keep reading." She gnawed on her lip as she tipped her chin at the piece of paper.

Orgasm Control

I am to achieve orgasm only by express permission of my Dominant.

Sweat trickled down his neck and back and his dick pulsed beneath his hockey gear.

"Keep reading." Her voice was barely a whisper.

Punishment will be given for the following offenses:
Cockiness/rudeness
Disobedience
Incorrectly addressing the Dominant
Failing to properly serve
Achieving orgasm without consent
Any other punishable offense as dictated

Punishments are intended as full and complete penance for offenses. Punishments should always fit the crime, and would be executed with full understanding that once over, the issue is over.

"You are making this incredibly difficult Mackenzie."

"I know. I'm sorry. But I really couldn't wait any longer. I needed to see you. I needed to give this to you. I needed you to know that I'm not okay. Tu me manques, mon Guerrier."

The contract went on to describe her hard limits, which included beastiality, age play, and gun play and her soft limits which included fisting, slapping, and temporarily being given away to another Dominant.

A steady trickle of showered and dressed players started to leave the locker room, but Kenzie held her ground, determination flaring in her intense stare.

The Submissive's pledge

I will work hard to correct any insecurities or inhibitions that interfere with my capability to serve you. I will maintain honest and open communication.

I will reveal my thoughts, feelings, and desires without fear of judgment or embarrassment.

"Excuse me, Coach Swift?"

Austin jerked his head up and met Mackenzie's eyes once more. Her eyes were questioning and her eyebrows raised.

"Yes, Mackenzie. What can I do for you?"

He rubbed the page between his finger and thumb. Was he ready to disclose his relationship with the team trainer to his Coach?

"Do you have a sec?"

He had been ready for a while and was waiting for her to catch up, but seeing her words in black and white cemented something inside his chest. He nodded.

"Sure, what is it? Austin, why are you still dripping sweat in the corridor? Get your ass in there and get changed."

"It's my fault he's here, Coach. I... uh..." She cast a fearful glance behind her, but most of the team had already left, and those who had not were still in the locker room. "I wanted to disclose a personal relationship between myself and Austin."

Coach's eyebrows shot up.

"We're uh... we're dating. I checked my contract and there is no clause about disclosing the relationship to my superiors, but I wanted to bring it to your attention."

After a long moment of silence, Coach Swift spoke. "Are you both going to conduct yourselves professionally?"

They both nodded.

"And keep your canoodling out of the workplace?"

Mackenzie snorted out a laugh. "Canoodling?"

Coach raised an eyebrow, but didn't say anything.

"Yes, sir. The height of professionalism in the workplace."

"Absolutely no canoodling." Austin nodded solemnly and Mackenzie laughed harder still. He'd missed her smile, her warmth, her presence. He couldn't quite believe she was standing in front of him, presenting him with a well thought out and signed contract for the future of their relationship.

The contract said they could revisit terms in six months. She was already planning long term and flexibility for their relationship. She'd admitted her wrongdoing, and while they still had some things to talk about, her gesture settled his aching heart.

"If you fuck up and chase away our best trainer I'm going to have some things to say to you, Morgan." Coach Swift's stern face was almost enough to make the rookies cry.

"That will not happen, Coach. I am already in love with her."

Mackenzie's squeak-strangled-hiccup would have been adorable if she had not broken out into a full-on coughing fit. When she recovered, her watery eyes were wide and her face, flushed.

"I see. Well, don't fuck it up. And get your ass in the shower." Coach waved his clipboard and strode away muttering something half to himself about young love.

"You told him you love me."

"Because it is true. I do love you."

She twisted her hands in front of her body. "I want to be strong enough to tell you what I need from you. And a not small, competitive piece of me wants to be the best submissive you've ever had."

He reached out to cup her face but she scowled at him. "You already are."

She placed her hand on her chest. "You make my heart do funny things."

"And you remind me that I have one."

Her breath hitched and his name escaped on her gasp. "I have so many feelings and thoughts right now but they're hard to convey. But I think I'm starting to understand what you mean when you talk about our energies aligning. There's a warmth in my chest that wasn't there before we talked. I've had this tightness in my chest since we... since you left."

She cleared her throat. "My fear of losing you deepens every time I fall just a little harder."

"Love is a dangerous thing in many ways." He grazed his knuckles over her jaw.

"It's not really the love I fear."

"Without the love, you would not fear the loss."

He dressed in record time. Kenzie waited for him next to his car and when he crossed the parking lot, he dropped his kit bag on the ground and grabbed her face with both hands.

"Austin, I'm so—"

He swallowed her apology with hungry lips and a demanding tongue. She whimpered and softened against him.

Whistles and riotous cheering startled them apart. Linc leaned against his bike, Finn, Will, and Russ stood next to

Russ's SUV, clapping and hollering. Finn gave them both two thumbs up with a wide grin on his face.

She dropped her forehead to his chin. "Guess the dating cat is out of the bag."

"Is that a problem? I can go over there and smack them around until they forget what they saw if you prefer."

She laughed, but shook her head. "It's okay. I don't mind people knowing. I just didn't want us to get in trouble. Or for it to cause friction for you... y'know, at home."

He cupped her face. "Mackenzie?"

"Yes, Sir?"

"Get in the car before kissing you is the tamest thing they watch me do to you."

Her audible gulp made him smile before she climbed into the car. On the ride home she was restless, shifting in her seat and nibbling on her thumbnail.

"Are you okay?"

"Can I ask you something?"

"Anything." He pulled up to a red light and she turned to face him.

She shifted in her seat again. "Can you tell me what you saw in me that made you think I'd kneel for you and let you tie me up and stick things in my butt?" Her face was serious, a frown pinching the space between her brows.

"I just... I don't remember a time when I wouldn't walk through fire for you. I've never felt a need to submit before, but it somehow felt like a natural progression. Even though I was anxious and scared I wouldn't be what you thought I was, or what you needed, I never once questioned the idea of being your submissive. It just was. Was there something in me that you saw?"

The light turned green and he pulled the car into traffic. "Your awareness of what others need. Wanting to take care of everyone. Always being concerned. Remembering important dates and events with ease. Wanting to know what you could do to help. Nobody is beneath your desire to serve, unless they earned their place there."

He fell quiet for a moment, letting his words sink in. "When things go awry you justify them before anyone else even has the opportunity. You are quick to assume you are to blame. 'What have I done?' is more prevalent than 'What have they done?' Even when it is clear you are not to blame. It is not something I looked for, however, for better or worse that is a sign that you could be conditioned to react as desired and is one of the easiest signs to notice in a potential partner."

She chewed on her nail. He reached out and covered her hand with his.

"Qualifying statements like 'I know this is a dumb question.' We vs they statements, or we vs you – like assuming I would be the one to be unhappy, that you couldn't give me what I need." He paused and slipped his fingers through hers, holding her hand on her thigh.

"These are not things that are wrong with you. These are small signs that started painting the vision of potential submission. The more I asked, the more you responded. It was also not hard to identify a need to be cared for, to be close to that person you were with. And lastly your word choices – you are powerful, but you do not always believe it. It is easy to tell how strong your belief is simply by how you phrase things."

Her cheeks darkened. He brushed the back of her hand with his thumb as they got closer to his apartment.

"As for whether you would like certain toys, tools, or activities? That has been an educated adventure. Those are things you do not really know until you start down that path. Your reactions to things tells me plenty about you. I have said before, your breathing, especially during intense conversation, is always my biggest indicator."

"Is there anything about us that isn't intense?" Her light

laugh lifted his soul. It had been just over a week of not seeing her, a week of not laying his hands on her, feeling her body react under his fingertips, stroking her hair or reading to her.

He pulled into his allocated space in the parking garage under his apartment block. A week was more than enough. He needed her. He needed her to know that he'd forgiven her, to tell her that he was proud of her, and to pour his love into her.

She'd presented him with the precious gift of a signed contract, and he felt like signing it with her cum.

CHAPTER 28
Mackenzie

Mackenzie twisted the bottom of her shirt as Austin switched off the ignition. "My parents are in town, my sister, too. They came to see me."

A muscle in his jaw popped in the dim light of the underground parking lot. "How did that go?"

"It's going to be a long road. We're going to take it slowly. They know I'm not going back to Texas, and they don't seem to want to force me. It's going to take time and patience, but if they truly have changed then I want to give them a chance to be part of my life again."

He cupped her cheek and she leaned into his warmth. "I am very proud of you."

Tears welled in her eyes. "Thank you. I'm not used to having boundaries. It feels…" She shrugged. "Uncomfortable."

"Nothing great ever happens in our comfort zone."

"Garrett told them about you. They'd like to meet you sometime. And Bea, my sister, she wants to see a game."

"And all of that can be arranged. However." He cracked his door open. "I need to be inside you, Mackenzie. So unless you have any objections, I need you to get out of the car."

A whoosh of air escaped her body as every light on her switchboard lit up and started flashing. "Yes, Sir."

He took her hand and led her up to his apartment. Slipping off her shoes she took in his space. Minimalist, Zen, clean.

"You look surprised."

"I shouldn't be, but I guess I am. It's very... green?"

"In the absence of a garden, I opted for house plants."

"I kill everything – even succulents and cacti. What's the bowl on the coffee table? Is it a giant pestle and mortar?" She gestured to the dimpled gold-colored metal bowl with a wooden handle sticking out of it on top of one of the few pieces of furniture in the room.

He chuckled, slipping his coat off and hanging it up. "That's a Tibetan singing bowl. It is a type of bell that vibrates and produces a rich, deep tone. They are said to promote relaxation and offer powerful healing properties. I use it for meditation."

Her home was by no means overcrowded, but Austin seemed to be a minimalist in the extreme.

"My Feng Shui is freaking you out, isn't it?"

"Lil bit. I'm afraid I'm going to get everything dirty by just breathing on it."

He removed her coat and hung it next to his before leaning closer to her ear. "Don't worry, Love. You can be as dirty as you wish in our play room."

Our. Fuck. A shiver rolled through her muscles, making her gasp. "We're going to play in there?"

He nodded.

"Now?"

He nodded again.

Her heart skipped in her chest as a fresh wave of heat spread through her body. He guided her through the apartment with his hand on her lower back. "We can stay out here if you are not ready yet."

"I want to see it." Her nipples pressed against the fabric of her bra, and she knew without checking that her underwear was beyond damp.

He opened the door and flicked a switch on the wall to his right. On one of the pebble gray walls, two almost floor-to-ceiling mirrors hung a couple feet apart. In one corner of the room stood a huge, dark wooden bed with a cage underneath. Tall, solid wood posts in each corner, slats across the top, metal bars above the headboard, and an extra two posts with stocks between them at the foot of the bed. A chest sat next to the end of the bed, a plush, dark gray blanket folded neatly on top.

She swallowed hard. How many women had he had in that bed?

In another part of the room stood a Saint Andrew's cross and next to it a black bench shaped like a person on all fours, legs opened wide. The bench had black leather padding where a person's chest, thighs, and shins were supposed to rest. Thick black straps with silver buckles hung over the padding where ankles, knees, torso, and head got fastened to the bench.

She walked to it and ran her fingers over the cool leather, noting no padding or rests for her arms, only metal bars with black leather cuffs on each side.

A similar bench sat next to it but it was more compact, a long area for her body and a ledge on either side for her legs. The feet of the bench were tall, metal, and had loops, seemingly for hooking handcuffs and restraints to the bench. "For spanking?"

"Among other things. But yes, ma'am, it's called a padded spanking bench."

"It looks... expensive."

"That is not your concern."

"How much did you pay for this, Austin?" She tossed him an inquisitive look over her shoulder but he shook his head.

Facing the bed was a three seater black leather couch next to a black mini fridge. Support beams lined the ceiling and metal hooks protruded from the wood at various points throughout the room.

Perpendicular to the sofa sat a black, microfiber curved chaise with connector clips on the sides and rings along the edge at the bottom. "What's this?"

"It's called a Black Label Esse. It's designed for Kama Sutra-inspired positions."

Her eyes widened and she reached out to touch it.

"It's ergonomic, so it cradles your head and neck, it supports your back. It has twenty four connector points."

"Will you let me cuff you to it and have my wicked way with you?"

His brow quirked. "Not likely. But I would not rule it out some day."

She was taking it as a win. An array of whips, paddles, spreaders and chains hung on hooks next to a chest of drawers. She trailed her hand across the wood. "What's in the drawers?"

"Plugs, clamps, dildos, vibrators, restraints..." He pulled open a drawer filled with various sizes and textures of butt plugs. Rubber, glass, and metal all shone under the spotlight over the piece of furniture.

"I've only had one other woman in here, Mackenzie." He closed the drawer. "And all of the toys in here are brand new. Nothing belongs to her."

Her eyes widened. "That must have cost a fortune."

"That is irrelevant. I did not want you feeling uncomfortable."

Something that looked like a saddle caught her eye in the far corner of the room. "What's that?"

"It's called a Sybian."

"What does it do?"

"It's a masturbation device."

Her jaw dropped open. "I'm supposed to ride that thing?"

He nodded, heat flashing in his eyes. "Yes, Love. There are a number of attachments that can be added to the rod, which vibrates, rotates, and may also stimulate the clitoris externally."

"A sex machine..." She couldn't help but walk toward it. "Is it loud?"

"Not particularly. There's a reason it sits on thick matting."

"You just sit on it and it..."

"It fucks you, yes, Love."

She walked back toward the door, and pulled her shirt over her head.

"Mackenzie, you do not have to be in this room if you are not ready."

"And if I'm ready?"

"Kneel for me."

Remaining quiet, she slipped off her leggings, braided her hair over one shoulder, and removed her underwear before kneeling next to Austin's feet. He slipped his hand around her neck and pulled her head against his thigh before caressing her jaw and sliding his thumb into her mouth.

When he didn't move, she dragged her tongue from the base of his thumb to the tip before rolling her tongue 360 around his digit, then repositioning it in the middle of her tongue and sucking it back into her throat. Tipping her head so she could meet his gaze, his face was unreadable.

"What would you like to try, Love?"

"Isn't that topping from the bottom?"

"Perhaps. But I would still like to know the answer to the question." He dragged his thumb over her bottom lip before removing his hand from her face.

"I'd like to try spanking."

"With my hand?"

"Yes, Sir. And if it goes okay, maybe we could try something else? A paddle or a crop or something?"

A glint in his eye fanned the flames low in her abdomen. "That can certainly be arranged." He held out his hand and nodded at her as though encouraging her to take it. He guided her across the room, helping her onto the bench with the space to kneel with her knees pressed together.

"Lean forward. Hold on here."

She followed his instructions, her head and arms lower than her ass. "Sir?"

"Yes, Love?"

"Can I have a plug please?"

A pleasant hum sounded from behind her. "Yes, ma'am. Rubber, glass, or metal?"

"Glass."

"Small, medium, large or extra-large?"

"Medium."

A drawer opened and closed behind her. "Spread your cheeks."

She released her hands and gripped her ass cheeks, shuddering when a drop of cold lube dripped onto her puckered hole. He pressed the plug into her ass and she sighed as it slid into place.

He rubbed his hands together, the sound of friction as he brushed his palms, her racing heart, and her breathing were the only noises in the space. Gliding his hands over her butt cheeks he groaned.

"Such a perfect ass, Mackenzie." He kneaded her cheeks one at a time, then both. She leaned into his warmth. "Check in."

"Green."

"I am going to slap you. Each slap is going to have a

number. If you want to remain on the number, you repeat it back to me, if you want a harder smack, you say the next number."

"One." His palm met her skin. It took a moment for her to feel the sting and warmth spreading across her cheek.

She jiggled her hips and groaned. "Two."

"Two."

Another smack, another fraction of a second before the prickle, another moan. "Three."

"Three."

A third thwap against her ass, another blissful wave of pleasure rattling through her body.

"Check in."

"Four."

"Mackenzie, check in."

"Green. Four."

"Yes, ma'am."

Clenching her thighs together she braced herself for the impact of his palm on her skin.

Instead of the smack, his hands kneaded her cheeks again and rubbed at her hot ass. "Relax, Love."

"Yes—"

The crack of his hand meeting her skin made her cry out.

"Five."

"Are you sure, Mackenzie? You do not have to push yourself so hard on your first time."

She nodded and gritted her teeth. "Five."

Another smack, another wail, another wave of heat rushing to her core. "Six."

Six made her grunt and throw her head back, but she couldn't go beyond. He repeated the process for the other cheek, and she got to seven before she was a needy, wet mess of desperation, pleading with him to get inside her.

"Now?"

"Please. Right now. Here. Please, Austin." Her breathy pleas would previously have made her feel embarrassed about how burning her need was to have him inside her.

"Yes, ma'am." Without any more warning, he stepped up behind her and nudged her lips open with the tip of his cock, dragging his head through her wetness. "So fucking wet for me, Mackenzie."

Her legs trembled with want and she gnawed on her bottom lip as she nodded. "Yes, Sir."

"Did my Love enjoy having her ass smacked?"

She nodded again and both palms collided with her ass cheeks as he thrust inside her at the same time.

"Use your words, Love."

"Y-y-yes, Sir. I liked being spanked, Sir."

A sharp tug on her hair jerked her head back as his hips drove hard and fast against her ass. "Please come inside me, Austin. Please?"

She couldn't reach her clit, nor could she move to try, if she let go of the bench his aggressive thrusting could have upended her bringing her, Austin, and likely the damn bench onto the ground. She gripped the handles tighter and let him take her.

"Check in." His words were ground out between clenched teeth.

"Green." Her answer came out a roar as he relentlessly slapped against her ass, her braid curled around his fist. She screamed his name as his grunts and heavy breaths behind her drove her wild. His hips drove her against the frame of the bench, but she didn't care. She needed to take everything he had to give.

"Such. A. Good. Girl." His words were punctuated by his bucking hips as she moaned at his words.

She'd never come from her g-spot before, but something

was building low in her belly. She was going to pee. "Austin... Austin you need to stop, I'm going to pee."

"No, Love. You are not going to pee, you are going to squirt."

"I'm going to pee." Heat scraped over her skin as he pounded into her from behind.

"I do not care if you pee. I am not stopping unless you use your safe word. Do you wish to use your safe word?"

She couldn't bear the thought of him stopping and withdrawing from her. "No, Sir. Please don't stop."

If he didn't care, neither would she. She closed her eyes and hissed out a breath as he drove her closer to whatever the fuck was happening between her legs. She cried out as he gripped her hips and fucked her harder. His dick combined with the plug in her ass had her feeling fuller than she'd ever been before. Pressure mounted everywhere.

Another smack pulled a scream from deep within her chest and something trickled down her thigh. "Come inside me, Austin. Please." Her pants and wails weren't quiet, neither were her pleas for him to let go and fill her.

A few more thrusts made him come with her name on his lips and it was the sexiest sound she'd ever heard. His hands skimmed across her still burning flesh. "Check in, please, Love."

"Green." She heaved in a deep and steadying breath.

"Do not move. I will clean you up."

After a few minutes, he'd cleaned her, carried her to the bed where he placed her gently on top of the sheets and circled her nipples with the tip of his fingers. He kissed her forehead before brushing his nose against hers. "I am so fucking proud of you."

She slipped her fingers into his hair and dragged her nails down his scalp before kissing him deeply. He broke apart the kiss, but kept his lips on her skin, scorching a trail down her body.

"Arms above your head, grip the bars and do not let go. Do you understand?"

"Yes, Sir."

"If you move, I will stop what I am doing and reset."

"Yes, Sir."

He settled between her thighs, shouldering her legs so they draped over his back and sinking his face into her pussy with a rumble. After a few minutes of sucking and swirling his tongue over her clit she bucked her hips, riding his face as she crested the wave.

Gripping his hair with both hands she pressed herself against his face, inching closer to release when he stopped and his head snapped up.

"Noooooo. Why?"

"Where are your hands?"

She hadn't even noticed she'd let go of the bar above her head. She stared at the hard, chocolate eyes peering back at her from her crotch, getting lost in their depths.

"Mackenzie." His squelchy snarl would have made her laugh if it wasn't for the heat behind his glare. She was so fucking wet.

"Yes, Sir?"

"Hands. On the fucking bar. Now."

She jumped. "Shit. Yes, Sir." Resetting her grip she nodded. "It won't happen again, Sir."

"That might have cost you your orgasm, Love." He dove back into her pussy, lapping and grinding his tongue against her clit while his fingers worked her g-spot.

It took only minutes before the familiar tingle vibrated deep inside her. "Austin, please... please let me come."

He shook his head, sucking her clit into his mouth like a fucking vacuum cleaner.

She cried out, but didn't let go of the bar. "P-p-please. I need to come, Sir."

Another shake of his head, sending shockwaves through her limbs as he grazed the bundle of nerves between her legs with his teeth.

"Ten seconds." His mumbled command only drove her closer to the edge. She was on the precipice of a sheer cliff face, white knuckle gripping the jagged rocks and praying she didn't fall. "Count out loud."

"Ten." Her heart raced so hard she thought her chest might explode.

"Nine." His tongue fluttered against her clit like it owned her every breath.

She sucked in a shuddery breath. "Eight."

"Seven." Her legs trembled.

"Six." She was pretty sure he was drowning. Had she ever been so wet?

"F-f-f-fiiiiiiiiiiiiiiiiive." She huffed out air, gripping the bar over her head so hard her hands ached.

"Four. Four. Four. Four." She whispered four like her orgasm wouldn't hear her if she didn't say it too loudly.

"Come for me, Mackenzie."

She'd never come on command before, but holding her climax back with everything she had made it easy to let go when he demanded it and give him what they both needed.

Letting go of the bar overhead she thrashed her hips against his face and snaked her fingers into his hair, not letting him move. The harder she came the harder she pressed his head into her pussy. "D-don't stop. Please, Austin, please don't stop."

She tensed her thighs on either side of his head, which served only to spur him on more. He rumbled against her clit and a second wave hit her full force. "Fuuuuuuuuuck."

He pressed her hips to the bed with both hands as she

writhed against him, twisting and thrashing against his unrelenting tongue as he rode out her orgasm with her.

Her body twitched and jerked as her climax receded. When her ass hit the bed, she shrieked at the cool, wet surface. Austin kissed his way up her stomach, dotted kisses over both her breasts, and trailed his tongue along her collarbone before capturing her mouth in a deep and soulful kiss.

"I need a nap." She tried to pull his head to hers so she could cuddle, but he shook his head.

"Not here. We do not sleep here. Let me clean you up and I will take you to my bed, okay? Can you manage a snack and some water?"

She shook her head and tried to mumble 'No, Sir,' but parts of her were already asleep. Movement pulled her to the edge of consciousness as he cleaned her up and carried her to his bed. The cool sheets he lay her on made her shiver, but he was there, strong, warm arms wrapped around her as sleep dragged her under.

She didn't know what she'd done to deserve such a man, but she felt like the luckiest girl in the world. His thumb brushed along the side of her face as he kissed her forehead. "Sleep, Love. I will be here when you wake up."

CHAPTER 29
Austin

"Maman, what are you doing here?" He stepped aside to let Maman into his apartment, tugging his low-riding sweats up and slipping the t-shirt he'd grabbed on his way to the door, over his head.

Father stepped into the room behind her. Shit.

"Do we need a reason to visit?"

Yes. "No. I just wasn't expecting it."

"Obviously, otherwise you wouldn't have been sleeping in the middle of the day."

Maman rose an eyebrow, a knowing smile teasing her lips. "Je ne pense pas qu'il dormait. Is someone else here, mon Chou?"

There was no use denying it. He had made grilled cheese and was about to wake her up. "Oui, Maman, ma copine."

"I knew there was someone stopping you from joining the company." Father shook his head and made his way into the dining room. "Is there enough food for all of us? Or should we order in?"

They were staying for lunch? Joy of fucking joys. "Of course. Here." He plated the grilled cheese and handed them to his parents. "I will go and wake Mackenzie and make some more when I return. Help yourselves to the soup too, if you'd like."

He made his way to the bedroom, knelt on the bed and bent over Mackenzie, brushing loose strands from her slept-on braid out of her face. "I need you to wake up, Mackenzie." He kissed her.

"I haven't brushed my teeth yet." Her mumbles between kisses were adorable.

"I do not care."

She slid both hands around his neck and kissed him until her eyes flickered open and her tongue met his with a hunger that gave him a semi.

"Easy, Love. My parents are in the dining room eating grilled cheese and I really do not need to be pitching a tent when I walk back out there."

She gasped and her eyes flew wide. "Your *parents*? *Here?* Why didn't you tell me they were coming? I'd have given them a better impression than post-sexed and exhausted to the point I needed a nap in the middle of the day."

He chuckled. "You needed to sleep. And I did not know they were coming, otherwise I would have prepared you." He gritted his teeth. "I apologize in advance for my father. He is... difficult."

A frown creased her beautiful face and he traced the ridges between her brows with his thumb. "Do not worry, I imagine he will be perfectly polite to you."

He pushed back up off the bed. "Would you like for me to wait while you get dressed so we can walk in together?"

She shook her head. "I'm good. I'm not afraid of the big, bad wolf." She winked at him. "But I would definitely like some grilled cheese."

"Consider it done."

Back in the dining room, Maman and Father chatted in hushed voices.

"Mackenzie will be with us in a moment. Does anyone need more grilled cheese?"

"Non, merci, mon Chou."

"Who is she?"

"She is not a local."

"That doesn't mean I wouldn't know her, son."

Son. He rarely broke out the s-word unless he wanted something from him.

Father sighed. "I am not naïve enough to think I can commandeer control of your heart anymore. But I came to implore you to reconsider your decision not to step into the company when you graduate."

"Your business does not need a psychology major, Father." Austin put together another grilled cheese sandwich and re-started the stove.

"You have a business minor, Austin." He pointed a triangle of grilled cheese at him. "What about part time? Name your terms."

He flipped the sandwich in the pan. "Why are you pushing this so hard?"

"I have wanted you to work by my side since the day you were born. I know I'm pretty terrible at communicating it, but I am proud of you and believe you could do great things under my wing until you are ready to take over and lead by yourself."

Speechless, he slid the sandwich out of the pan and onto the chopping board, slicing it in half. A warm hand splayed onto the bottom of his back and he turned to kiss Mackenzie on the forehead and hand her the sandwich on a plate.

She beamed up at him. "Every girl in the whole world should get forehead kisses and grilled cheese cut diagonally. Thank you."

"You're welcome. Mackenzie Abbott, I'd like for you to

meet my parents. Malcolm and Delphine. Maman, Father, this is Mackenzie."

She put her plate onto the dining table and extended her hand with a warm smile. "It's a pleasure. My friends call me Kenzie." Her eyes flitted to Austin and her cheeks heated. "Austin always gives me my full name."

"It is nice to meet you, Kenzie." Maman shook her hand and returned her smile. "Sit. Join us. Tell us all about yourself. Chou has kept you to himself for long enough."

Mackenzie's laugh was light and airy. "We've been keeping it quiet until we knew things were long term. We work together and it's..." She picked up a triangle of grilled cheese and they spoke at the same time. "Inappropriate."

"You work for the team?" Father had finished his sandwich and was scooping tomato and basil soup into his mouth.

"Yes, sir. I am a trainer. Physiotherapist."

Recognition glinted in Father's eyes. "You're the one who helped Austin get back onto the ice after his shoulder?"

She nodded and took a bite. "He helped me too." She touched her finger to her lips, probably searching for any crumbs of cheesy goop. "I got injured a few years ago. I used to be a figure skater. He coaxed me back onto the ice."

Maman reached over to pat his hand. "He is a good boy."

"What if I sponsor a hockey program? Or donate tuition to a couple of the Snow Pirates next year. Would you be any more inclined to join our ranks?" Father wasn't giving up without a fight.

Austin paused, sandwich on its way to his mouth. "Bribery?"

"Strategic negotiation." He shrugged. "Whatever it takes. Six months... a year... a trial period."

Mackenzie picked at her grilled cheese and Maman glanced between the two men.

"Are you sick? Dying?" There had to be another reason for his vehement persistence.

Father dropped his spoon into the empty soup bowl. "I want to keep the business in the family, Austin. Is that so hard to understand?"

Austin shook his head, but he still couldn't imagine working in the same space as Father without feeling an overwhelming urge to murder him, thirteen times a day. At least.

"You've made comments about the company since you were ten years old. Ideas, suggestions, good things we could do with our money to help those who don't have any. Now's your chance. Put together a business plan, where you see the company going in the next five to ten years."

"You think I'm naïve and full of airy fairy ideas."

"And you think I'm an asshole hard ass who gets on your case too much. But together we can maybe do something good, do something better, and help a bunch of people in the process. Hell, start up a charity committee if that's what you want to do. I don't care. I just don't want you to miss out on an opportunity to shine because you can't get past the fact you think I hate you."

It was the realest conversation they had ever had and it was happening with an audience. Maman seemed to be holding her breath, and the weight of Mackenzie's stare pressed against the side of his face. It would never work, they would kill each other.

The quiet, confident support on Maman's face, coupled with the warmth of Mackenzie's gaze cemented something in his chest. With Mackenzie by his side, he could face anything with confidence. "What about we make a plan together? One we can all agree on and feel good about."

❋

Sabrina cleared her throat. "Are we really sure he should be handling sharp objects?" She gestured at Finn, who wielded an ax with a wild gleam in his eye, grinning like Jack Nicholson in The Shining.

"Hey! I resemble that remark."

"I mean... yeah... she's definitely not wrong." Linc took a sip of his beer. "He looks like he's a serial killer picking his next victim."

"I'm not sure it was a good idea to give any of you free rein with a fucking axe." Mackenzie gasped and slammed her hand over her mouth while the group cracked up into a blend of giggles and outright laughter.

"I said the quiet part out loud again, didn't I?"

He leaned over to her and kissed her forehead. "It is okay, Love. I am in agreement. It was probably not our wisest idea to come ax throwing."

"But it's fun." Finn spread his feet hip width apart inside the assigned cage, gripped the ax with both hands above his head and launched it at the target with a 'whoohooo!'

"You're way too excited about this, Finn." Cleo shook her head.

"He doesn't get out much, let him have his moment." Molly drained her beer and stood to take her turn.

"I'm more concerned about *her* having an ax than I am, *him*." Lincoln spoke behind his hand.

"I heard that, Lincoln Scott." She pointed the ax at him. "Don't think because you're dating my best friend you're above being diced into tiny pieces and buried where no one will ever find you."

Finn's eyes widened and he swiped a flat hand back and forth in front of his neck. "She'll do it, man. She really will."

Austin chuckled. "How about we make it interesting?" He spoke low and next to Mackenzie's ear and the only outward sign that she'd heard him was the tiny ripple that passed through her as she shuddered.

Without taking her eyes from Molly, she nodded. "I'm listening."

"A wager."

She gnawed on her lip, but her eyes twinkled in the bright lights. He had her. She never backed down from a challenge.

"What are the stakes, Sir?" She side-eyed him, but did not turn her head.

"If you throw better than me – overall, not just one shot – then we will go to Protocol tonight and Phoenix can flog you."

She gasped. She had been toying with the idea of public flogging for a few weeks, but he had not been convinced she was ready.

"And if I lose?"

"You know neither of us ever truly lose, Love. But if I win, we try something new off the list that you might have rated a three."

She squirmed next to him, but did not blink. "Deal."

Three hours later, topless, tied, and tranquil, his love stood, knees buckling from exhaustion. Her hair hung in braids over both shoulders, her back, red and raised with welts from Phoenix's leather bull flogger.

"Check in, Love." She turned her head so her chin was level with her shoulder.

"Green, Sir."

"Phoenix?"

"All good, here. Another round?"

He expected her to shake her head, to decline, and step down. But once again she surprised him and reset her body, feet firm, head straight. "Yes, ma'am."

Sweeping her braid behind her ear he leaned closer to her. "Such a good girl."

She moaned as the leather straps smacked against her

reddening skin. He had underestimated her at every turn from the moment they met. He'd thrown down challenges, and she had risen to meet each one with a strength and determination that made him dizzy.

She was the sunshine to his shadow, the gentleness to his inflexibility, and he couldn't wait to take her home and make her fall apart on his tongue.

CHAPTER 30
Epilogue

"Omg, this is so exciting!" Bea's hand gripped Kenzie's thigh so tightly she was concerned blood would stop flowing to the muscles.

Prying her sister's hand off her leg, she patted her. "While I'm glad you're enjoying your first ever hockey game, I need my thighs to walk. So can you find something else to death grip, please?"

She'd taken the night off from work, Austin's dad had pulled some strings to procure a fancy suite for all of them to watch the game.

The final whistle of overtime blew and Bea huffed out a sharp breath. "What now? We just leave and go home with two goals each?"

"Overtime." Delphine sat on the far side of Bea and patted her leg. "It is going to get tense."

Bea squeaked. "It's already tense."

Mama and Daddy laughed behind them. "She ain't wrong, though. I mean, it's no Houston Livestock Show and Rodeo, but I appreciate the athleticism and skill in front of me right now."

She rolled her eyes. That was high praise from her father. On the bench, Austin's head turned and she met his stare. She nodded, they could do it.

Fifteen minutes later she was proven right when Lincoln lit up the lamp with the game winning goal and the place went wild.

"Are we eating?" Bea patted her stomach.

"I made reservations for all of us. It's our last night in town and we had hoped to have one last meal with everyone before we left. We barely got to talk to Austin before he had to leave for training." Mama was smitten with him from the moment she met him. She was already naming her grandbabies and planning their return trip, and the one after that.

Kenzie had even overheard Mama talking to Daddy about buying a place in Minnesota so they could visit more. And considering she basically hung the stars in the sky as far as Daddy was concerned, Kenzie expected an announcement of a new investment property being picked up by the family in the coming months.

She smiled. While they'd left such a huge gap in her life for so long, and despite the fact she'd changed a lot since she'd left Texas, so many things were exactly the same.

Bea still planned to marry Garrett's brother and keep the families united, but Mama and Daddy swore Kenzie would never have to be in his company again beyond the wedding activities if she didn't want to. They couldn't apologize enough. Austin planned to go with her to the wedding, as both her date, and her heavy.

"Let's go. We'll meet you at the restaurant, okay, Kenzie?"

She nodded, a warmth spreading through her chest at the sight of her parents, and Austin's, helping each other into their heavy coats and chatting like old friends. "We'll catch up."

Bea slid her arm through Kenzie's and squeezed. "I've

missed you, Sissie." She kept her head facing forward, but her eyes shone with unshed tears. She leaned her head on Kenzie's shoulder. "I'm so glad I stalked you."

She laughed, blinking back tears of her own. "Me too."

Austin

His heart hammered in his chest as he laced his fingers in hers and led her to the elevator of his apartment complex.

"You sure you're okay?" She peered up at him as the elevator ascended the levels, dinging as it passed each floor.

Slipping his hand around her waist he pulled her to his side and kissed her temple. "Yes, Love. I am okay."

He was not okay. His stomach was in knots. He had never offered any of his previous submissives a collar before, not even his long-standing ex. Something had kept him from the commitment. But the more time he spent with Mackenzie, the more he was convinced she was the one.

In his apartment, he silently led her to the play room, kicking off his shoes at the door, he indicated she should do the same.

She shirked her coat off her shoulders and he draped it with his over the back of the sofa. Concern wrinkled her brow and her intense eyes searched his face. Brushing the pad of his thumb across her lips, he exhaled, willing the tension oozing from his muscles to dissipate.

"Mackenzie." He dropped his forehead to hers. "I think I determined why I dislike 'my woman.'"

One of the guys at the office had referred to Mackenzie as his woman, which had driven him into irrational irritation.

"Being a woman is something that roughly half of the world's population does without a thought. Anyone could be 'my woman.' It does not take any special skills, it does not hold any meaning. I have had women before, and there will be more, with you."

He sucked in a breath. "You, however, are more than

simply 'my woman.' You are my Love. Not my loved one. Not my lover. But my Love. That is a title that you earned and deserve, that I freely give to you regularly. I may not always include the "my". But it is always there and implied."

"Yes, Sir."

"I have owned you for quite some time. Some days I cannot remember a time when I did not. In some ways you could say that early on it was my job, but I have held many jobs prior that did not carry the same weight."

He grabbed the hem of her shirt and raised it over her head, gliding his fingers across her skin as he removed the fabric.

"Ownership is not a responsibility I take lightly. As time evolved, so did that definition of ownership. Physical safety. Emotional safety. Sexual safety. Taking ownership of your growth and health."

Supporting her head in both his palms he met her eyes. "I hold those responsibilities of my own free will, and have always endeavored to push you for more. Challenging and rewarding you. I refused to call you "mine" with no qualifiers for some time. Claiming parts of you, claiming an orgasm. Claiming you as my good girl. Those things came naturally. Stating "you are mine" took a conscious shift in how I defined what that meant internally."

She swallowed but stayed quiet.

"Historically, calling a submissive "mine" meant they were mine to do as I pleased with, within the terms of our contracts. Mine to use and abuse for my own benefit, and hopefully they would get what they desired too. For the most part, aftercare was simply a clause in a contract. Often followed to the letter. They provided an outlet. And fulfilled a physical need."

He dotted kisses along her collar bone as he reached

behind her and unclasped her bra. "Owning those pieces of you was easy. It comes without thought. I desire those things for you, and I enjoy the role I hold. Coming to terms with the fact that I loved you was much more difficult."

He dropped the bra onto the shirt next to her feet on the floor. "Some days it still is. I worked hard to not have any vulnerabilities. Eventually, though, I had to admit to myself that the reason I was struggling to call you "mine" was because the additional dynamic of loving you changes the entire meaning behind that ownership."

Her jaw trembled as he brushed his lips across hers.

"I take responsibility for, and pride in your accomplishments and strides. It is why I take your days of struggling as hard as I do. In many ways I see those moments as failure on my end. Above all else I desire to keep you safe, and have from day one. Not just from outside threats, but by initially trying to build up and maintain walls to keep you from getting close to me."

He tucked his thumbs into the sides of her pants and tugged, guiding the fabric to the floor. Once she had stepped out from the fabric, he remained on his knees and she hugged his head to her stomach.

"I am under no misconception that I will not ever hurt you. I know I will. I know I have. But I truly do not want to. I never have. I do not know what the future holds, but keeping you safe is at the center of everything I do with you. You are mine to protect. Mine to nurture. Mine to challenge. Mine to reward as I see fit."

Her fingers scratched his scalp, trailing a path through his hair down to his neck and back up around the curve of his head. "Can anyone else ever fill the space you hold in my mind and heart? Doubtful. But I cannot say it is impossible. Can someone else take care of you as well as I desire for you?

Doubtful. But again I cannot say it is impossible. Monogamy is a strange space for me."

He kissed her stomach. "I want you to be happy. That is where my primary role and responsibility is. To ensure your safety and happiness. Knowing that you will be happier if you are challenged, if you are healthy, if you are taking care of yourself. There is a direct correlation between your submission, your response, you showing me that you want to do the things I desire for you and both your and my happiness."

She smiled and the insecurity and anxiety tangled in his chest unwound as he stood.

"I do own that. I do everything I can to ensure you know that I am your safe place. To ensure you know that you can say and think anything you want. To make sure you know that you can do anything you want. And to support you in whatever journey and adventures you choose to take."

He opened his hand and moved it downward with his fingers together. In response, she dipped her head and sank to the floor, kneeling at his feet.

He caressed her hair before tugging the hair tie and letting her hair fall loosely around her bare shoulders. "So beautiful, Mackenzie."

He stepped away to pick up the box he'd left out on the arm of the couch.

"I got you something."

The corner of her eye twitched as he lifted the red box in his hand. Taking off the lid ruffled the black tissue paper underneath.

"We have talked about the different types of collars, so it might not come as a surprise. I wanted a physical symbol of ownership that denotes your role as my submissive." He pulled the long, inch-thick piece of purple leather out of the box and put the box next to him as he knelt in front of her.

"This is a play collar." The metal clinked as he held it up

between them. "When placed around your neck, it will signify a change in habit from the everyday world, and will bring your mind to the present moment. As such, your behavior will change appropriately."

She slanted her head and studied the collar silently. A smaller strip of purple leather overlaid the middle of a larger piece. A D-ring hung from each side, diamanté studs lined the center of the collar, and an O-ring dangled from the center.

"The second typical purpose of this type of collar is to serve as a signal to others that you are under a Dominant's protection, and ward off unwanted attention or casual pick-up play from other Dominants. But mostly, it is to remind you that you are loved and cherished."

"I cannot demand your submission. But I can protect the hell out of it. If you desire me to own your submission, I accept that wholeheartedly. I am more than happy to call that mine. But I also need to ensure you are aware that it is ultimately yours to take back as you see fit if you were to need to."

He waited for her nod, before reaching behind her with the collar to affix it around her neck. She nibbled on her lip as tears coursed down her cheeks. Her fingers roamed the stiff collar around her throat, skating over the metal studs and rings.

"I love you, Austin."

"I love you, too, Mackenzie." Hooking his finger into the O-ring at the front of her collar he pulled her to him and kissed her deeply, getting lost in her as their tongues collided. It was not a collaring ceremony in front of their friends and family, but he had told her how he felt and knew she understood the depth of feeling and importance attached to it. And he was every bit as much hers as she was his.

Need more from Austin and Mackenzie? Click here to get your bonus epilogue!

For those of you interested in what happens next for Addison, Paige, Thor, and the rest of the gang from Protocol, the series starts here.

Keep reading for a sneak peek between the covers of book 5 in the Snow Pirates series, Two for Tripping!

CHAPTER 31
Quinn

The vibrations rattled through the stage under her feet and into her muscles as Quinn belted out one of her karaoke faves: *I Still Haven't Found What I'm Looking For.* Sure, she was no Bono, but the lyrics shifted something in her every time she sang them.

If there was a time in his life when even the legendary Irish singer Bono didn't know what the hell he was doing, she wasn't going to hold it against herself that she still hadn't found what she was looking for either.

Or she'd at least try. Things like that were easier in theory than practice.

Clutching the microphone with both hands, her gaze skimmed the bar. She didn't need the lyrics on the screen, not for U2, not for Heart, Alannah, Madonna, Roxette, or Stevie. She sang them all with reckless abandon.

Tuesday nights were only ever busy in Pucks because of karaoke. And, while the place wasn't exactly booming, she had a modest audience of drunken freshmen who sang along with her. One guy even held up an unlit lighter, swaying in his chair while yelling that he loved her and wanted her to have his babies.

Flattering though he was, she didn't date younger men. In fact, she hadn't dated anyone in a long time, something she thought might change with each passing Tuesday. Surely she'd find *someone* compatible at some point, right?

If Clary Fairchild managed to find Jace, Alec, and Izzy all at the same time outside a bar in the very first episode of Shadowhunters, there had to be some point in time where Quinn would meet a regular guy.

She didn't even need for him to be a hot Shadowhunter kicking demon ass on the regular, just an everyday guy who wasn't a douchebag. She wasn't asking for much. At least, she didn't think so.

Just someone who perhaps enjoyed karaoke, sci-fi, an occasional game of Mario Kart, and who could carry a conversation beyond 'nice tits' and sending dick pics so she knew what he was equipped with and where he wanted to put it.

Why did guys think dick pics were hot?

Jen the bartender held up a glass, offering a refill when she made eye contact and Quinn nodded. She'd been singing Tuesday night karaoke in Pucks for just over a year, and as she stared down her sophomore year at the University of Minnesota, she knew that wouldn't change any time soon. It was her happy place.

Two women sat at the end of the bar drinking pink cocktails from tall glasses with orange slices hanging on the rims. They made come-to-bed eyes at a guy slouched over a half full glass of something golden. If there had been ice cubes in the tumbler in front of him, they'd long since melted.

His hair was mussed from running his fingers through it, and the collar of his shirt was open and tugged to the side. He turned toward the two chatting women, giving Quinn a perfect line of sight to his face. Frozen in place, goosebumps crept along her skin.

William Morrison. Will. Team captain of the Minnesota Snow Pirates. Former captain. 5 feet 11 inches, 180lbs, right handed shot on the ice, birthday July 6th. And the deliciously hot guy who all but made her forget her damn name when they'd met at Cleo's first book signing. He'd bought her books, like some kind of fictitious too-good-to-be-true man that only exists in women's fantasies – and romance novels. Then she'd lost the receipt with his number on it, and never seen nor heard from him again.

Yup. She'd absolutely – and shamelessly – memorized his stats from the team website. She'd also memorized the curve of his jaw and the precise shade of his cognac brown eyes. She'd crushed on him, hard, but considering she hadn't heard from him and he'd just graduated, she figured that ship had sailed.

Yet there he was, leaning on the bar in front of her, the weight of the world pressing his shoulders forward. His heavy presence almost had her stumbling over her lyrics as she belted out the final few lines of the song. Who was the shell of a man in front of her? And where was the geeky, awkward, smiling team captain she'd met in the bookstore?

She placed the microphone back in the stand and curtseyed to her adoring fans before stepping off the stage.

The two women had moved onto their next drink, chatting back and forth with animated hands and hushed whispers. Their cursory glances at Will suggested one of them was winding up to shoot their shot with him.

Deciding to save them both from potential embarrassment, or worse, ire from Will whose fuck-off vibes were so loud she couldn't fathom how the women hadn't picked up on them, she sidled up to him. She bumped her shoulder against his before sliding onto the empty stool next to him.

"So... what's a guy like you doing in a dive bar like this?"

A small smile tugged at the corner of his mouth. Under his eyes were dark circles, and the bags and red lines behind his heavy eyelids suggested he hadn't slept well for a while. She wanted to hug him.

"And where is your posse? Isn't it a well-known fact that hockey players travel in packs?"

"Hey."

It wasn't a 'fuck off,' but it wasn't a chatty Cathy answer either. She'd take it.

She hooked a thumb at her chest. "Quinn. I mean, hey. I'm Quinn. We met at Cleo's book signing a while back."

When he canted his head an inch and narrowed his gaze, she nodded and took it as an invitation to continue. She had nowhere to go but to his recent success. "Big fan. Congrats on the championship by the way. It must have been a huge deal for you to leave on such a high note. I know it totally sounds like an excuse, but I lost the receipt with your number on it."

The more he stared, the more her cheeks sizzled. Did she have something on her face? Was there something stuck in her hair? She reached up to pat down her wayward auburn waves, unable to stop the word vomit bubbling in the back of her throat.

"Anyway. You were about to have company." She gestured to the two women behind her. "And I... eh... you don't really seem to be in the mood for company, so I... uh..."

"Thought you'd join me instead?" His eyes dropped back to the half-empty glass in front of him.

"Yeah. I thought I'd save you." She winked. "You can thank me later."

Behind the pain and sadness in his brown eyes, his sparkle was nowhere to be seen.

"We can just sit for a little bit."

He nodded but didn't answer. Jen placed Quinn's gin and Sprite on the bar in front of her and accepted her credit card.

"Wanna keep a tab open?"

Quinn nodded and swirled her straw around the slice of lime in her highball glass. "Thanks, Jen."

Jen widened her eyes and jerked her head at Will before mouthing, 'get it girl.'

His eyes drifted to the left of the bar, fixating on something she couldn't see as she ached to fill the silence expanding between them.

On stage, someone with all the audacity in the world butchered *Love Shack* by the B-52's. Had they no respect for the classics? She cringed at the shrieking.

She shook her head and sipped her drink, ignoring the glares from her now-nemeses across the bar. She wasn't normally someone to cock-block another woman, but the sadness seeping from Will's every pore had driven her to act.

If she had to dole out a case of blue balls to a member of her gender to spare Will from even a second more of pain and discomfort, she'd take one for the team.

"I haven't seen you since the book signing." Neutral territory. It wasn't quite 'Let me count the ways,' but she didn't want to spook him.

He didn't tear his eyes from whatever was holding him captive next to the bar, but he nodded and took a drink. "Things have been..." He rotated his wrist, swirling the golden liquid around in the glass. "Crazy."

"I get that. Graduation, am I right?" She took a drink. "I mean, not that I'd know yet, obviously." She cringed again. What the hell was wrong with her? She was a conversational queen, she could make friends out of strangers, but the reserved hockey hottie was apparently her kryptonite.

She swallowed and tried again. "I was starting to feel like I'd dreamt you up like one of my book boyfriends." She snorted, coughed to cover her snort, and choked on the fizzy Sprite that had somehow made its way up her nose.

His lips twitched, but his line of sight was still off to the side of the bar. A picture of Gordie Howe hung on the wall, and the more she stared at it, the more she realized it was crooked. Was that what had been holding his attention?

She tried to avert her gaze, but once she'd seen it, it was all she could see. How could he just sit there, knowing it was crooked and not get up to fix it?

Slipping off the stool next to him, she circled the bar and righted the picture. "That straight?"

Over her shoulder he nodded through a small smile. "A hair more and you're good."

It wasn't much, but she'd take it. She slid the picture frame a tiny bit further before seeking reassurance from him.

"Perfect."

She settled back onto the chair next to him and signaled another round to Jen, who stuck her tongue out and winked before throwing a double thumbs up. Quinn rolled her eyes.

"You sounded great." He gestured up at the stage. "Perfect song choice."

"U2 fan?"

He shook his head. "A fan of any song that doesn't make me feel like an epic fuck up for not having my shit together beyond college graduation."

Wow. Not so reserved after all. "I'll drink to that." She clinked her fresh glass against his.

His eyebrow quirked like he was surprised at her answer.

"There's no rulebook for adulting, William. We all just gotta fuck around and find out."

Wrinkles appeared on his forehead. "Did you just call me William?"

She hiccupped a gasp. "Shit. I guess I did. Sorry. I didn't even think. It just came out."

He picked up his fresh glass, and drained half of it in one go. "I like it."

When his eyes met hers it swallowed the short distance between them. Something warm swam with his sadness, something that sparked in her chest.

His fingertips, cold from cradling the glass, brushed along the curve of her jaw as her eyes fluttered closed. Palm cupping her cheek, his fingers weaved into the loose strands of hair falling around her face.

After a moment, neither of them had moved, so she opened her eyes again to find him studying her.

As she opened her mouth to ask him what he was doing, his lips crashed against hers. He tasted of whisky and his lips were cold from his drink. He smelled of apple and cedarwood, a dizzying, warm, comforting aroma that curled around her.

She gripped his shoulder and his kiss grew more urgent, his tongue spearing at the seam of her lips, demanding entry. When she parted them on a sigh, he invaded, sweeping his tongue against hers and cradling the side of her face in his other hand.

One of the women behind her muttered "bitch," Jen hissed out a "yesssssss," and if Quinn's eyes had been open she probably would have noted a monumental fist pump from her bartending friend.

She couldn't wrap her arms around his neck, but instead layered her hand over his, still on her cheek. She stroked his fingers with her thumb as he kissed her until she was breathless. She tasted a lifetime together, a future, the same connection she'd been hit with at the bookstore when they'd first met. The same tingle that started at the tips of her fingers and traveled all the way to the base of her spine. It scared the fuck out of her.

Dropping his forehead against hers, he sighed, not letting go of her cheek. Her heart swung like Miley Cyrus on her freakin' wrecking ball. What the hell was that?

They sat in silence for a moment, or perhaps twenty, foreheads together, his warm hands holding her face, and her chest rising with startling calmness considering the crazy dance her heart was doing.

Dropping a kiss on her nose, he finally spoke. "Ask me anything." He leaned back and reached for his drink.

She smirked. "Anything?"

He shrugged.

"Okay, favorite TV series."

"The West Wing." There wasn't a beat of hesitation before he answered.

Be still her quickening heart. "I love The West Wing."

His eyes narrowed. "Who's your favorite character then?"

"Donna." She took a drink. "I love her character arc. How she falls in love with her boss and sticks around despite him neglecting to see her true worth because she's constantly hoping he'll see *her*. But then she discovers her own worth and…"

She sent her hand into the air like a plane taking flight. "Beautiful. And I like CJ. Obvs. What about you?"

"Toby."

"Interesting." She smiled. "Intelligent, quiet, grumpy, and a secretly soft underbelly, eh? How did you get into it? It's quite a dated favorite, pretty old and not something you would have watched as a kid."

"My parents are *huge* fans. They re-watch it every single year. When we were old enough to watch, it became an annual family thing. Molly loves it too. Though she has a crush on Ainsely Hayes. What about you? How did *you* find the West Wing?"

A lump formed in her throat. "My gramps. He's to blame for my entire pop-cultural upbringing."

As though he sensed her sadness, he cleared his throat. "What's next?"

She smiled at the President Bartlet reference. "Star Wars or Star Trek?" She held her breath.

There had to be something wrong with him. He'd bought her books in a bookstore, he was delicious, smelled good enough to eat, complimented her on her karaoke, and he'd kissed her like he owned her. Not liking sci-fi was where the line was, it had to be.

"Wars."

Her stomach fluttered. "Trek. But I'm not averse to Star Wars. I'll watch it. Left handed or right?" He was right handed, the internet had told her so, but it was a fun question to ask all the same.

"Only left handed people ask that question." He pointed his drink at her like it was an accusation.

"Guilty."

"I'm right handed. You didn't answer the first question, what's your favorite TV show?"

"Shadowhunters."

"Never seen it."

She gasped dramatically, smacking the back of her hand against her forehead. "You haven't?" She held up her wrist, showing him the small rune tattoo just under the ball of her thumb.

"What does it mean?"

"Fearless."

His eyes darted between hers. "I can tell."

Something flickered in her chest. "Favorite song?"

"I always envy people who can just pick a song or a book and declare it their favorite."

"What about a genre?"

He shook his head. "I like just about everything except gangster rap."

"I love the oldies."

He pursed his lips. "How old?"

"70's, 80's, 90's."

"Suitably old. Great decades."

"Another round?"

"Please." Will answered for both of them and Jen's waggling eyebrows had another snort bursting from her before she could smother it with her hand. Smooth. Real smooth. Sure, he'd kissed her once, but there was still plenty of time for her to chase him off by, well, being herself.

"Crunchy or smooth peanut butter?" She jabbed a finger at him.

"Smooth."

"Orange juice – smooth or with bits?"

"Uhhh... freshly squeezed and not store bought?"

She scrunched up her face. "You're telling me oranges don't come in cartons from the store? Lies."

His chuckle was golden and made her want to jump up and down with glee. The tension in his muscles was easing, the sadness on his face, too.

She folded her arms. It was make or break time. "And where do we fall on the whole pineapple on pizza debate?" She arched her eyebrow and steeled herself to do battle.

"I don't get why everyone has a problem with pineapple on pizza. I mean. I don't love it. It's not my favorite thing. I don't worship at the temple of pineapple or anything. But I won't crucify you for it either."

She heaved out a breath. "Right answer. Wait – there's a temple of pineapple?"

Another chuckle, longer and more relaxed than the first. Melodic and smooth. "What were the stakes? I feel like I'm on trial."

She grinned. "I don't know that I can be friends with someone who likes crunchy peanut butter, and hates pineapple on pizza. I'd have had to wash my hands of you." She brushed her palms together.

His nostrils flared. "Is that so?"

She nodded.

He leaned closer to her, gliding the pad of his thumb along her jaw. "You'd be done with me even though our kisses taste like that?"

She tilted her head. "Taste like what? I've already forgotten how it tasted. You'll have to remind me."

"Liar."

Her cheeks were hot and her pulse fluttered faster and faster the more he stared at her.

"But I can definitely remind you." He pulled her to him by her waist, an urgency holding her in his grip and a fire burning low in her belly.

Mid-kiss, she pulled back. "How do you take your steak?"

He burst out laughing. "Right now? That's what you need to know right in this moment?"

She shrugged and slipped her hands around his neck. "If you like your steak cooked until it's a hockey puck, or still mooing, we're going to have issues and I need to stop this train."

"I don't. Now, if it's all the same to you, I'm not quite finished kissing you yet."

Her stomach dropped to her feet, her heart took flight, and her fingers burrowed into the soft hair at the nape of his neck.

She wasn't finished kissing him either.

Read Quinn and Will's story now!

Author Note

I went to Catholic school as a kid. In fact, both primary school and grammar school were convent schools, run by nuns. As such, we were raised believing kissing got you pregnant, sex before marriage would get you a one-way-ticket to hell, 'the gays' and anything other than straight up missionary was the devil's work.

Don't let anyone play with your butt – it's not the poop we fear, but the demons that obviously live there and could be released by going against the godly flow of traffic.

I've known I was bisexual since I was about eight years old and I kept it hidden like some nuclear, dirty secret that needed to be kept from everyone until I was well into adulthood. And even then, I didn't really come out. I'd drop it into conversation with people I trusted and hoped no one reacted poorly.

I had my first kiss at seventeen, to my first boyfriend – a guy I was allowed to see once a week, every Saturday for a few hours while supervised by either his parents or mine. Even through college I was constantly aware of the shame surrounding my sexuality. When I kissed girls it was when we were drunk and being dared to by the guys, because it was 'so hot' and as though the only way I was 'allowed' to like girls was if it came with the permission and approval of the penises in the room.

When *Fifty Shades of Grey* came out, the world went crazy. Not necessarily because of the kink, but because someone finally had the balls to stand up and say, hey, this thing happens and it's totally okay if you're a kinky fucker like we are. E.L. James opened the door, the door to discussion, the door to kink, the door to generations of women saying, "I love having things stuck in my ass," or I love being tied up and whipped, or I love being forced to come repeatedly until I forget my name.

She gave us permission we didn't realize we needed. Permission to accept ourselves and our kinks as we are. To be unapologetically ourselves. She gave us permission to not only explore those niggling tingles deep in the recesses of our soul that we spent years ignoring but to own them like a badge of fucking honor.

I've never been one to shy away from writing those subjects society deems 'icky' or taboo, and with Austin, this was no different.

Hot damn, y'all... *fans self* I think this is by far my hottest book to date, right? My pants are on fire and I'm here for it. We all knew Austin was a Dom from the get-go. I mean it was pretty obvious in previous books that he had the Dom-Vibes goin' on but I wasn't really sure where Mackenzie was going to take me and when she came out as even more vanilla than vanilla pods, I was totally here for it.

A kind of 'coming of age' but for kink, finding herself after a difficult marriage where she'd been made to feel like a freak, dirty, and ashamed was a beautiful transformation to write. I wanted to shine my own flashlight on the fact that no matter what you're into, you have every right to be that way. It doesn't make you dirty or unclean, it doesn't make you an aberration, or a deviant and it's not something you need to push down, hide, or run from.

I didn't want to write a hard-ass Dominant (Yet! I'm saving that for my new Protocol series, where Thor, Slade, Sterling and Phoenix will all be making appearances in upcoming stories) because that's not who Austin is. When I started planning, I knew he would be softer, he would adore his submissive with his whole heart and soul and love her fiercely. I knew he'd push his newly discovered submissive out of her comfort zone, challenge her and control her without being an asshole.

So many people don't realize that pleasure Doms actually exist. They hear the word *Dominant* and they think 'raging douche canoe.' They hear 'owning' and shudder with discomfort because they don't realize that – like in the case of Mackenzie and Austin, ownership doesn't mean master/slave. It can be phrased with such care that it is like wedding vows: you are mine and I am yours, in sickness and in health, etc.

I wanted to write about the softer side of kink, where Dominants nurture their submissives, and submissives push themselves to be the best versions of themselves under the guidance and direction of someone who loves them.

I wanted to take some of the fear out of a D/s relationship and show that it's not all hardcore pain and torture.

Kink can be whatever you want it to be.

A D/s relationship can mean whatever you and your partner decide it means.

Don't let society, or the media's definition of something deter you from trying it.

Let your freak flag fly!

Acknowledgments

Each book brings with it its own special set of challenges, and this one was no different. While I had a more complete outline and a better idea of what was going to happen in Austin and Kenzie's story than probably any of my other books, I had a short turnaround to get it to the editor.

Books 4 and 5 of the Snow Pirates series needed to be done and out of the way ASAP so I could give all my attention to another commitment for the latter half of the year – which in the end didn't actually pan out. At the time, though, it was pedal-to-the-metal and a hard graft to get it done on time to send to my new editor. Yup, because I don't do things by half! LOL!

Couple this with the fact that from early on there were indications this book was going to be even longer than all my others, my son getting Covid in January, my best friend arriving for a surprise one-week-long visit (that I needed more than I care to admit), my husband leaving his job and starting a new one, then getting Covid in February... and... and... and (you get the idea.) We had ourselves a ball game. Longest book plus *life* plus shortest turnaround time – y'all, that's a recipe for disaster.

Or rather it would have been, had I not surrounded myself with the very best gang of people to help keep my eyes on the prize.

Tracie and Clare – My early morning sprint bitches and queens of the universe. Thanks for pushing me, for listening to me grouse about how I didn't want to write some days, and for kicking my ass to write more on the days the words flowed. I couldn't have made my deadlines without you guys and your aggressive encouragement, passive aggression (aggressive aggression) and support – not to mention the 2kg bag of Hot Tamales that showed up at the door to fuel those last few thousand words!

Heather – Thank you for checking in on me in the author cave every now and then and making sure I'm still eating and bathing, and for dragging me outside into the – albeit cold – sunshine for a cuppa and a breather. The cake you brought round for my birthday fueled many of the words in this book, so you basically wrote it yourself! Thank you for supporting me through two bouts of C-19 in the house and for offering to help if we needed it. The offer alone meant the world to me.

JP – My mentor and friend. Thank you for reminding me of my inner strength at a time I felt like I had none left. Your continuing support and encouragement helped me get this book written, but your faith in my ability to conquer even the hardest of hard things helps me get up in the morning.

My Alphas – Savannah, Erika, Robynne, and Ivy – thank y'all for taking time to give this a once over with your constructive eyes. As always, your feedback and head pats meant the damn thing actually got published and not set on fire, or thrown in the Irish Sea – y'all the real MVPs.

My Betas – Micky and Corinne: typo queens and two of my biggest fans – thank you!

Jennie Hack for giving me Kenzie's shitty ex's name Garrett.

HUGE thanks to my editor Jami Nord and my cover designer Kate Farlow over at Y'all That Graphic.

My ARC readers, my Facebook reader group *Margaritas,*

Men, and Mischief with Lasairiona, and to each and every one of you readers who picked up this book: a bazillion thank yous. I truly hope you loved it enough to pick up the next one.

Resource: Dom Drop Article: www.sofiagray.com/blog/the-thing-we-dont-talk-about-dom-drop

Also by Lasairiona McMaster

Two for Interference - Minnesota Snow Pirates book 1

Freezing the Puck - Cedar Rapids Raccoons book 1

Two for Tacos - A Snow Pirates Novella

Control - The Protocol Series (Writing as: Lasairiona Lewis)

www.Lasairiona.com

About the Author

Lasairiona McMaster writes sassy, classy and badassy women and strong, yet vulnerable men. She challenges reader's expectations by openly dealing with mental health issues, often exploring tough-to-handle topics and 'taboos' and books with a whole lotta heart.

She can either be found enjoying a gin and lemonade by the Irish sea, or baking sweet treats in her kitchen while singing at the top of her lungs. When she's 'home' in Texas, and isn't eating fresh-popped popcorn while buying things she has absolutely no need for in Target, she can be found at Chuys eating her body weight in chips and queso and washing it down with a margarita swirl. She loves to make friends out of strangers.

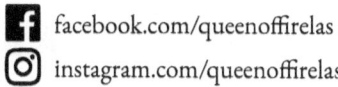

facebook.com/queenoffirelas

instagram.com/queenoffirelas

www.ingramcontent.com/pod-product-compliance
Lightning Source LLC
Chambersburg PA
CBHW020134130526
44590CB00039B/158